The History
of the Mongol Conquests

The History
of the Mongol Conquests

J. J. Saunders

Department of History,
University of Canterbury, Christchurch

Routledge & Kegan Paul   London

First published 1971
by Routledge & Kegan Paul Ltd
Broadway House, 68–74 Carter Lane
London EC 4V 5EL
Printed in Great Britain by
The Camelot Press Ltd
London and Southampton
and set in Plantin (110) 11 on 12 point

ISBN 0 7100 7073 X

Contents

TO MY GRANDSON MARK

Illustrations

Plates

Maps

Glossary

All the names listed are Turkish unless otherwise stated.

Adak, Azak, Ayak	leg, foot. Sea of Azov (Azak) at *foot* of Don.
Agha	elder brother, in Ottoman Empire chief or master, later used as a military title. Cf. Agha Khan.
Ak	white.
Alp	hero.
Altin, Altun	gold. Altin-yish, 'golden mountains'.
Anda	sworn (adopted) brother (Mongol).
Aral	island.
Arslan	lion.
Ata	father, ancestor.
Atabeg, Atabak	'father-guardian'.
Bahadur	hero. Other forms are *baghatur, batur, ba'atur,* in modern Mongolian *bator,* as in Ulan Bator, 'Red Hero'.
Balik	town. Cf. Khan-Balik, 'Khan's City', i.e. Peking.
Balish	Persian 'cushion'; gold and silver coin circulating in the Mongol Empire; 1 gold balish =2,000 dinars, 1 silver balish=200 dinars.
Beg, Bey, Bek	lord, chief, governor, commander. Feminine *begi* or *beki* in Mongol, *begum* in Mogul India. Probably a loan word from Persian *bag,* 'divine', title of Sassanid Shah.
Beki	shaman (Mongol).

Besh	five. Cf. *Besh-balik*, 'Five Towns'.
Bilik	sayings or maxims, especially of Chingis Khan.
Bökö, Böge	strong.
Bolar	Mongol name for Great Bulgaria on the Volga, *not* Poland.
Borte	wolf (Mongol).
Buka, Buqa	steer, bull.
Chagan	white (Mongol).
Choban, Chopan	shepherd.
Dalai	ocean, hence universal, supreme (Mongol). Cf. *Dalai* Lama of Tibet.
Darugha, Darukhachi	commissioner, police chief, leading official in Mongol-controlled town or district. From *daru*, to press or seal (Mongol).
Deniz, Teniz, Derya	sea.
Dokuz, Toquz	nine. *Toquz-Oghuz*, 'Nine Clans'.
El, Il	submissive, subordinate. Cf. *Il*-khan State in Persia, subordinate to the Great Khan.
Elchi	envoy, ambassador.
Erküt, Ereke'ün	Mongol name for Christians, perhaps from Greek *archon*, 'priest'.
Gurkhan	'universal lord'. *Gür* or *kür*, wide, general. Title of thirteenth-century ruler of Turkestan.
Hui-hui	Chinese name for Muslims, perhaps derived from *hui-ho*, Chinese for 'Uighur'.
Idikut	'holy majesty'. Title of some medieval Turkish princes in Central Asia.
Ikhshid	prince, lord. Title of Persian origin assumed by some Turkish rulers; name of Turkish dynasty which governed Egypt from 933 to 969.
Ilig, Ilak	king.
Kand	town. Often found as second part of place-names like Samarkand, Yarkand, Tashkand (Tashkent). Iranian word adopted into Turkish.
Kara	black. Cf. Kara-Korum, 'Black Rock'.
Keler, Kerel	Mongol name for Hungary, from Hungarian *király*, 'king', itself derived from Karl (Charlemagne).
Keshik	Mongol imperial guard.
Khan	king, prince, chief. Most common sovereign title in medieval Asia. Probably shortened form of *khagan*, *kaghan* or *kha'an*.

Khatun	queen, princess, lady.
Kizil	red.
Kök	blue, sky.
Köl	lake. Cf. Baikal, 'rich lake'.
Kum	desert, sand. *Kizil-kum*, 'red desert'.
Kuriltai	national assembly, diet (Mongol).
Möngke	eternal, common title of Tengri, the sky-god.
Naiman	eight (Mongol); name of tribe probably composed of eight clans.
Nökör, Nöker	comrade, knight, free warrior (Mongol). Plural *nököt* or *nököd*.
Nor	lake (Mongol). Cf. Lop-Nor.
Noyan	general, commander, official (Mongol).
Obok	clan.
Oghul	son, child, descendant, prince of the blood.
On	ten.
Ordu	camp; in English 'horde'.
Ortak, Ortaq	a partner, member of a company of merchants.
Paiza	tablet of authority, of gold, silver or wood.
Sarai	palace (Persian).
Sira	yellow (Mongol).
Solangqa	Mongol name for North Koreans.
Su	water.
Tagh	mountain.
Tajik or Tazik	Turkish name for Persians and Persian name for Arabs; hence *Ta-shi*, Chinese name for Arabs.
Tamgha	seal, die, tribal badge.
Tanga	small silver coin in use in Mongol age.
Tarkhan	commander with right to fixed share of booty.
Tarsa	Muslim name for Asian Christians, from Persian *tars*, 'fear', i.e. 'God-fearers'.
Tash	stone. Cf. Tashkent, 'Stone City'.
Tegin	prince. Cf. Alp-tegin, 'hero prince'.
Tengri	heaven, sky, God.
Timur, Temür	iron.
Toghril	kite (rather than falcon).
Tumen	10,000; hence an army division.
Ulus	people, land, territory.
Yabghu, Jabghu	prince.
Yam	post-station (Mongol).
Yarlik	decree, order, law.
Yasa	code of law, specifically that of Chingis Khan (Mongol).

Yasun	bone; *chagan yasun*, white bone, i.e. noble; *kara yasun*, black bone, i.e. commoner (Mongol).
Yer	earth.
Yil	year.
Yurt	territory, appanage.

A note on chronology

The commonest systems of reckoning time in Mongol Asia were by:

(1) The Muslim era, the starting-point of which is 16 July 622 AD, the year of the Prophet Muhammad's flight or emigration (hijra, hegira) from Mecca to Medina. As the Muslim year (AH = Anno Hegirae) is a lunar one of 354 days, it is steadily catching up on the Christian solar year of $365\frac{1}{4}$ days. Mongol public documents (at least outside China) were usually dated by this era, e.g. the Great Khan Küyük's letter to Pope Innocent IV bears the date AH 644 = AD 1246. On this method of chronology and the Christian era equivalents of Muslim dates to AD 2000, see W. Haig, *Comparative Tables of Muhammadan and Christian Dates*, London, 1932, and C. H. Phillips, *Handbook of Oriental History*, London, 1951.

(2) The Twelve-Year Animal Cycle, widely used among the Turkish-Mongol peoples and also to some extent in China. Each year was named after an animal, always in this order: mouse/rat, ox, tiger/panther, hare, dragon/crocodile, snake, horse, sheep/goat, monkey, chicken, dog, pig/boar. This system has obvious drawbacks: thus, when we read that the *Secret History* was completed in the Year of the Rat, we are uncertain whether this refers to AD 1228, 1240, 1252 or 1264. See E. Chavannes, 'Le cycle turc des douze animaux', *T'oung Pao*, 1906.

(3) The Christian Nestorians, who were so prominent in Asia

in Mongol times, used the Greek or Seleucid or Macedonian era, so called after Seleucus Nicator, who secured Babylonia out of the wreck of Alexander the Great's empire in 312–11 BC. It is usual to deduct 311 years from the Nestorian date to get the ordinary Christian era equivalent (e.g. 1586 Nestorian era = AD 1275), but this gives no precise reckoning, since the beginning of the Seleucid era is not exactly fixed and lies somewhere between 313 and 309 BC.

A note on transliteration

The problem of transliterating Oriental names in English is well-nigh insoluble, yet some principles ought to be followed and in general the form adopted should be that nearest in sound and spelling to the original. Consistency has often to be sacrificed to clarity.

In the Mongol history five principal Asian languages are involved: Mongol, Chinese, Turkish, Persian and Arabic. A whole group of dialects is classified as Turkish: only a few have a written literature.

As the Mongols were illiterate before the time of Chingis Khan, their names were first written down in other languages and some became fixed in that form. Thus the Conqueror's name is properly spelt Chinggis, but as Arabic has no ch, the Arabic form is Jinghiz, which in the eighteenth century became transformed in the West into Genghis. Mongol names in such forms as Hulagu, Mangu and Uljaitu represent the Perso-Arabic spelling: I have preferred the forms Hülegü, Möngke and Öljeitü as being closest to the original.

Mongol and Turkish ö and ü are pronounced as in German.

Persian has the same alphabet as Arabic, with the addition of four letters: p, ch, zh and g. Some of the letters they have in common are pronounced differently in the two languages. Thus the Persian town Ispahan is Isfahan to the Arabs, and the Persian historian Vassaf is called Wassaf in Arabic. The Persian province of Azerbaijan is sometimes spelt Adharbaijan, but the dh is pronounced z and so spelt in Arabic.

Arabo-Persian kh is pronounced like the ch in Scottish 'loch', but Mongol ch as in English 'church'; the dh, as noted, as z in Persian and the gh like the French r, a virtual gargling.

Chinese names are very difficult to represent in a romanized alphabetic form: I have usually followed the Wade-Giles system and shown the aspirate by an apostrophe, e.g. T'ang. In Chinese, ch is pronounced nearly as dj, and ch' like the ch in 'church'.

In Czech and cognate Slavonic languages, I transliterate the letters ž, č and š by zh, ch and sh respectively.

Genealogical tables

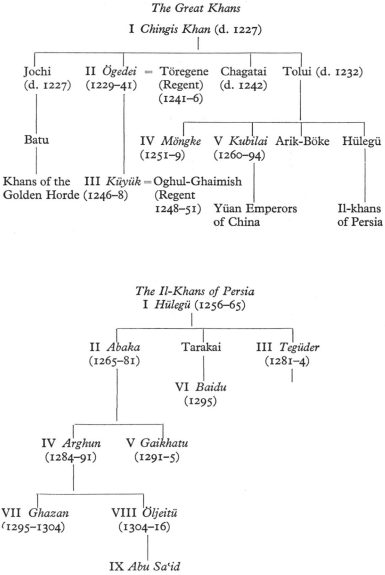

The Great Khans

I *Chingis Khan* (d. 1227)

Jochi (d. 1227)

II *Ögedei* (1229–41) = Töregene (Regent) (1241–6)

Chagatai (d. 1242)

Tolui (d. 1232)

Batu

IV *Möngke* (1251–9)

V *Kubilai* (1260–94)

Arik-Böke

Hülegü

Khans of the Golden Horde

III *Küyük* (1246–8) = Oghul-Ghaimish (Regent 1248–51)

Yüan Emperors of China

Il-khans of Persia

The Il-Khans of Persia
I *Hülegü* (1256–65)

II *Abaka* (1265–81)

Tarakai

III *Tegüder* (1281–4)

VI *Baidu* (1295)

IV *Arghun* (1284–91)

V *Gaikhatu* (1291–5)

VII *Ghazan* (1295–1304)

VIII *Öljeitü* (1304–16)

IX *Abu Saʻid* (1316–35)

The Mongol Emperors of China

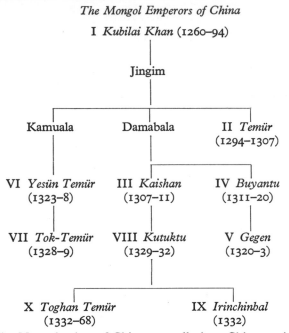

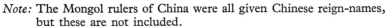

Note: The Mongol rulers of China were all given Chinese reign-names, but these are not included.

The Khans of the Golden Horde

(only the more prominent included)

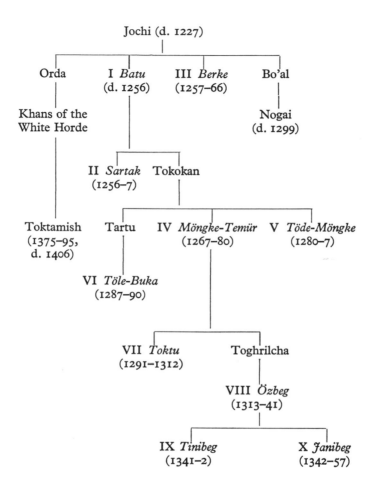

Preface

The Mongol conquests of the thirteenth century turned the world upside down; they spanned the globe from Germany to Korea, they destroyed kingdoms and empires wholesale, and left the greater part of the Old World shaken and transformed. Yet the literature of the subject is surprisingly meagre. Few documented studies (as distinct from popular, romanticizing biographies)[1] exist of the amazing career of Chingis (or, as he is better known Genghis) Khan; no scholarly life of his famous grandson Kubilai Khan, immortalized by Marco Polo and Coleridge, exists in any Western language,[2] and even the best general histories of the medieval world deal very cursorily with these tremendous events. The reasons for this strange neglect are probably the vast scope of the subject and the daunting character of the linguistic problem. In bulk, the original sources are not unmanageable, but they are extant in so many languages that only a linguistic prodigy could claim a mastery of them all. He who would undertake to write a history of the conquests that fully measured up to the exacting standards of modern scholarship must be fluent in Chinese, Mongol, Japanese, Russian, Persian, Arabic, Armenian, Georgian, Latin and several forms of Turkish. Such a Mezzofanti would be hard to find. However, during the last 200 years or so a small but able band of scholars, who have cultivated intensely small portions of this vast field, have published critical editions, translations, commentaries and learned annotations and so have built up a substantial body of accurate knowledge.

The French were the honoured pioneers; more particularly, the French Jesuit missionaries at Peking, who did so much to introduce China to Europe in the age of the Enlightenment. Father Antoine Gaubil published in 1739 the first reliable Western life of Chingis (*Histoire de Gentchiscan*), based on the Chinese sources,[3] and the posthumous *Histoire générale de la Chine*, by Father Joseph de Mailla, which came out in thirteen volumes at Paris between 1777 and 1785, is essentially a translation of the *T'ung Chien Kang Mu*, the fullest single collection of Chinese historical records, which was put together over a period of many years. This valuable publication instructed contemporary European writers like Voltaire and Gibbon in the Eastern side of the Mongol conquests, and the fact that it has been recently reprinted (1969) indicates that its usefulness is not yet exhausted. In the post-Napoleonic age the French Sinologist Abel-Rémusat examined the relations between the Mongol khans and the Western kings,[4] and the earliest general survey of Mongol history was compiled by Mouradja d'Ohsson (1780–1855), who came of a family of diplomats and savants of Armenian origin and ended his career as Swedish minister in Berlin; exploiting for the first time the rich Perso-Arabic sources, his *Histoire des Mongols* from Chingis to Tamerlane was published in four volumes in 1824. It impressed Goethe among others, and is mentioned with respect in the *Conversations with Eckermann* (12 October 1825); it was comprehensive and critical, has needed relatively little subsequent correction, and remains to this day the best treatise on the subject in any European language. The second edition, much enlarged and improved, dates from 1834; a third followed in 1852. Regrettably, it was never translated into English, but a reprint of the 1834 edition has been announced.

D'Ohsson's *History* stimulated fresh research: this was the age of Ranke and the critical evaluation of source material. The narratives of the great Franciscans Carpini and Rubruck, who travelled through Asia in the 1240s and 1250s at the height of the Mongol conquests, were printed in full in the original Latin in 1839. The indefatigable Austrian orientalist Baron Josef von Hammer, who possessed more industry than criticism, wrote the first detailed studies of the Golden Horde of Russia (1840) and the Il-khans of Persia (1841–3), the French savant Étienne Quatremère translated the section of Rashid ad-Din's History embracing the reign of

Hülegü (*Histoire des Mongols de la Perse*, 1836) and the part of Makrizi's voluminous history of Egypt dealing with the early Mamluks (*Histoire des sultans mamelouks*, 2 vols, 1837–45), whose conflict with the Mongols of Persia was of such decisive importance in world history, and the German scholar Franz von Erdmann produced a critical if ponderous life of Chingis (*Temudschin der Unerschütterliche*, 1862), based mainly on the Persian historian Rashid ad-Din. England was slow to contribute to Mongol studies, but between 1876 and 1888 Sir Henry Howorth (1842–1923) brought out in four volumes a massive *History of the Mongols*, one of the most disappointing, or at least exasperating, works in historical literature. Howorth was a man of immense industry and vitality and ardent interest in Asian antiquities, but he was expert in no Asian language and his book is a huge, ill-digested repertory of facts from second-hand sources, with little attempt at critical discrimination and inexcusably destitute of an index or even a table of contents. (A posthumous supplementary volume, with an index to the whole work, came out in 1927.)

Before the nineteenth century closed, the Russians, who under the last Tsars had absorbed into their empire one by one the Turkish khanates of Central Asia, had made impressive intellectual conquests in historical studies. Barthold's *Turkestan down to the Mongol Invasions* (1900) is a classic work, and indeed almost everything he wrote threw fresh light on the rise and fall of the nomadic empires of inner Asia. Vladimirtsov tackled the crucial and difficult question of the social and economic background of the conquests, and translations into English of his life of Chingis (1930) and into French of his *Régime social des Mongols* (1948) carried his findings to the West. The debates these two great scholars opened up have not yet been concluded, but more recently Russian attention has been diverted to archaeological investigation on numerous prehistoric and medieval sites in Turkestan, Mongolia and Siberia and to studies of nomadic art, inquiries which are enabling us to reassess the life and culture, trade and contacts, of many pastoral peoples of the Turco-Mongolian family who have left little or no written record. All too slowly the history of Central Asia is emerging from obscurity.

Yet such written records as we have of the Mongol age have not yet been adequately published or elucidated. Our primary authority on Chingis, the *Secret History of the Mongols*, has not

3

yet received the honour of a critical edition, though Professor Cleaves is understood to be preparing one at Harvard; specialists are not even agreed on its approximate date;[5] incomplete translations in French and English exist, but to the non-Mongolist this precious and artless memorial of the Conqueror is available in full only in the German of Erich Haenisch (*Die geheime Geschichte der Mongolen*, 1948). Of the great Persian historians of the conquests, Juvaini can now be read in Boyle's excellent translation (*History of the World Conqueror*, 1958), but only fragments of Rashid ad-Din's wonderful universal history (*Jami 'al-Tawarikh*) have appeared in the languages of Europe, chiefly Russian and German. Some of the Armenian, Georgian and Egyptian Arabic chronicles are accessible in French or English; the Latin travellers have been carefully edited and re-edited, and the fascinating narrative of Marco Polo, a library of medieval lore on Asia, has been supplied with a full scholarly apparatus in the richly annotated edition of Yule and Cordier, which has not been wholly superseded by the later work of Moule and Pelliot.

The mention of this last name affords, however, an opportunity to honour the most erudite and laborious worker in the field of Asian antiquities. The daunting linguistic knowledge of Paul Pelliot (1878–1945), combined with a shrewd and unfailing judgment, illuminated every corner of the history of medieval Asia, and what had been confusion and uncertainty he nearly always left clear and unclouded: even his occasional errors were sometimes more instructive than other men's verities. He wrote no general survey, but bequeathed a rich library of articles, reviews, notes and essays to light the path of all who came after him. Of those successors, I may mention two distinguished Germans, Otto Franke, whose *Geschichte des chinesischen Reiches* (5 vols, 1930–52) accurately traces the story of ancient and medieval China down to the advent of the Ming in 1368, though the treatment is perhaps more narrowly political than is now the fashion, and Bertold Spuler, who has compiled with the same Teutonic thoroughness the histories of the Golden Horde and the Il-khans which have superseded the century-old pioneer work of von Hammer. The Mongol invasion of Europe in 1237–42 has been treated in detail by scholars of the nations which endured it, but those who are ignorant of Russian[6] and Polish, Czech and Magyar, are unable to profit from researches in which patriotism has sometimes,

I much fear, triumphed over strict academic detachment.
I am aware that to treat a subject of this scope and nature as I
have done is a risky undertaking and may even be deemed fool-
hardy. But when I reflected that English historical literature is
almost destitute of books on the Mongol conquests, which made
so significant an epoch in world history, and that a considerable
volume of specialist work has been produced in recent years which
never reaches the educated public, I felt that some attempt, on the
lines of René Grousset's *L'Empire des Steppes* (1939), an excellent
piece of French *haute vulgarisation* now, however, thirty years old,
might be justified. As no one can claim competence over the whole
range of medieval Asian history, I have not been afraid (as Gibbon
once said) to borrow the aid of the strongest glasses. My principal
obligation is to Professor J. A. Boyle of Manchester, the translator
of Juvaini, who patiently read most of the typescript and corrected
me on many points of Persian and Turkish history and philology.
Professor Owen Lattimore scrutinized and commented critically
on whatever I wrote on Eurasian nomadism. In Dr Igor de
Rachewiltz, of the Australian National University, I found a most
valuable and generous guide through the intricacies of Mongol
China, who has also supplied some of the deficiencies arising
from my total ignorance of Japanese. Sir Gerard Clauson clarified
for me several obscure questions of Turkish antiquities. Professor
Vernadsky of Yale courteously answered my queries on the
Golden Horde. Dr Bawden, Reader in Mongolian at the London
School of Oriental and African Studies, while protesting only a
general acquaintance with medieval Mongolia, none the less
revealed by his most useful advice and comments how a firsthand
knowledge of the land today can illuminate much of its past. But
I must add the traditional qualification: none of these distinguished
scholars is in any way responsible for such errors of fact or per-
versity of interpretation as may have escaped their notice and
proceeded from my own ignorance.

In so far as the specialists who have recently examined and re-
evaluated the contemporary literature on the Mongol conquests
have reached a consensus, they may be said to have rejected the
old theory of wholesale destruction and to have stressed the more
positive and constructive achievements of the last of the great
nomad empire-builders. Edward Glanville Browne, writing in the
peace and security of late-Victorian and Edwardian England, saw

5

in the Mongol invasions 'a catastrophe which changed the face of the world, set in motion forces which are still effective, and inflicted more suffering on the human race than any other event in the world's history' (*A Literary History of Persia*, 1906, II, 426–7), but Wilhelm Barthold replied, in the year of the Russian Revolution, that 'the results of the Mongol invasions were less annihilating than is supposed' (*Mussulman Culture*, Eng. tr. 1934, 111), a judgment which is now commonly accepted, for a generation which has lived through world wars and revolutions and genocide on a hideous scale is more impressed by the recuperative powers of human societies than by the destructiveness of armies commanded by fanatical nihilists. Yet however we choose to judge the results, we must still stand amazed at the Mongol military achievement. Our theologically minded ancestors could find no other explanation than that the dreadful 'Tartars' were sent by God to punish the nations for their sins: a more secular age, while striving for a more rational judgment, may yet be pardoned for continuing to speak of 'the Mongol miracle'.

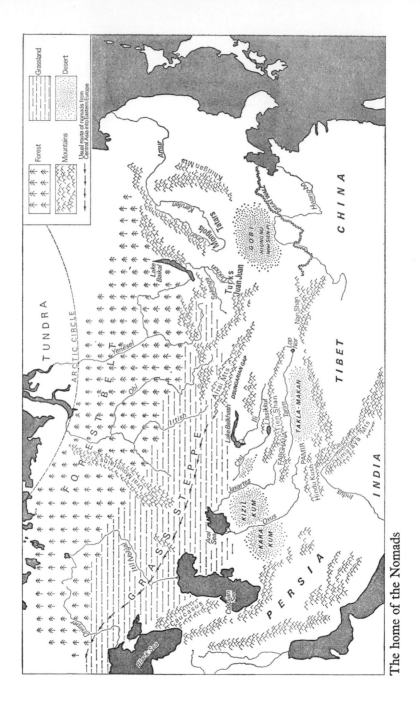

The home of the Nomads

I

Eurasian nomadism

The geography of the vast continent of Asia may be said to fall into four divisions: (1) the *taiga* or northern forest; (2) the steppe or treeless pasture; (3) the desert; and (4) the river valleys of the south (Hwang-ho and Yang-tse, Ganges and Indus, Euphrates and Tigris), on whose rich alluvial soil the great civilizations (Chinese, Hindu, Sumer-Babylonian) have arisen.

Of these, the first is a high broken plateau sloping away to the Arctic Sea and drained by the mighty rivers of the Ob, Yenesei, Lena and Amur, of which the second and third flow into Lake Baikal, a stretch of water 400 miles long surrounded by steep hills. In this thickly wooded land, the mountain sides are clothed with pine forests; shrubs and grasses grow on the plain; the rainfall is abundant, but the climate is bleak and harsh, and near Yakutsk the soil has been found to be permanently frozen to a depth of 446 feet.[1] A scanty population of fishers and hunters endure these forbidding conditions, but the Samoyedes, a tribe of Finno-Ugrian speech, who may possess some admixture of Mongol blood, were doubtless driven here by stronger peoples from the steppes of the south, and have played no part in history. By contrast, the Tungus, who inhabit eastern Siberia and the Amur basin, have at times emerged from their forests, taken to horse- or cattle-raising in the region between Korea and the Khingan mountains, and under a variety of names (Sien-pi, Chin and Manchus) have threatened or conquered the empire of China.

9

The third division is a dreary waste which runs with intervals from the Gobi,[2] between Manchuria and the Great Wall, through the Takla-makan of the Tarim basin to the Kizil-kum,[3] south-east of the Aral Sea, the Kara-kum,[3] east of the Caspian, and the Great Salt Desert of Persia. Here none of the rivers reaches the sea; they lose themselves in the sand or flow into salt marshes, like the Tarim into Lop-Nor. The Gobi is a cheerless solitude of sand, rock or gravel, 1,200 miles long, inhabited, in popular belief, only by demons, whose thunderous wailings are more plausibly attributed to the noise of shifting dunes, dislodged by strong winds. Vegetation is confined to scrub and grassy reeds; the climate is extreme; icy sandstorms blow furiously in winter and spring; rain falls but seldom, though after a brief shower the desert floor suddenly blooms with small green plants. The Takla-makan is a smaller Gobi, so swept in summer with choking dust storms that travel across it is tolerable only in the winter. The Dasht i-Kavir, or Persian desert, 800 miles wide, consists less of sand than of salt swamps, but being dotted with oases, its crossing is rendered more hazardous from the raids of bandits than from lack of water.

The second division, the steppe, the peculiar home of the pastoral nomad, extends irregularly across the Eurasian land-mass from Manchuria to Hungary. A rough distinction is made between the high steppe and the low, corresponding to the ancient classification of the Greek geographer Ptolemy, of 'Scythia intra Imaum' and 'Scythia extra Imaum', the Imaus being the Himalayan mountain barrier, of which the Pamirs constitute, as it were, the knot or node.[4] The true 'roof of the world', the Pamirs rise to heights of over 12,000 feet, with broad, canyon-like valleys between the peaks; to the east, the ranges of the T'ien Shan, or Mountains of Heaven, and the Altyn Tagh, with its continuation the Kun Lun, enclose the Tarim Basin; to the north, the T'ien Shan are separated by the Dzungarian Gap[5] from the Altai, or Golden Mountains, beyond which lie the steppes of Mongolia. West of the Pamirs, or rather of the T'ien Shan, the land falls away to the lower level of the Kirgiz, or Russian Turkestan, and the flats of southern Russia, drained by the Volga, Don and Dnieper. At either end of the vast steppe area, a mountain range intersects the open pastures: in eastern Asia, the Khingan Mountains separate the Mongolian from the Manchurian steppes, and in Europe, the Carpathians divide the Russian steppes from the Hungarian Alföld.

The true steppe is a treeless pasture, a grassy plain between the mountains, unsuited to agriculture unless expensively irrigated, but admirably adapted to the breeding of cattle, sheep and goats,[6] the sub-alpine valleys of the Altai providing exceptionally fine grazing-grounds. The vegetation consists chiefly of rich grass; the surface of the soil varies from gravel to salt and loam; the climate, though severe, and in the high steppe, appallingly cold in winter,[7] is dry and therefore bearable, and the shepherds of these regions often live to extreme old age. Though the grazing-lands of Mongolia and Kirghiz are more extensive, the heart of the steppe country has always been the pastures along the northern edge of the T'ien Shan and the southern edge of the Altai. Through the low passes between these two chains of mountains, nomad horsemen have again and again galloped out of Asia into Europe, from the days of the Scythians to those of the Mongols.

Pastoral nomadism is not an intermediate stage on the evolutionary path from hunting to farming. It is a highly specialized way of life, involving the domestication and control of a variety of animals and the utilization of vast tracts of land with sparse rainfall in such a way as to provide support for men and beasts. The nomad (his Greek name means 'cattle-driver') enjoys the freedom of the open country, of wide spaces and changing scenes, and often despises the peasant, who is rooted to the land he tills and is condemned to a life of arduous and at times painful physical toil. The flesh of his flocks and herds provide him with food, their skins with clothing and covering for his tent; yet he is the prisoner and at times the victim of the seasons, and a severe winter may prove fatal. In every age nomadic society, though it commonly prefers trade to rapine, has been frequently predatory; the contest for the best grazing-lands has set one tribe against another, and the greed for luxury or manufactured goods beyond the reach of their simple economy has repeatedly driven the pastoral peoples to ride out of the steppes and plunder the fields and cities of their sedentary and civilized neighbours.

In this long struggle, the nomad derived an inestimable advantage from the taming of the horse, a revolutionary innovation possibly achieved by the Scythians of the Russian steppes at the beginning of the first millennium before Christ. The operation was conducted in two stages, doubtless separated by a long interval of time: the wild horse was first domesticated, so that it could draw a light car or war-chariot;[8] and later a new species was bred with a backbone strong enough to carry the weight of a rider in battle.[9] The speed with which the nomad horseman could move gave him for 2,000 years the mastery of the Eurasian steppe and rendered him a formidable threat to the settled societies of the south. His principal weapon was the bow, made of horn (wood being unobtainable on the treeless steppe), which the archer learnt to shoot from horseback, and the invention of the stirrup (perhaps originally a Chinese device) enabled him to fire at the enemy while riding away from him.[10]

The nomad had no permanent home; the felt-covered tent in which he lived was easily dismantled, packed, loaded on an ox-wagon, and transported to a new location, where it was as easily re-erected, and his loyalty, which had seldom a territorial basis, was given to his clan and leader.[11] That leader was no hereditary monarch, but a warrior chief whose prowess had been tested in many a raid and skirmish; yet something more than skill in the use of arms was required of a man who must hold together a tribe of many discordant factions, direct the seasonal migrations of the flocks of hundreds of families and effect a smooth and harmonious distribution of the grazing-grounds of his people. The quality of such leadership inevitably varied, and as a weak chief, whose authority had fallen into contempt, might helplessly bewail the disintegration of his confederacy, so a strong one might attract the obedience of distant clans and build up a powerful following. Nomadic empires rose and fell with astonishing swiftness, but the essential features of the pastoral societies of the steppes remained unchanged for ages, and the description by Herodotus of the Scythians of the fifth century before Christ will apply, with trifling variations, to the Mongols of the thirteenth century after Christ, 1700 years later, as they are depicted in the pages of John of Plano Carpini and William of Rubruck. Incapable of social or economic progress, the nomads trod from age to age the same round; their animals provided them with a sufficiency of food and drink, supplemented by some easily grown vegetables; to engage in mining or manufacture would have impeded their free and seasonal motions; the blacksmith was commonly their only artisan, and whatever wrought or metal objects were in demand among them for use or display were purchased or stolen from their civilized neighbours.[12]

The religion of the nomads was a simple nature worship. To men who passed their lives on the open steppe, the sky and the heavenly bodies were objects of awe and veneration, and Tengri, an old Turkish name meaning the eternal blue firmament, is descriptive of an almost personal god, from whom all power was derived.[13] To some nomads, Tengri, a holy protector, was in direct contact with his people: to others, such contact could be established only through the medium of *shamans*, who in ecstatic trances ascended to heaven and learnt the will of the deity.[14] From poverty and a deficiency of suitable material, nomad religion functioned without altars or temples, but sacrifices were sometimes offered at cairns of stones, and hills, from which an uninterrupted view of the sky could be obtained, enjoyed a sacred character. As the most valuable of their possessions, the horse was a common sacrifice; when a man died, his horse was killed and buried with him, that he might ride it in the next world, and above his grave disembowelled horses were often impaled on stakes, presumably in honour of Tengri.[15] A widespread legend, reported by the Chinese as far back as 150 BC, told of the existence in the depths of central Asia of a divine breed of 'heavenly horses' who sweated blood and could never be caught by men; to the mountain where they lived, people brought their mares to be impregnated by these divine stallions, whose offspring inherited their singularity.[16]

The culture of the nomads was understandably poor. Though in the course of time some of their dialects might be committed to writing, they have left scarcely any written memorials; the Orkhon inscriptions of the eighth century, in archaic Turkish, and the *Secret History of the Mongols*, which dates from the thirteenth, are the sole historical documents of an illiterate race, whose jejune annals have been compiled by their civilized enemies. But in the field of art their achievement was noteworthy.[17] They carved from bone, horn or hard wood a variety of objects—bowls and cups, plaques and plates, brooches and bracelets—in animal or geometrical patterns; their spirited representations of lions and tigers, horses and deer, eagles and falcons, display an enviable skill and accuracy, and their art-forms have been diffused, by conquest or influence, over a great portion of the Old World from China to Britain.[18]

CMC

The languages of the Eurasian nomads fall into four categories.[19] (1) The Iranian, or Indo-European, akin to later Persian, was once spoken as far east as the oases of the Tarim basin and Lop-Nor and perhaps even in Kansu; Sogdian and Tokharian are forms of it which have been disinterred from the sand-buried ruins of Turkestan in modern times, and the speech of the Scythians and the Sarmatians was of the same family. (2) Turkish, an agglu-tinative tongue, which perhaps originated in the Altai region, is far older than its name, which is traceable no further back than the sixth century. In the millennium 500–1500 Turkish-speaking peoples pressed further and further westwards and supplanted Iranian throughout Central Asia while the conquests of the Seljuks and the Ottomans carried Turkish into Azerbaijan, Anatolia and south-east Europe. In eastern Asia Turkish survives only among the Yakuts of the Lena valley, the most northerly users of the language. (3) Mongolic, an archaic tongue, probably arose in the forest country north-east of Lake Baikal, but although the conquests of Chingis made it familiar over a wide area, it never displaced Turkish as the principal language of the heart of Asia. (4) Tungusic was a group of dialects confined to eastern Siberia, the Amur basin and Manchuria, only one of which—Manchu—has been reduced to writing. It is needless to stress that speech and race are not necessarily coterminous; in the constantly shifting patterns of nomad politics, a subjugated tribe or confederacy may adopt in time the language of its conquerors, or the conquerors may adopt the language of their subjects, so that a people of Mongol blood may become Turkish-speaking, or an Iranian community become turcicized, and in some cases the paucity of evidence leaves us unable to determine either the speech or the race of a people who attained a temporary mastery of the steppes. Notwithstanding the intensive researches of philologists, no organic relationship has yet been established between the Turkish and Mongol branches of speech, and a 'proto-Altaic' language, from which both may be supposed to have sprung, has still not been discovered.

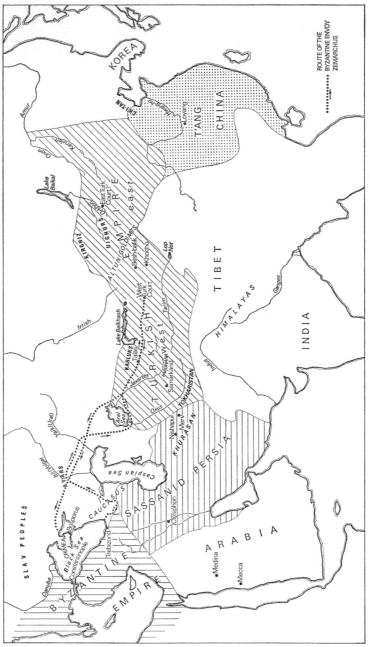

The first Turkish Empire about AD 600

2

The Turkish rehearsal for the Mongol conquests

Bibliographical Note The sources for the beginnings of Turkish history are almost wholly Chinese and Byzantine. The Chinese documents on the eastern Turks were collected, translated and annotated by Stanislas Julien, 'Documents sur les Toukiue', *Journal Asiatique*, 1864, those on the western Turks by E. Chavannes, *Documents sur les T'ou-kiue occidentaux*, St Petersburg, 1903, with additional notes and errata in *T'oung Pao*, 5, 1904. On the former, see also Lius Mau-tsai, *Die Chinesischen Nachrichten zur Geschichte der Ost-Türken*, Wiesbaden, 1958. All the Byzantine notices concerning the Turks are assembled in G. Moravcsik, *Byzantino-Turcica*, 2 vols, Buda, 1942–3, reprinted Berlin, 1958. The Orkhon inscriptions, discovered in 1889, were published with a French translation by V. Thomsen, *Inscriptions de l'Orkhon*, Helsingfors, 1896.

The best general account is W. Barthold, *Histoire des Turcs d'Asie centrale*, Paris, 1945, adapted from lectures given in German at Istanbul in 1926 and published as *Vorlesungen über die Geschichte der Türken Mittelasiens*, Berlin, 1935. Barthold's article 'Turks' in *EI* is a brief summary of his views. R. Grousset, *L'Empire des Steppes*, Paris, 1939; 4th ed. 1952, Chap. 1, gives an admirable survey of the subject. Two recent monographs are J. Hamilton, *Les Ouighours a l'époque des cinq dynasties*, Paris, 1955, and R. Giraud, *L'Empire des Turcs célestes*, Paris, 1960. A good deal of historical as well as philological information is

17

contained in G. Clauson, *Turkish and Mongolian Studies*, London, 1962. See also William Samolin, *East Turkistan to the 12th Century*, The Hague, 1964 (*Central Asian Studies* No. 9), Louis Bazin, 'The Turks of Central Asia in the 8th Century', *Diogenes*, 1963, and Denis Sinor, 'The Historical Role of the Turk Empire', *Journal of World History*, I, 1953.

The first nomads to build up a formidable empire in Asia were the Turks, and their extensive conquests may be fitly compared with those of the Mongols seven centuries later. The Hiung-nu controlled no more than Mongolia and the adjacent regions; the Scythians and Sarmatians were masters only of the plains of Russia; the Huns of Attila ruled from the Danube to the Volga; the Ephthalites or White Huns governed from the Aral Sea to the Hindu Kush, but the decrees of the Turkish *kaghan* were obeyed over the Eurasian steppes from the Great Wall of China to the Black Sea. I shall here discuss how this people so swiftly rose from servitude to empire, the peculiar circumstances which enabled them to triumph by dividing their neighbours and enemies barbarous and civilized, how their own feuds and factions undermined the fragile structure and brought it to ruin, and the nature of the legacy they bequeathed to their successors.

In the fifth century of the Christian era the pastures north of the Gobi were dominated by a people known to the Chinese as Juan-Juan. Their native or private name has not been recorded, and their Chinese designation has been plausibly explained as a contemptuous double derived from a verb to squirm, because the civilized officials of China likened them to wriggling vermin. They were perhaps of Mongol speech and origin; their chiefs were certainly the first to assume the royal titles of *khan* and *kaghan*,[1] which were later destined to decorate half the thrones of Asia. They warred, as such barbarians always did, with the Chinese, whose provinces north of the Yellow River were governed, as was not infrequent, by sinized princes of barbarous origin, the Tobas or T'o-pa, who reigned under the Chinese dynastic name of Wei. Among their slaves or dependants was a clan of smiths or ironworkers whom the Chinese annalists style *T'ou-kiue* or rather *T'u-chüeh* and aver were descendants of the Hiung-nu. Their proper name was *Turk*, a word which had been variously explained as an abstract noun meaning 'force' or 'strength' and a concrete noun meaning 'helmet', from the shape of a hill in the Altai range which was their earliest habitat.[2] The Turkish forges supplied the Juan-Juan with arms, but if occasion demanded, the smiths could use them in defence of their own rights and claims. Towards the year 546, the Juan-Juan, already weakened and divided by quarrels among the ruling family, were threatened by the revolt of a subject tribe; the Turks loyally fought for their suzerain; the rebellion was crushed; and the Turkish chieftain Bumin (the first of his race to be named in history) sought as the reward of his services the hand of the kaghan's daughter. Such a request from a slave was treated as an insolence and haughtily refused; Bumin swore revenge; what the Juan-Juan had denied him was prudently offered by the Tobas, who had long awaited an opportunity to annihilate these dangerous foes. The combined forces of the Tobas and the Turks fell upon the Juan-Juan; their power was broken; their kaghan committed suicide, and his title and empire were appropriated by his former slave. Bumin was clearly a leader of merit, but his personality is dim, and he lived but a short while to enjoy his triumph. The Juan-Juan were destroyed in 551; Bumin died in 552 or 553 and his newly acquired territories were partitioned between his son Mu-han, who reigned in Mongolia with the title of *kaghan*, and his brother Istemi, who received the pasturelands of the lower Irtish and the valleys of the Yulduz, Ili, Chu and Talas, with the subordinate rank of *yabghu* or prince.[3]

The Chinese records paint a portrait of the new masters of the steppes not radically dissimilar from that of their predecessors. The tribal totem of the Turks was the wolf; the father of their race, like Romulus and Remus, had been suckled by that animal, and a wolf's head in gold was affixed to the pole of their standards. The newly elected kaghan was carried nine times round the camp on a carpet of felt, and at each circumambulation received the obeisance of his officers. His tent opened to the east, out of respect to that portion of the sky where the sun rose, and he paid an annual visit to a holy hill to sacrifice to the spirits of his ancestors. In levying troops for war or cattle for taxes, the Turks carved the number required on a piece of wood, to which they added, as a mark of authenticity, an arrow with a golden barb sealed with wax. At a man's death, his relatives each killed a sheep or horse, rode seven times round the tent in which the corpse lay, uttering mournful cries, and gashed their faces with knives, a mode of 'blood-weeping' observed at Attila's funeral. The Turks (concludes the reporter) were happy to perish in battle and blushed to die of disease.[4]

The rapidity with which the Turks supplanted the Juan-Juan may be in part attributed to the superstitious belief of the nomads that military victory was a sign of divine approval and that instant obedience should be tendered to those who so clearly enjoyed the favour of the gods. The news of the Turkish success flew over Asia; the friends, the allies and the slaves of the Juan-Juan deserted their standards, and a few broken remnants of the defeated confederacy escaped westwards beyond the Urals into Europe, where under the name of Avars, they settled in the plains of Hungary, till they were annihilated by Charlemagne in the closing years of the eighth century.[5] The achievement of Bumin was considerable, and he was ever revered by his nation as the author, under heaven, of their fortune, but he lived only a few months as the prince of a united people, and at his death clan custom triumphed over political prudence. The new Turkish empire was divided into an eastern and a western khanate, a breach of unity ultimately fatal but masked for a time by the friendly relations and adroitness of the son and brother of Bumin, who quickly learnt to exploit the rivalries of the civilized states with whom they were now brought in contact.

In the east the disorder of China almost guaranteed the continuance of Turkish rule; since the fall of the Han in the third century, that great country had known little peace and no unity; and the Chinese dynasties which reigned to the south of the Yang-tse or Hwang-ho were at perpetual war with the two Toba kingdoms of the north, which figure in the dynastic annals as the Eastern and Western Wei. In the west, the Turks, pressing beyond the Aral Sea to the Oxus, clashed with the Hephthalites or White Huns, who since 430 had been in possession of the ancient Greek kingdom of Bactria and the eastern marches of the Iranian world, whose recovery was the constant aim and hope of Persian policy. Istemi, the *yabghu* of the west, dealt with the Hephthalites as his brother had dealt with the Juan-Juan. He offered alliance to Persia, then ruled by the mighty Khusrau Nushirvan; his friendship and a daughter were gratefully accepted; a joint campaign was organized some time between 563 and 567; and the Hephthalites, caught between two powerful armies, were ground to pieces. The victors divided the spoils; Khusrau regained the long-lost province of Khurasan, and Istemi was gratified by the annexation of Sogdiana, a rich and fruitful land beyond the Oxus through which the silk of China passed on its way to the markets of the west.

In the 2,000 years of nomad domination, few of the shepherd kings of Asia were indifferent to economic advantage. The rudest barbarian quickly learnt that it was preferable to tax rather than to plunder the merchant and manufacturer, and that to police the roads, repress brigandage and encourage the flow of commerce were the surest means to the prosperity of his kingdom or tribe. The silk of China had long been in demand in the West, and the road through the oases of Central Asia had been for centuries a principal highway of world trade. But before the precious cargo could be unloaded at Antioch or Alexandria or Constantinople, it must pass through the territories of Persia, the hereditary enemy of Rome, and in the constant wars between the two great powers, a trade embargo often stopped the flow. In the reign of Justinian, an attempt was made to introduce the manufacture of silk into Greece, so as to render the Empire independent of supplies from the Far East, but the Roman business houses were still unwilling to forgo the importation of the more finished products of China. The arrival of the Turks in western Asia opened up new and favourable prospects. Maniakh, a Sogdian chief with, one may suppose, a financial interest in the silk trade, suggested to Istemi that he should seek direct contact with the Romans and himself offered to lead an embassy to Constantinople. The offer was accepted; the mission was despatched; the envoys reached the imperial capital and presented their credentials to Justin II, the nephew of the great Justinian, in 568, and the Byzantine world received its first impressions of a people who nine centuries later were to proclaim Turkish sovereignty over the city of Constantine.

The Chinese at the eastern end of the steppe-country, the Greeks or Byzantines at the western end, are our principal sources of information concerning the manners and laws, the wars and the history, of the illiterate tribes they despised and feared, and the reports of the ambassadors of Justin and his successors lift the curtain on the Turks and display in vivid detail the customs of their court and the motives of their policy.

To the emperor Justin, Maniakh brought the offer of friendship and alliance in the name of his suzerain Istemi; he reported the ruin of the Ephthalites, and represented the common interest of the two sovereigns in maintaining an uninterrupted commercial intercourse. The Byzantines were not unimpressed; they may have suspected that with the disappearance of the Hephthalites, relations between the Turks and Persians would grow strained, and it would be sound policy to ally with a Power that might soon be in conflict with Khusrau. Zemarchus of Cilicia was deputed to accompany Maniakh on his return and convey the greetings of his imperial master to the Turkish *yabghu*, and the report of this shrewd and observant diplomat, preserved in the historian Menander Protector, is a precious picture of early Turkish life and manners.[6] After a long and tedious journey, they reached the Sogdian frontier, where the Turks offered them iron for sale, and proceeded to the court of Istemi at a mountain called Ectag, the Turkish Ak-tagh, or White Hill, which was perhaps the T'ien Shan rather than the Altai.[7] After passing between two fires, to neutralize the malicious designs of evil spirits, they were conducted into the presence of Istemi, whom they found in a tent hung with coloured silks, seated on a golden chair to which two wheels were attached. He received them courteously; detained them, in barbarian fashion, to a series of drinking bouts, and displayed before them, with childlike pride, in separate pavilions, his treasures, which included a throne supported by four golden peacocks and masses of silver plate and dishes set out on wagons. Byzantine hopes or expectations were realized; the Turks and Persians were on the verge of war, and Istemi invited Zemarchus to accompany him on a campaign of military demonstration. At Talas they found an envoy from Khusrau; at a dinner party the Turk, by placing the imperial ambassador by his side and ostentatiously conversing with him in the friendliest fashion while he snubbed and slighted the Shah's representative, indicated his policy and preferences. A Byzantine-Turkish treaty of alliance was ratified; Zemarchus with a Turkish escort, made his way back across the Emga, Yaik (Ural) and Volga; evaded a Persian ambush while crossing the Kuban, and after stopping to visit an Alan chief in the Caucasus, reached the Black Sea port of Trebizond, whence he took ship for Constantinople.

Yet Zemarchus may well have brought back some disturbing

impressions of the military might of the new sovereigns of the steppes, and if Istemi told him the spirits of his ancestors had warned him the time was ripe for the Turks to invade the whole world,[8] the Byzantine government might feel impelled to take precautions in face of these alarming ambitions. The fugitive Juan-Juan or Avars had reached the plains north of the Black Sea; they besought the protection and friendship of Constantinople, and the Byzantines, true to the tradition of balancing one barbarian horde against another, granted their application. The Turks were annoyed; when Istemi died in 575 and the emperor Tiberius, who governed in the name of the mentally sick Justin II, sent a mission under Valentine to congratulate his son and successor Tardu, the latter violently upbraided the Byzantines for their treachery and threatened vengeance. 'You have as many tongues as I have fingers,' he cried, 'tongues of deceit and perjury,' and he despatched an army to chase the Avars farther west and seize the Byzantine-protected settlements in the Crimea. A squadron of Turkish cavalry, operating from the Kuban valley, crossed the Kerch strait in 576, captured the city of Bosphorus, the ancient Panticapaeum, and in 580 appeared under the walls of Cherson, a self-governing Greek city whose remains are to be seen a few miles from modern Sebastopol. The Persian war halted further aggression in Europe; the Turks evacuated the Crimea in 590, and eight years later Tardu, who had now assumed the title of *kaghan* and brought the eastern khanate under his control, patched up the quarrel with the Byzantines and in a message to the emperor Maurice greeted him as a friend and styled himself the master of the seven races and seven climates of the world.

The boast was vain; and had scarcely been uttered before the tide of Turkish dominion began to ebb. In fifty years the Turks had mastered the Eurasian steppe and negotiated as equals with the sovereigns of civilization, but unlike the Mongols of a later age, they were met by challenges to which they could make only a feeble or inadequate response. The decline and fall of their power may be attributed to the following combination of circumstances.

(1) Bumin, their founder, died before he could consolidate the realm he had won, and the fatal expedient of dividing his heritage destroyed the unity and concord of the nation. The formal breach between the eastern and western Turks occurred in 584, when

Tardu snatched the title of *kaghan* and the vassal laid claim to suzerainty.

(2) The unity of China was restored at almost exactly the same time as that of the Turks was lost. Under the new and native dynasty of the Sui, which ascended the Dragon Throne in 589, the traditional policy of Chinese officialdom was revived; the barbarians who roamed beyond the Wall were alternately opposed by arms and enticed by wealth and office within the ambit of civilization, and their domestic enemies were bribed or cajoled into repudiating their leadership. When Tardu tried to seize the eastern khanate, the tribe of Tölös or Tölesh (the ancestor of the Uighurs) rose in revolt and overthrew him in 603, whereupon his kingdom was shattered to pieces.

(3) The premature fall of the Sui might renew Turkish hopes, but their supplanters the T'ang, who reigned for close on 300 years (618–907), carried the Celestial Kingdom to new heights of glory. Li Shih-min, the son of the founder of the dynasty, was a soldier of outstanding ability whose deeds are recounted at length by the imperial annalists. In an encounter with the Turks, a heavy rainstorm burst, and the bows of the barbarians, wet and swollen, were difficult to draw. 'Comrades!' cried the young prince, 'the whole steppe is now nothing but a lake. Night is falling and it will soon be dark. This is the moment to march. The Turks are to be feared only when they can fire their arrows. Let us set on them, sword and pike in hand, and drive them back before they can put their defences in order!'[9] His men responded, and the Turks were routed and thrown back into Mongolia. Two years later (626), Li Shih-min ascended the throne under the title of T'ai-tsung; he prosecuted the war with vigour; the *kaghan* Hsieh-li fell a prisoner into his hands; the Turkish chiefs did homage to the Son of Heaven, and for over fifty years (630–82) the eastern khanate was a Chinese dependency. 'The sons of nobles [we read in the mournful annals of the Turks] became slaves of the Chinese people and their chaste daughters became their chattels. The Turkish nobles abandoned their own titles, adopted those of China, and submitted to the Chinese *kaghan*.'[10] The shadow of the T'ang fell across High Asia; the four oasis-cities or 'kingdoms' of the Tarim basin—Kashgar, Khotan, Yarkand and Kucha—received Chinese garrisons, and Chinese arms, carried as far west as the Pamirs, might seem ready to envelop the western branch of the Turkish nation,

had not a new power, that of the Arabs, made its appearance in western Asia.

(4) The project of a Turco-Byzantine alliance had never been realized, and the defeat and death of Tardu in 603 left the demoralized western Turks in no condition to profit by the last great duel between the Byzantines and the Persians, which dragged on from 603 to 628, a struggle which ruined the Sassanids and gained for the Arabs an easy entry to the Iranian plateau. The Arabs invaded Persia in 633; the last Sassanid shah was killed near Merv in 651, and the Caliph's armies crossed the Oxus in 667. For the first time Arabs and Turks came into armed conflict. Had the Turks been a strong and united people, they might have excluded the Arabs from Transoxiana and seized some valuable fragments of the defunct Persian monarchy, but their loose confederacy had split (c. 638) into two groups, each of five tribes, divided from each other by the Chu river; the chief of one of the tribes, the Turgesh, usurped the title of *kaghan*, and fixed his *ordu* or camp at Suyab, near modern Tokmak west of Lake Issik-kul; the example of successful revolt was contagious; every city or region was governed by its own *yabghu* and at least one by a *khatun* or queen, and the Arabs moved into a divided and distracted world until the rival imperialisms of the Caliphs and the T'ang met on the high Pamirs.

For the Chinese had struck deep into the realm of the Western Turks in 656; the *kaghan* was beaten in a battle west of the Issik-kul, and the land was reduced to the status of an imperial protectorate. Yet within a few years the Turks both in east and west had restored their fortunes and they enjoyed a last era of success and brilliance. In 665 the western Turks rebelled against their Chinese-appointed khans; in 670 the Tibetans invaded the Tarim basin and cut or disrupted China's communications with the west, and in 682 the eastern khanate recovered its independence, in circumstances recounted in the famous Orkhon monuments erected in the next age, under a new *kaghan* appropriately named Kutluk or 'happy', whose minister Tonyukuk, celebrated by his countrymen as the wisest of the Turks, had been educated in the secrets of Chinese statesmanship.[11] The ruling house of the T'ang had fallen into dissension on the death of T'ai-tsung; in 690 the throne was seized by his former concubine, the famous Dowager Empress Wu,[12] who with the help of the Uighurs ejected the Tibetans from the Tarim oases, but she failed to crush the Turks, who in the twenty-five-year reign of Kutluk's brother and successor Mo-ch'o (691–716),[13] were the scourge of China. In 699 that able and ambitious prince won recognition from his western kinsmen as supreme *kaghan*, and the unity of the nation was briefly restored. He perished in 716 in an ambush on the banks of the Tula river in Mongolia, and his nephews Kül-tegin and Bilge,[14] who seemingly exercised joint power, were the last effective *kaghans* of the ancient Turks. The subject tribes revolted against the brothers; the aged Tonyukuk dissuaded Bilge from invading China, then vigorously governed by Hsüan-tsung (713–55), urged him not unnecessarily to add to the number of his enemies, and perhaps negotiated in 722 a peace with the T'ang. Kül-tegin died in 731, and his brother erected on the shores of the Kocho Tsaidam lake in the Orkhon valley a funeral eulogy, the oldest specimen of Turkish writing and a precious monument of Turkish antiquities. Such evidence of rising culture might seem to presage for the Turks a more civilized future, but when Bilge was poisoned by a minister in 734, the khanate finally fell to pieces. Three rebel tribes—the Uighurs, the Basmil and the Karluks—divided its territories among them; the last members of the house of Bumin sought refuge in China, and the title of *kaghan* was appropriated by the chief of the Uighurs, who reigned in Mongolia for almost a century (744–840).

Almost simultaneously the domination of the Turks in the West came to an end. The ambitions of the Turgesh had long undermined the western khanate, and all the Turkish tribes were caught between the Chinese and the Arabs, now contenders for the mastery of Central Asia. The Arabs crossed the Oxus in 667; their advance, delayed by the civil wars within the Caliphate, was resumed early in the eighth century by Kutayba b. Muslim, who in ten years (705–15) overran the whole of Transoxiana, penetrated Farghana, and threatened Kashgar.[15] The Turks, divided and distracted, begged for Chinese help, but the T'ang were engaged with the aggressive Tibetans, who had seized the region of Gilgit in the Hindu Kush, and not till 747 did the emperor Hsüan-tsung despatch his Korean general Kao Hsien-chih to re-establish Chinese power along the Silk Road and stop the onrush of the Arabs. The Turks were little more than spectators of the mighty clash of two rival imperialisms. At Talas in the high

Pamirs,[16] on a summer day in 751, the Arabs, with some aid from the Karluks, destroyed the forces of Kao Hsien-chih, and the Chinese relinquished for ever their hold on the land later to be known as western Turkestan. Thus two centuries after the overthrow of the Juan-Juan by Bumin the Turkish confederacy was shivered into fragments and the steppes were abandoned to a multitude of tribes who spoke indeed dialects of Turkish but speedily lost all memory of the great days of the *kaghans*.

In the general context of world history, the episode of the first Turkish empire possesses considerable significance. (1) The Turks had shown that it was possible for a well-organized nomad confederacy to seize control of almost all the Eurasian steppe from Mongolia to the Ukraine. The means by which they did so are obscure; their success was not attributable to the employment of new military techniques, nor were they led to victory by an outstanding conqueror of the calibre of an Attila or a Chingis Khan; but they must have developed a political and military system superior to that of the Hiung-nu, the Sien-pe or Hsien-pei, the Ephthalites and the Juan-Juan, whose domination of the steppe was more limited or ephemeral. (2) The Turks were the first barbarians to create a kingdom so extensive as to touch at different points the four great civilized societies of the day: China, India, Persia and Byzantium. Their relations with these states were sometimes friendly, sometimes hostile, but in peace or war the flow of trade and ideas through the heart of Asia ran deeper than in past centuries, and under the protection of the *kaghans*, merchants and missionaries travelled the roads in ever increasing numbers. Through this Turkish channel Nestorians,[17] Manichaeans and Buddhists passed from western to eastern Asia, though curiously there was no religious traffic in the opposite direction. (3) Stimulated by these contacts with literate peoples, the Turks learnt to write; the Chinese ideograms were indeed beyond their needs or capacities, but a kind of runic alphabet was borrowed from some Iranian community of Central Asia, possibly the Sogdians;[18] inscriptions were carved in durable stone by hired Chinese craftsmen, commemorating the deeds of illustrious *kaghans* or their counsellors, and these funerary monuments, more modest and realistic than such memorials commonly are,[19] have been uncovered in modern times on the banks of the Orkhon, the Yenesei and elsewhere in Mongolia,[20] and provide us with the oldest written examples of the Turkish language. From this time onwards the Asian nomads ceased to be wholly illiterate, and the art of writing was slowly diffused over the vast spaces between China and Persia. (4) Under the rule of the Turks, not only writing, but a new system of reckoning time, was widely adopted in Asia. At some unknown date and place, perhaps early in the Christian era, a lunisolar chronology, based on a cycle of twelve years, in which each year was named after an animal (mouse or rat, ox, tiger or panther, hare, dragon or crocodile, snake, horse, sheep or goat, monkey, hen, dog, and pig or boar), always in the same order, was brought into being and at least as early as the sixth century is found in use in China.[21] The Turks adopted it; examples are found in the Orkhon inscriptions,[22] and the expansion of Turkish power carried it westwards beyond the Altai to the Urals.

As the Turks created the biggest Asian empire before that of the Mongols, a comparison between these two great agglomerations of nomad power may afford some useful lessons. They both rose with remarkable rapidity; both drew advantage from the disarray of their neighbours and enemies;[23] both aspired to universal monarchy,[24] and both proved that an army of light cavalry, of trained professional mounted archers, could sweep from the field the clumsy levies of ill-equipped and undisciplined peasants, mere temporary soldiers bereft from their farms, who for long constituted the defence forces of civilized states. But here the comparison ends; for the Turkish achievement fell far short of that of the Mongols. Whatever might be the merits of Bumin, he is a shadowy figure notably inferior to the mighty Chingis, and indeed no Turkish *kaghan* attained the stature of an Ögedei, Küyük, Möngke or Kubilai. Though the Turks often raided China, and broke into Transoxiana and the Crimea, they never subjugated a civilized kingdom, whereas the Mongols fastened their yoke on China and Persia and reigned from Syria to Korea and from Russia to Annam. The Turks disturbed, without seriously damaging, the urban bureaucratic states along whose borders they ranged: the Mongols shook the globe, overturned empires, razed cities, and killed more human beings than any conquerors before them.[25]

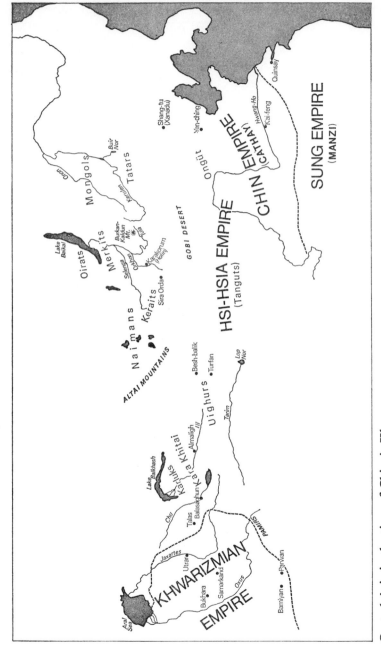

Central Asia in the time of Chingis Khan

3

From Turk to Mongol 750–1200

Between the dissolution of the first empire of the Turks and the rise of Chingis Khan lies an interval of four and a half centuries, during which no one tribe or confederacy attained supremacy over the steppes. That interval was filled with the local and temporary dominance of the Uighurs in Mongolia; their expulsion into the Tarim basin, whence their cultural influence penetrated deep into the Turco-Mongol world; the disorders in China after the fall of the T'ang (907), and the subdivision of that empire into the rival domains of the Tanguts, the Ch'i-tan, the Chin and the Sung; the spread of Islam into the lands of the Western Turks and the collapse of the Arabo-Persian barrier against Turkish expansion after the overthrow of the Samanid dynasty in 999, and the entry of the Kara-Khitay, or Black Cathayans, into Muslim Transoxiana, which presaged the irruption of the pagan Mongols into the same regions a century later.

The Uighurs, whose name is said to mean adhering to, uniting, coming together,[1] replaced the Eastern Turks in Mongolia in 744; their *kaghan* resided at Ordu-Balik ('Camp City'), on the upper Orkhon, near the ancient seat of the Hiung-nu and the future Karakorum of the Mongols; he was the loyal friend and ally of the T'ang, a circumstance which curiously led to his conversion, with that of his people, to the faith of Mani, as narrated in a trilingual inscription in Chinese, Turkish and Sogdian, erected in his capital about the year 820.[2] When rebellion broke out in the city of Lo-yang, in Honan, the T'ang emperor claimed the succour of his vassal, who had already assisted him against the Tibetans; an Uighur army, co-operating with the imperial troops, retook the disloyal city (757); the *kaghan* was rewarded with titles of honour and pieces of silk; but the revolt was renewed, and a new *kaghan*, after some hesitation, marched once more on Lo-yang, which was captured and pillaged (762). In the city he encountered some Manichaean missionaries; he listened with sympathy to the exposition of their creed and carried them back with him to Mongolia, and the title 'emanation of Mani', conferred on him in the inscription, proclaims his adhesion to the syncretistic religion of Irak. The Uighurs were the first Turks to adopt a religion of civilization; the Manichaean clergy acquired great influence in their councils, and the Chinese annalists assert that the *kaghans* took no decisions without the concurrence of the *mojaks* or priests.

The propagation of Manichaeism in the heart of Asia is a strange chapter in the history of organized religion.[3] The prophet Mani, after a long ministry in Persia and India, died in prison in 276 in his sixtieth year, condemned by the Sassanid Shah and the Zoroastrian clergy, but his teachings spread rapidly in east and west; his dualistic theology, which ascribed an equal power and status in the universe to a good and an evil God, might satisfy minds who found it difficult to reconcile the existence of an omnipotent Creator with that of manifold evil, and the cult of Light, which was borrowed from the Gnostics, might be assimilated by these Asian shepherds to that of Tengri, their peculiar deity of the sky. In its original homelands, the spread of this attractive and eclectic faith was checked by the vigorous and unrelenting resistance of three rivals. The Zoroastrian State Church of Persia strove to crush a dangerous heresy which threatened the power and privileges of the Magian priesthood; the Christians, after their victory in the Roman Empire in the reign of Constantine, employed the civil power to put down a creed which treated Jesus as a pantheistic emanation of Light, and when Islam arose in the East in the seventh century, the Muslims refused to the followers of Mani the toleration they accorded to Christians and Jews, and a remorseless persecution drove them eastwards beyond the frontiers of the Caliphate along the trade routes of Central Asia into the provinces and cities of a more tolerant China.

When the Uighurs accepted the religion of Mani, they lifted

32

themselves above the barbarous level of a Turkish tribe. The Manichaean scriptures, a curious medley of prayers, prophecies, tracts and epistles, were composed in the Aramaic or Syriac language, and the same script was soon employed to reduce to writing the Uighur dialect; the ancient runes of the Orkhon monuments were abandoned, and a Turkish literature arose, fragments of which were unearthed early in the present century from the sand-buried ruins of Turfan. The scribes wrote on silk, leather and paper, in a beautiful calligraphy; the books were illuminated and carefully bound, and the instruction of the common people was pursued by the medium of art, such as fresco paintings depicting white-garbed priests, the sacred tree, and even the prophet Mani himself. With the ardour of converts, the *kaghans* exploited their friendship with China to induce the T'ang sovereigns to permit the preaching of the faith and the erection of temples in the principal cities of the empire, and traces of Manichaeism were found in the province of Fukien as late as the seventeenth century.[4]

The Uighurs might have become a literate and perhaps an agricultural people,[5] but they did not grow in strength, and they were ejected from their Mongolian settlements in 840 by the Kirghiz, a primitive race of Siberian Turks from the Yenesei valley. Migrating southwards, one group moved (about 860) into western Kansuh, where it survived until conquered by the Tangut in 1028, but the larger and more fortunate settled along the oases to the north of the Tarim river, their principal colonies being at a place called by the Chinese Kao-ch'ang and by the Turks Khotcho,[6] some twenty miles east of modern Turfan, and Beshbalik ('Five Towns'), a former Chinese administrative centre[7] which, after falling to the Tibetans in 791, was taken over by a Turkish tribe whose princes bore the title of Iduk-kut, or 'holy majesty',[8] both town and title being annexed by the Uighurs. This area remained a centre of Uighur power till the days of Chingis Khan; from the ruins around Turfan a surprising quantity of paintings and manuscripts have been unearthed, mostly dating from the ninth and tenth centuries, and revealing the presence of Buddhists and Nestorians as well as Manichaeans.[9] The Uighurs, by seizing control of a long section of the famous Silk Road, enriched themselves by the profits of commerce, and their culture rose with their prosperity.[10] The Manichaeans had introduced

33

them to the arts of peace; the representatives of the other and rival creeds (and the Uighurs displayed a kindly tolerance of them all) added their quota, and Uighur literature was enhanced by translations of prayers and homilies and such pieces as the life of Hsüan or Yuan Tsang, the celebrated Chinese Buddhist pilgrim of the seventh century,[11] until these literate Turks were well qualified to be the educators of the Turco-Mongol world.

While the Uighurs were enjoying a new prosperity, their fellow Turks on the northern borders of China were shaken and weakened by the disturbances and upheavals which followed the fall of the T'ang, an event which reverberated throughout Asia. After a glorious reign of nearly 300 years, the strength and capacity of that dynasty were exhausted; it failed to protect the poor and curb the powerful; the peasants, the mainstay of every Chinese régime, were alienated; from 878 onwards rural uprising shook the State, and in 880 a peasant army, led by a former mandarin, Huang Ch'ao, drove the emperor from his capital. In his extremity, the latter besought the help of the Sha-t'o, an offshoot of the Western Turks, who had fled before the Tibetans from their original home near Lake Barkul and settled in northern Ordos,[12] and their young leader, Li K'o-yang, a loyal and valiant soldier, retook the city and was rewarded with a post in the imperial government. But the T'ang was moribund, and for the next sixty years rival groups of sinized Turks struggled to snatch the throne; their usurping chiefs assumed the names of past dynasties to confuse or conciliate the native Chinese, and the vast empire was plunged into the miseries of civil strife. A general or bandit (the two are often synonymous in such times) deposed the last T'ang emperor (907) and proclaimed himself sovereign of the dynasty of the Later Liang; in 923 the Sha-t'o, under a son of Li K'o-yang, ejected him and founded the dynasty of the Later T'ang, in memory of their former suzerains; in 936 a third claimant ascended the throne (as he called it) of the Later Chin, a fourth could not prolong its existence for more than four years (947–51) even by assuming the honoured name of Han; and the Chou, the last of the *Wu-tai*, or Five Dynasties,[13] was swept aside by the Sung, which in 960 gathered under its sway the greater part of China and reigned for more than 300 years (960–1279) over a diminishing kingdom. But even the Sung were unable to restore the unified domain of the T'ang; the northern provinces

34

had been occupied by the Ch'i-tan, a people who ruled from Peking under the name of Liao,[14] but whose proper name, under its Arabo-Persian form of Khitay, was vaguely conferred by foreigners on the whole country (the medieval 'Cathay') and is still the Russian name for China.

In the Chinese annals the Ch'i-tan first appear in the early years of the fifth century as roaming north of the Great Wall in the regions of Jehol and Liao-tang. They were probably a Mongol-speaking race, and though a nuisance to China during the whole of the T'ang era, made no serious attempt to settle south of the Wall until the chaos following the fall of that dynasty tempted them to do so. Early in the tenth century, an able chief whom the Chinese call A-pao-chi, organized his people, gave them a tincture of Chinese culture, and fixed the dignity of khan in his clan, the Yeh-lü, a name which was adopted, like that of Caesar in Rome, as a title of honour by all his successors. In 924 he led his warriors into Mongolia, drove the Kirghiz northwards into the valley of the upper Yenisei, and offered the Uighurs the re-possession of the ir ancient homeland. The offer was declined; and no Turk ever again reigned in Mongolia. The arms of A-pao-chi were carried eastwards into the kingdom of Po-hai or Korea, and the Jürchet, a Tungus people of Manchuria, were reduced to vassalage. He died in 926, after an unsuccessful attempt to conquer Hopei, and his widow, a formidable dowager, placed her two sons on horseback at the tribal *kuriltai*, or assembly, and cried to the nobles: 'Seize the bridle of the one you think most worthy!' She reigned at the side of Te-kuang, the son they chose, and in difficult affairs of state she regularly consulted the spirit of her late husband. The Yeh-lü Te-kuang promised the support of the Ch'i-tan to the pretender who usurped the name Tsin; the support was given, a reward was claimed, and a portion of the provinces of Hopei and Shansi, together with the city of Peking (then called Yen-chu) was handed over to these slightly sinized barbarians, who were thus installed to the south of the Great Wall. The Ch'i-tan were now better placed to interfere in the domestic struggles of China, but their temporary seizure of K'ai-feng, the imperial capital, in 947 provoked a violent national reaction, which in 960 carried to the throne the dynasty of the Sung, who were destined to be the focus of Chinese resistance to the barbarians down to the days of the Mongols.

35

The Sung might have driven the Ch'i-tan beyond the Great Wall but for the presence and threat of another competitor, the kingdom of Hsi-Hsia in Shensi and Ordos, which was founded about 990 by the Tangut, a people of Tibetan race who recognized the Ch'i-tan as their suzerains and the Chinese as their enemies.[15] Twice the Sung sought in vain to recover Peking; their attention was distracted by the menace of the Hsi-Hsia, and early in the eleventh century the Ch'i-tan took the offensive, marched to the Yellow River, and besieged K'ai-feng. The Chinese opposed a furious resistance, and eventually the Ch'i-tan were glad to sign a peace (1004), which fixed for a century the frontiers between the two states, the line of division running through the provinces of Hopei and Shansi. The Ch'i-tan had neither the strength nor perhaps the desire to occupy all China; they were content that the Sung should reign over the south so long as they retained control of the northern steppes. In China they were never assimilated;[16] the mass of their people continued to follow a pastoral life; the tribe remained the basis of their social organization, and they had little contact with the native peasants and artisans whom they despised. Their interests and ambitions lay outside China proper, and particularly in the Tarim basin and the Altai region, but their attempts at expansion in this direction proved fatal to their rule. Their cavalry rode westwards as far as Lake Issik-kul, but they were repulsed from the walls of Balasaghun,[17] in the Chu valley, and their neglect of their Chinese territories was punished by their defeat and expulsion by a new enemy, the Jürchen of Manchuria.

The Jürchen or Ju-chen,[18] the ancestors of the modern Manchus, were a forest people of Tungus speech, whose primitive barbarism had not been softened by contact with China. A Sung ambassador who visited them in 1124 in their home in the wooded hills of the Usuri valley in north-eastern Manchuria, described their savage chief reclining on a seat of tiger-skins and applauding the gyrations of dancing-girls who flashed mirrors around on the spectators.[19] The Sung, who never reconciled themselves to the loss of the northern provinces, pursued the traditional policy of calling in one barbarian horde against another; the Ju-chen were set against the Ch'i-tan, but the success of the newcomers exceeded the desires of those who summoned them. The Ch'i-tan were overwhelmed, and their last king taken prisoner; Manchuria and Jehol became the nucleus of a new barbarian realm, which the Ju-chen styled the Chin, or Golden,[20] kingdom and which assumed in time a Chinese façade. The Sung, who had hoped to regain all China, merely exchanged one foe for a worse one; the Chin speedily quarrelled with their former allies; more aggressive than their predecessors, they pushed southwards towards the Yellow River and the Yang-tse; K'ai-feng fell in 1126, the Sung emperor and his heir were carried prisoners to Manchuria; a new emperor failed to hold Nanking, Hangchow and Ningpo, all of which had been lost by 1130, but the cavalry of the invaders was hindered and confused by the intricate network of canals and rivers in the thickly populated area of the Yang-tse estuary, and were obliged to retire. The Sung recovered Hangchow, which was henceforth their capital, and launched a counter-offensive which won back large stretches of territory between the two great rivers. A peace treaty concluded in 1138 conferred on the Chin the legal title to the provinces of Hopei, Shangtung, Shansi, Shensi, and Honan. Not only had the Sung failed to retrieve Peking and the north, which were to remain in barbarian hands for more than two centuries, but they were compelled to yield to the Chin more Chinese territory than the Ch'i-tan had controlled at the height of their power. China was split into three sovereignties, the Sung in the south, the Chin in the north, and the Hsi-Hsia in the north-west, and all ere ultimately swept away in the Mongol deluge.

The Ch'i-tan and the Chin had successively broken through the barrier of Chinese civilization: the Western Turks at the same time broke through the barriers of Arabo-Persian civilization in Transoxiana. The eastern defences of the Caliphate were manned first by the Arabs and then by the Persians, who enjoyed a renaissance under the native house of Saman, who reigned at Bukhara from 875 to 999 and whose authority extended from the southern shores of the Caspian to Kashgar. Zealous devotees, the Samanids laboured to spread the faith among the nomads beyond the Oxus, and about 960 the Seljuk clan of the Oghuz Turks,[21] who pitched their tents near Jand, on the Jaxartes,[22] were converted to Islam, a change as momentous as the conversion of the Franks under Clovis to Christianity nearly five centuries before. Distrustful of the loyalty of their native levies, the Samanids, following the earlier example of the Caliph Mu'tasim, introduced Turkish slave troops into their military establishment and these

37

hardy barbarians were easily tempted to intervene in the dynastic quarrels of their employers and to grasp at political power. In 962 a Turkish commander seized the fortress of Ghazna, in Afghanistan, and set up an independent principality, an event which transformed the history of Asia, for that principality was governed from 998 to 1030 by the celebrated Mahmud of Ghazna, a conqueror who carried the faith of Islam by force of arms into the heart of Hindustan. His blows were also directed against his former suzerains; the Samanids were destroyed in 999; their fall was a victory of Turan over Iran, and Turkish military power was henceforth dominant in Muslim Western Asia.[23]

In their aggression against the Samanids, the Ghaznavids were assisted by another Turkish people, who have been dubbed by modern scholars the Kara-Khanids, on the ground that their earliest chief, Satuk, reigned under the name or title of Bughra Kara-Khan. Like the Seljuks, they were probably an offshoot of the Oghuz, but the details of their kings, conquests and conversion to Islam are meagre and obscure, a want of knowledge especially to be regretted, for the Kara-Khanids changed for ever the character of Central Asia. Before their day, that region was Iranian and of mixed religion; after them it was Turkish and largely Muslim, and the name Turkestan may be fittingly applied to it.[24] They first appeared in these parts about the middle of the tenth century; Satuk died in 955, and a Turkish people of 200,000 tents who embraced Islam in 960 *may* have been the Kara-Khanids.[25] Notwithstanding that they controlled the oasis markets of the Tarim basin, they cast covetous eyes on the rich, urbanized province of Transoxiana, held by the Samanids, the discontents of whose subjects were skilfully exploited by these astute barbarians. Bughra Khan Harun, the grandson of Satuk, crossed the Oxus and seized Bukhara in 992, but the final ruin of the Samanids could be accomplished only by an alliance of the Kara-Khanids and the Ghaznavids. The conquered realm was divided between them, with the Oxus as boundary, which gave Khurasan to Mahmud and Transoxiana, with the wealthy cities of Bukhara and Samarkand, to the Kara-Khanids. In the manner of allies, they shortly quarrelled, but a Kara-Khanid attempt to annex Khurasan was repelled by Mahmud, whose Indian elephants struck terror into the enemy, in a battle near Balkh in 1008, and the Ghaznavid conqueror followed up this victory with the occupation in 1017 of

Khwarizm, a fertile land of orchards and cotton fields to the south of the Sea of Aral.[26]

The death of Mahmud in 1030 was followed by the rise of the Seljuks, who in the course of a few years, under such leaders as Toghril Beg, Alp Arslan and Malik Shah, erected the greatest Turkish empire since the sixth century. Their defeat of Mahmud's son Mas'ud at Dandankan near Merv in 1040 delivered Khurasan and Khwarizm into their hands; in 1055 Toghril was called to the aid of the Abbasid Caliph in Baghdad and received the title of King of the East and West; his successor Alp Arslan destroyed the Byzantine army at Manzikert in Armenia in 1071 and opened Asia Minor to Turkish penetration, and under Malik Shah (1072–92) the Seljuk Empire embraced nearly all Muslim Asia. The Ghaznavids retained some fragments of their kingdom, chiefly in India, but the Kara-Khanids were reduced to the status of Seljuk vassals. Their realm had divided into a western and an eastern half; both were distracted by family feuds, and when Malik Shah crossed the Oxus and captured Bukhara and Samarkand, they had no choice but to submit and do homage to the conqueror. By 1092 the power of the Seljuks extended from the Mediterranean to Kashgar. But on the death of Malik Shah the empire broke up; provinces became appanages of members of the ruling family, and the Sultan reigned over a loose federation of principalities. Sanjar, the last Great Seljuk, in a long reign of forty years (1117–57), ruled directly only over eastern Persia, but he was responsible for the defence of Transoxiana, which the Kara-Khanids still governed, however, feebly, as his subordinates. That duty he was, however, unable to discharge, and Transoxiana, during his reign, fell to the Kara-Khitay, a pagan people, and for the first time a Muslim land was lost to the infidel.

In the days when they dominated North China, the Ch'i-tan or Khitay were drawn, perhaps by commercial interest, westwards towards the Tarim Basin with its rim of market oases. When the Ju-chen displaced them at Peking, the more enterprising of their leaders migrated in this same direction, arriving in Kashgaria as early as 1128. Onc group of refugees, under the Yeh-lü Ta-shih, settled at Imil, east of Lake Balkash; the local Kara-Khanid chief, who ruled at Balasaghun, summoned them to his aid against the Karluks; and in a manner drearily familiar, the saviours imposed themselves on the saved. Yeh-lü Ta-shih, assuming the arrogant

title of Gur-Khan, or Lord of the World,[27] set up in eastern
Turkestan the kingdom of the Kara-Khitay, or Black Cathayans.[28]
The heart of his power lay in the region of Kashgar and Issik-
kul; his rule was a centralized absolutism, copied no doubt from
Chinese administrative practice; no fiefs or appanages disrupted
the State and dissipated its authority, and the influence of China
is attested by the fact that all the princes of his dynasty are known
to us only by their Chinese names.[29] The Gur-Khan professed
Buddhism,[30] tolerated Christianity in its Nestorian form, and
perhaps in private performed the rites of his ancestral shamanism.
Having reduced to vassalage the eastern Kara-Khanids, he invaded Transoxiana, whose terrified princes besought the succour
of their Seljuk suzerain Sanjar; but the Sultan was decisively
routed (September 1141) on the field of Katwan; Bukhara and
Samarkand fell to the conquerors; Khwarizm was forced to
submit, and the Oxus became the western boundary of the Kara-
Khitay realm. The advance of Islam into Central Asia was halted;
Turkish power received a severe blow; a Muslim land was occupied and polluted by infidels, and mosques were replaced by
Buddhist temples or Nestorian churches. The news of this heavy
Muslim loss travelled westwards into Latin Christendom, whose
Crusading armies were about to be driven in 1144 from the fortress
of Edessa; a hope was kindled that an ally against the Saracen had
arisen in Asia, and the Gur-Khan, a Buddhist pagan, was subtly
transformed into Prester John, the rich and powerful Christian
priest-king who, legend reported, had advanced as far as the Tigris
with the intention of bringing massive reinforcement to the
Franks of Jerusalem.[31]

The hopes of the Christians were disappointed; Edessa fell, and
the Latin territories in the Levant were confined to a narrow strip
along the Syrian coast. But the Muslims mourned the loss of
Transoxiana; the holy law required that they should fight the
unbelievers and regain the land for Islam; for some years no
champion of the faith was visible, but from the middle of the
twelfth century the devout might see such an avenger in the
Khwarizm-Shahs, who erected a short-lived empire in western
Asia on the eve of the Mongol conquests. The shahs rose by a
familiar progression from governors to kings; the founder of their
house was a servant of the Seljuks; as viceroys of a rich province
they built up a following of soldiers and officials, and Atsiz, the

first of them to win notice and repute, alternately declared himself dependent or independent as the fortunes of his nominal master, Sultan Sanjar, rose and fell. He died in 1156, and the Sultan in the following year, and Atsiz's successor Arslan (1156-72) aspired to fill the vacuum created by the death of the last Great Seljuk. The title 'shah' which they adopted, inherited or retained implied a claim to sovereignty over the lands of ancient Iran, but they were in practice the vassals of the Kara-Khitay, nor could they prudently renounce allegiance to the pagans so long as they were threatened by the Karluks, a tribe of Turkish nomads who roamed the steppes north of the Caspian, and by the Ghurids, who from their mountain strongholds in Afghanistan ruled over the Indus valley and eastern Persia. Yet by adroit diplomacy and successful war they raised themselves from petty dynasts to supreme princes. The Shah Tekish (1172-1200) enforced his hold on Khurasan; in turn he fought and submitted to the Kara-Khitay; he defeated and killed the last Seljuk at Rayy in 1194, and the advance of Khwarizmian power into western Persia alarmed the Caliph Nasir, who in a long reign of more than forty years (1180-1223) worked to restore the temporal lordship of the Abbasids over Irak and Khuzistan. He bade Tekish retire; Tekish demanded that the Caliph relinquish Khuzistan to him and be content with a purely spiritual dominion over the Muslim *umma*. The quarrel had not been pressed to an issue when Tekish died in 1200, leaving his realm and his ambitions to his son Muhammad, who was to experience in twenty years a more dramatic reversal of fortune than most princes of his rank had suffered even in the history of Asia.

Muhammad directed his first efforts to eliminating the power of the Ghurids, which stood between the Khwarizmians and the conquest of Persia and Irak. With the help of his suzerain the Gur-Khan, he destroyed their armies near Balkh in 1204; the capture of Herat in 1206 enabled him to push into the Afghan hills against Ghur itself; the Indian possessions of the enemy were conquered and consigned as a vice-regal domain to his son Jalal ad-Din, and after the fall of Ghazna, the old capital of Mahmud, the last Ghurid sultan was deposed in 1215. Strong enough now to defy his Kara-Khitay masters, Muhammad undertook with some assistance from local Muslim princes, to recover for Islam the lost lands of Transoxiana, but his success owed less to his own valour than to the rise of the Mongol power on the eastern frontiers of the Gur-Khan's dominions. Chingis had just subdued the Naiman, whose chief Küchlüg fled west to the Kara-Khitay kingdom, where he clearly planned to usurp the Gur-Khan's position. The latter was in no condition to defend Transoxiana, which was overrun by the Khwarizmians, but the native Muslims found the rule of their co-religionists harsher than that of the pagans; Samarkand rose in revolt against the Shah in 1212 and was ruthlessly punished by a three days' sack and a general massacre. Küchlüg, now virtually master of the Kara-Khitay realm, began to raid Muhammad's borders; operations against the Kipchak Turks of the steppes were also necessary, and in the summer of 1216 Muhammad found himself in brief conflict with the Mongols themselves, who were pursuing the defeated Merkits to the Kipchak country. The clash was indecisive; the Mongols, led by Chingis's son Jochi, professed to have no quarrel with the Muslims, and withdrew under cover of night. For a brief year or two Muhammad reigned without a rival in Western Asia; the governors and atabegs of the fragments of the defunct Seljuk Empire did homage; Persia submitted to his generals, and his name was pronounced in the *khutba* in distant Oman. Only the Caliph refused to accede to the conqueror's demands, a repetition of those put forward by Muhammad's father Tekish, namely, that Nasir should renounce his temporal power in favour of the Shah and accept a position similar to that held by his predecessors under the Buyids and Seljuks. Muhammad resolved on drastic measures; on the basis of documents found in Ghazna in 1215, he accused the Caliph of inciting the Ghurids against him, and haughtily demanded of his theological advisers if a prince who had fought so valiantly for the Faith had not the right to depose so unworthy an *imam*. They replied submissively in the affirmative; the Shah promptly declared the Caliph dethroned, proclaimed an Alid as Commander of the Faithful, and set his armies on the march to Baghdad. But his advance, in the winter of 1217-18, was held up by heavy snowstorms; a division was cut to pieces by tribesmen in the Kurdish hills, and after this humiliating setback, the campaign was postponed to the next season. By that time, Muhammad was fully entangled with the dreaded Chingis and his kingdom on the verge of ruin; Baghdad was saved, Nasir retained his throne and the allegiance of the Muslim world, and the existence of the Caliphate was prolonged for another forty years.

In the four centuries since the collapse of the first Turkish empire, the face of Asia had changed and perhaps on balance the area and strength of civilization had shrunk. The various branches of the Turkish race had spread over western Asia at the expense of the Iranian peoples, whose language and culture disappeared from the region which now acquired the name of Turkestan. Two civilized states (the T'ang in China, the Samanid kingdom in Transoxiana) disintegrated and fell, and successive waves of barbarians poured through the gap. Yet the superior culture of China and Persia was usually so attractive to the sons of the steppes that the continuity of its life was assured; the Turks as far east as the Altai and Kashgar accepted the faith of Islam and to a limited degree the arts and sciences of the Arabs and Persians, while the Khitay and the Chin speedily aped the dress, the manners and the attitudes of the mandarins of the Middle Kingdom. But the numerous invasions damaged if they did not destroy civilization; the impact of nomadic pastoralists on a settled agrarian society which they despised was commonly unfavourable, the structure of political organization was impaired, and the victorious career of the Mongols may be partly ascribed to the total absence in all the vast area between the Yellow Sea and the plains of Russia of a strong, centralized, civilized state capable of staying their advance.

4

Chingis Khan

Mongolia, which achieved immortal fame as the country of Chingis Khan, had since the expulsion of the Uighurs in the eighth century been peopled almost exclusively by tribes of Mongol speech and primitive manners. They followed the life of hunters and stock-raisers; indeed they had no choice, since the land is, or rather was, unsuited for agriculture or mining. The climate of the high plateau is harsh and continental, and in a year of two seasons, only three months can be truly described as summer. From June to August the steppe is a green carpet of grass and flowers, whose growth is promoted by heavy rains; in September the cold is already severe, in October snowstorms sweep across the land, by November the water courses are frozen, and until the following May snowfalls are frequent and winds blow with such ferocity as almost to lift a rider from his saddle. The height and rarified atmosphere sometimes induce giddiness and exhaustion, and the lack of oxygen often obliges the nomad to desist from his attempts to kindle a fire. The monotony of the steppe is notorious; as far as the eye can travel, it sees little but a flat wilderness, broken by occasional ravines and stony hills where no tree is visible. Beyond the steppe, the land rises into lofty ranges; larches and pines flourish on the mountain slopes, the cedar spreads its branches in the valley hollows, and at a lower level, poplars and willows push out along the river courses.[1]

The aboriginal inhabitants of this forbidding land had long

44

1   Temujin, later Chingis Khan, 1167–1227, with his sons Ögedei and Jochi on the right

2 *above* Chingis Khan seated in the mosque at Bokhara while two
Muslims stand before him surrounded by four Mongol soldiers
below Kubilai Khan crossing a river on a bridge of boats during the
conquest of Southern China

been displaced when the name Mongol is first encountered in the Chinese annals.[2] The true Mongols undoubtedly came from the *taiga*, or Siberian forest, the habitat of such fur-bearing animals as the bear and lynx, the fox and squirrel, since the legends of their race, embodied in the famous *Secret History*[3] put together in the imperial age of conquest, trace their descent from the union of a doe and a he-wolf, who met and mated at the source of the Onon river by the holy mountain of Burkan-Kaldun, the home of the sky-god Kökö-Tengri. The first *human* ancestor of the Mongols, Dobun the Wise, married Alan-Koʻa, a woman from a tribe of forest-dwellers settled along the western shores of Lake Baikal. By her he had two sons, but after his death she produced three further sons, as she told the elder ones, by miraculous impregnation by Tengri; the god entered her tent on a moonbeam, caressed her belly, and a ray of light penetrated her womb. The Mongol bards celebrate this divine bastardy, which may be said to have established an intimate connection between the god and his people, whose conquests were later undertaken at the behest and accomplished to the honour of the Eternal Heaven. As the national saga proceeds from legend to history, it links the affairs of the Mongols with the disturbances that followed the fall of the T'ang and the rise of the Chin and the Ju-chen. A Mongol chief died, leaving a widow and seven sons. Nomolun, the widow and the earliest of the spirited dowagers who from time to time governed the Mongol people, held the tribal *tuk*, a banner decked with yak tails, and fought the Jalair, a tribe who had been driven from the Kerulen valley by the Ju-chen and had encroached on Mongol territory. In this war she and six of her sons perished; the seventh, Nachin, survived along with a nephew Kaidu, then a child, who was concealed under a heap of firewood till the enemy had passed. When Kaidu came of age, the uncle loyally recognized him as chief; he gained fame and following as a warrior, and was the first Mongol to be granted by the Chinese about the year 1150 the title of khan. His grandson Kabul was invited to Peking by the Chin Government, who esteemed him a valuable ally against the Ju-chen; he was showered with gifts and recognized as King of the Mongols. Kabul was succeeded by Ambakay, another grandson of Kaidu's, in whose time the Mongols first came in conflict with the Tatars, a people of kindred stock whose name was destined to be for ever linked and confused with theirs.

The name Tatar is first found on an Orkhon inscription of the year 731.[4] The Tatars were, it seems, a Mongol-speaking people who lived in the vicinity of Lake Buyur, or Buir-Nor, into which flows the Khalka river, and Lake Kolun or Kulun, which receives the waters of the Kerulen. The land around the lakes, where it is not swampy, is semi-desert, but vegetation multiplies as one travels eastwards to the foothills of the Khingan Mountains; high grasses are succeeded by groves of elm and birch, and the peaks, which rise to a height of over 6,000 feet, are covered with forests of larch. Of the early fortunes of the Tatars, nothing is known, but by the eleventh century they were the allies of the Chin against the Ju-chen, and the Peking government was displeased to find them entangled in war with the Mongols. An opportunity arose to read the latter a severe lesson. Ambakay, perhaps sincerely, sought a peace with the Tatars; the reconciliation of the two peoples was to be cemented by a marriage alliance, but as the Mongol khan was escorting his daughter to the Tatar camp, he was ambushed by a group of Tatars from another clan, and conveyed a prisoner to the Chin, who put him horribly to death by impaling him on a wooden ass. His nation swore revenge, but that revenge was not exacted till some fifty years later, when the armies of Chingis entered Peking. Kutula, another son of Kabul's, was elected to succeed Ambakay; the *Secret History* represents him as the Mongol Hercules, with powerful hands like bear-paws and a voice that rolled like thunder through the mountain gorges, and relates with awe that he was capable of devouring a whole sheep at a sitting and emptying at a draught an enormous jar of *kumiz*. He fought with more vigour than success against the Tatars; once, fleeing from an enemy detachment, he plunged into a marsh and hid beneath the reeds, so that only his horse was visible. His pursuers, seeing no man but only the animal, cried scornfully, 'What is a Mongol without his horse?' and rode away. Kutula emerged, and retrieved his horse by pulling it out of the swamp by its mane. His nephew Yesugei captured a Tatar chief named Temujin, a trivial occurrence which would scarcely deserve mention had not the prisoner's name been conferred, in Mongol fashion, on his captor's son, just then born, who was destined to be better known under the title of Chingis Khan. The Tatar war ran its inglorious course; the Chin lent assistance to their allies or vassals; the Mongol tribal confederacy was broken; Kutula died defeated, and so crushed and demoralized was the nation that no khan was appointed to succeed him.

His lot being cast in these dark days of Mongol history, Yesugei never rose above the status of chief of a petty sub-clan, but he made a friend who was to prove in later years an invaluable ally of his house. After the exogamous custom of his race, he married into the Onggirat or Konkitat, a nomadic people who wandered by the shores of Lake Buyur, his wife being kidnapped by him from a Merkit chief who had just married her.[5] Though his following was small, it was sufficiently formidable for his aid to be sought by Toghril, a chief of the Keraits,[6] and a compact the two men made in the Black Wood by the banks of the Tula river may be considered the first of the alliances contracted by the house of Chingis with the Turkish peoples of the Eurasian steppes. 'In token of the service you have rendered me,' declared Toghril, 'my gratitude shall be manifested to your children and your children's children, may heaven and earth be my witness.' Of Yesugei's children, the first was born probably in 1167,[7] the Year of the Pig, on the banks of the Onon, and as prodigies always attend the birth of heroes, tradition narrates that the infant entered the world clutching in his right hand a clot of blood the size of a knucklebone. Three more sons and a daughter were born to Yesugei and his wife Ho'elun, and two sons to an inferior wife or concubine.

The Mongols were accustomed to seek wives for their sons outside the tribe, and betrothals were commonly arranged at an early age. When Temujin was nine years old,[8] his father resolved to marry him into the Onggirat, his wife's clan celebrated for the beauty of its women, whose chief offered him his daughter Borte, a girl of ten, destined to be the mother of emperors. During the betrothal period, the boy remained in the camp of his future father-in-law, and Yesugei, after entrusting his son to the care and protection of the Onggirat, prepared to return home. On the way back, he encountered some Tatars, who recognized their old enemy. Unaware of their identity, Yesugei asked them for a drink, which the vengeful Tatars gave him but mixed with a slow-acting poison. Three days later, he reached his *yurt* mortally sick, and realizing too late what had happened to him, he begged a friend to go to the Onggirat and fetch back Temujin, after making which request he died.

47

Temujin returned to his people, but the wayward Mongols refused to submit to the chieftainship of a boy, and the Taichi'ut clan, which had pretension to the vacant khanate, set the example of revolt. Yesugei's widow strove courageously to stem the tide and rally loyalty to her son, but she was repudiated by Ambakay's widows, excluded from the sacrificial communion, when sacred meats were offered to ancestors, and cast adrift with the seven children in a country where he who would claim no tribal protection almost invariably perished. For months, for years, the little group somehow survived in the harsh region of the upper Onon, living on berries and wild apples from the woods and fish from the streams. In this merciless school Temujin grew to manhood; he made friends with Jamuka, a boy of his own age from another clan whose early career was to be intertwined with his. Ho'elun's brood, reduced to desperate straits, were prone to violent quarrels, in one of which Temujin shot to death his half-brother Bekter, whom he accused of stealing the larks and other small birds they captured in order to keep alive. In time the Taichi'ut chief, a son of Ambakay, learnt with surprise that Temujin was not dead and instituted a rigorous search for a possibly dangerous competitor. The hunted youth fled into the woods, was forced by hunger to emerge after nine days, and was promptly captured; his life was oddly spared, but a *cangue* or wooden collar was placed about his neck and he was dragged around under guard from camp to camp. One night in the midst of a tribal feast, he made off and jumped into a river, where he lay concealed, the *cangue* serving as a buoy to keep him afloat; with the help of a youth from another clan, who removed his *cangue*, he evaded capture and succeeded in rejoining his family. His mother and brothers still eked a miserable existence, but Temujin had gained from his adventures a confidence in his powers, and when their horses were stolen (a loss which might have been fatal to them), he displayed extraordinary skill and courage in recovering them. The doings of this bold and enterprising youth were noised about the camps; such qualities were looked for in a chief or khan, and when Temujin resolved to claim the bride to whom he had long been affianced, the Onggirat raised no objection, and his marriage to Borte gave him a standing in the community. Encouraged by this modest success, he took a step which revealed the political acumen later to be displayed in a world theatre. Seeking out the Kerait chief Toghril, he reminded him he was the *anda* of his father Yesugei, and presented him with a valuable sable-skin coat which had been Borte's dowry. The reminder and the gift were effective; Toghril embraced the young man, solemnly took him under his protection, and with so powerful an ally, Temujin no longer had difficulty in attracting a following.

He acquired this ally at an opportune time. His camp was suddenly raided by a group of Merkits, who carried off Borte, perhaps in revenge for Yesugei's abduction of Ho'elun many years before. The Merkits, a powerful confederacy of three tribes, could put, we are told, 40,000 horsemen into the field. Temujin instantly appealed to Toghril; the Keraits, to the number perhaps of 20,000 men, came to his assistance; Jamuka brought his following to the succour of his *anda*, and the allied forces entered the valley of the Khilok, the Merkit homeland; the enemy were routed and Borte recovered at a place near Ulan Ude, in the present Buriat Soviet republic. But the retrieving of his bride was over-clouded by her pregnancy; whether Temujin or the Merkit chief was the father of her first child was uncertain, and if Jochi, who was born on her return journey to the Mongol camp, was always recognized as Temujin's son, his descendants, who reigned over the Golden Horde in Russia, seem to have been excluded from the succession to the grand khanate, as though his legitimacy were in question.

The victorious campaign against the Merkit, the first campaign in which Temujin participated, might have been expected to cement the union between him and his *anda* Jamuka. Such indeed was the immediate consequence, but within a year or so the friendship was clouded by jealousy and suspicion. As a member of the old royal family, Temujin might hope soon to be offered the khanate, but for the moment Jamuka exercised superior power. The Mongol chronicler avers that one spring, as the two leaders had broken camp and were riding ahead of their horses and flocks, Jamuka remarked that 'if we camp on the hill slope, the herders of horses will get what they want, if we camp by the stream, the shepherds will get their fill of food'. Temujin made no reply, but Borte warned him that Jamuka was seeking to divide the tribe to his own advantage, whereupon Temujin decided to separate forthwith from his colleague and the *Secret History* enumerates the clan who followed him and those who continued with Jamuka. On this *personal* rivalry, two distinguished Russians of the last generation[9] erected a theory of *social* conflict, and depicted Temujin as the chief of a horse-raising aristocracy and Jamuka as the champion of the democratic sheep-raisers. No nomadic tribe is based on a system of complete equality; the captives of war were invariably enslaved, and the strong and the enterprising as always rose to leadership and power as the directors of hired or servile labour. But the distinction between noble and commoner, or as the Mongols expressed it, between white and black *bones* (Yasun), was not a distinction of economic function; entry into the ruling class of *noyans*[10] (lords or masters) was probably dependent on military skill and prowess as much as on birth and descent. That shepherds as such were socially inferior to horse-herders is unproved; that the tribal pastures were held in common and not individually owned need not imply a system of primitive socialism; private wealth in the form of horses and sheep could be accumulated by the clan chiefs and was not resented, and such chiefs would be raised up and followed in so far as they were proved capable of leading the tribe to war and booty.

In a contest for the Mongol leadership, Temujin possessed the double advantage of birth and military prowess; the shamans or sorcerers were granted omens and visions as of a white bull following his wagon and bellowing: 'Heaven and earth have decided that the *ulus* [patrimony] shall be Temujin's!' and the clan chiefs decided that the khanate, so long in abeyance, should be revived in the person of Yesugei's son. At a tribal assembly he was offered the throne, and on accepting was raised on a carpet of felt and proclaimed under the title of Chingis Khan.[11] The khan was by tradition a battle warrior rather than an absolute monarch, but Chingis (as we may now style him) had no mind to exercise a limited authority, and his first step, to create a body-guard (*nököd*)[12] personally devoted and responsible to him, was an earnest of his authoritarian intentions. The break with Jamuka led at first only to a clash between clans of the rival leaders, and Chingis benefited by the brutality and incompetence of his competitor, who alienated sympathy by boiling to death in seventy cauldrons some prisoners he had taken. The misfortunes of his benefactor Toghril also strengthened his position. The Kerait chief was dethroned by a revolt of his kinsmen, and after wandering desolate in the desert of Gobi, he begged for help from Chingis, who perhaps in the year 1197 restored him to his throne. The Chin in Peking, irritated by the rising insolence of the Tatars, sought succour from Toghril and Chingis; their aid was successful, and Toghril, as the senior prince, received the Chinese title of *Wang* or king, and under his new denomination of Wang—or Ong-Khan —he might as a Christian be identified in the far west as Prester John.[13]

In his rise to military celebrity, Chingis was content to act as the loyal subordinate of the Wang-Khan; their joint campaigns against the neighbouring tribes were waged over the vast area of the steppes from the Altai to the Khingan, but their most dangerous opponent was the jealous and unstable Jamuka, who organized a coalition of all the discontented and envious, the Merkits and the Naiman, the Tatars and the Taichi'uts and even Chingis's wife's tribe the Onggirat, against the two allies who aspired to the mastery of nomadic Asia. Not all his fellow Mongols were loyal to Chingis, but his cool skill surmounted all difficulties; furious battles raged amid the rain and snow of a fierce Mongolian winter; the confederate tribes, whose movements were probably ill-co-ordinated, were beaten and dispersed; the Tatars were ruthlessly punished for the slaying of Yesugei by a savage massacre in the foothills of the Khingan in 1202, and Chingis and the Wang-Khan reigned unchallenged over a submissive land.

The mutual loyalty of the two had already been shaken by the conduct of the Wang-Khan, an ageing, feeble and indecisive prince, who on more than one occasion had displayed towards his partner a lack of gratitude, not to say treachery, most unworthy of an *anda*. Chingis dissembled his wrath, till he was stung by the refusal of the Wang-Khan's son to give his daughter to Jochi, a public rebuke and humiliation. A rupture soon came; the rivals prepared to fight for supremacy; the Wang-Khan offered command of his army to Jamuka, who declined the honour; the first clashes were indecisive, but Chingis's forces were temporarily outnumbered, and after despatching a letter of complaint to his former protector in which he addressed him still as 'the Khan, my father', he retired eastwards in the summer of 1203 to the lake or river of Baljuna, the exact location of which is doubtful.[14] Here he was hard-pressed by a superior enemy and forced to practise concealment, and reduced to drinking water pressed out of the mud of the river-bed, but his closest friends and warriors loyally

51

supported him, and in later years, when he was master of Asia, a man who could say he had been with Chingis at Baljuna was assured of high honour. Time was on his side; the coalition constructed against him by the Wang-Khan's son fell to pieces; more and more of the tribes crossed to Chingis's side, and finding himself with a sufficient following, he planned and launched a surprise attack on the Kerait forces which issued in total victory and the flight of the Wang-Khan to the Naiman country, where he was killed by a frontier guard. The Kerait people ceased to enjoy an independent political existence, and were distributed among the Mongol formations, a policy later pursued on a grander scale and calculated to blunt the danger of treachery or revenge on the part of defeated foes.

The fall of the Kerait left only the Naiman to dispute with Chingis the mastery of the steppes. His enemies, including the Merkit people and the ubiquitous Jamuka, all sought shelter in the Naiman camps, and were joined by the Önguts, a Turkish people of Nestorian faith who acted as wardens of the marches for the Chin to the north of the province of Shansi. To prepare for this decisive struggle Chingis summoned a *kuriltai* in the spring of 1204 to plan the campaign. An autumn battle fought near the site of the later Karakorum established the supremacy of the Mongols; after a fierce and hard contest the Naiman were crushed, their king died of wounds, his son Küchlüg fled westwards to the Kara-Khitay, and Jamuka, who had set first the Keraits and then the Naiman against his former *anda*, was captured and put to death. The remnant of the Merkits were subdued by Sübedei, who was to become the most brilliant of Chingis's commanders, and enrolled in the Mongol army; and Chingis, who now reigned unchallenged from the Altai to the Khingan, was proclaimed supreme khan of 'all who dwell in tents of felt' at a *kuriltai* on the banks of the Onon in 1206, from which his imperial rule is commonly dated.

The authority of Chingis was now securely based on his personal prowess in war, his hereditary descent from the ancient khans of Mongolia, and an invincible success which betokened to the people the benign approval of heaven. Chingis possessed the full nomad measure of piety or superstition; his devotion to the gods and spirits was exemplary, and he never embarked on a campaign without seeking a personal and private communion with

Tengri, whose approval was necessary before the army marched. But as the mightiest prince could commonly learn the will of heaven only through the intermediary of the *shamans*, an unusual degree of power was concentrated in the hands of this primitive clergy, and at the *kuriltai* of 1206 a certain Kokchu, whose father Monglik had once advised Yesugei and married his widow, rode to heaven on a grey horse and returning, informed the assembly that Tengri had consecrated Chingis as universal ruler. Such divine succour, guaranteed from such a source, was doubtless welcome, but Kokchu unwisely presumed on his power, sought to dominate Chingis and set his brothers against him, and expected to usurp a position of influence in the new Mongol government. Chingis was perhaps unaware of his schemes, but Borte warned her husband of the implications, and the new khan, once convinced of a novel and dangerous challenge to his authority and the unity of the ruling family, took ruthless action. As Kokchu emerged from Chingis's tent, he was seized by the guard and his back was broken, a mode of execution common among the Mongols, who were averse to the shedding of human blood on the ground. The fate of the *shaman* terrified the people; it perhaps diminished the fanatical veneration in which these magicians or holy men were held, and it certainly confirmed the unlimited autocracy of Chingis, whose realm was never distracted by conflicts between Church and State.

Once Mongolia was at his feet and the Turco-Mongol peoples had all submitted to his rule, Chingis ventured to strike at the sedentary societies beyond the steppe and desert and the Great Wall, and unlike the earlier barbarian leaders, his aim was conquest rather than simple plunder. Of the three kingdoms into which China was divided, that of the Hsi-Hsia, Tibetan in race and Buddhist in religion, was the smallest and weakest; Chingis, though as yet without the capability of besieging fortified towns, ravaged the open countryside so destructively as to force his enemy to seek terms and acknowledge his suzerainty, and the discomfiture of the Tanguts gave him control of the routes linking China to the west and enabled him to attack his real enemy the Chin from the west as well as the north. The breach with the Chin, the traditional foes of the Mongols, was a natural development. Chingis received an embassy from Peking notifying him of the accession of a new sovereign, upon which as a vassal he was expected to kow-tow before the envoys. Instead, he cried: 'Is such an imbecile worthy of the throne and shall I abase myself before him?' and prepared for war, after calling on God to recognize the justice of his cause and avenge the blood of his uncle Ambakay. As usual, he did not move until he was satisfied that the political and diplomatic situation was favourable to him. The Önguts, a Turkish people who guarded the northern frontiers of the Chin empire, were won over to his side, and could be relied on to open the way for the Mongols into the heart of China, and the Ch'i-tan who were of Mongol speech and race, eagerly grasped at the opportunity to revenge themselves on their supplanters in Peking. The campaign against the Chin assumed the character of a national or race war, in which the Turco-Mongol peoples of the north were united against the Tungus-speaking occupants of the northern provinces of China.[15]

The struggle thus opened in 1211 was to continue for twenty-three years, and ended only in 1234, after Chingis's death, with the total destruction of the Chin régime. It began with a series of raids deep into the country south of the Great Wall; a more systematic plan of conquest was then devised, with three armies advancing into Hopei and Liao-ning, and when Peking was threatened, the Chin court decamped southwards to K'ai-feng. This desertion doubtless discouraged the defenders; Chingis had by now enrolled a corps of engineers skilled in siegecraft; Peking was closely blockaded, the governor committed suicide, the walls were breached, and the Mongol army poured into the northern capital (1215).[16] The palaces and public buildings were looted and burnt; many of the inhabitants were massacred; the fate of Ambakay was avenged, and the first out of many civilized capitals felt the savage fury of uncivilized nomads who feared and hated a way of life they could not understand. Thereafter, the war languished; Chingis was drawn away to the west in the campaigns against the Kara-Khitay and the Khwarizmians; the Chin recovered some of the lost territory, and the conflict degenerated into a tedious war of sieges, in which engineers of alien birth were more prized than the native Mongol archers.

The conquest of China was interrupted by developments in Central Asia of which Chingis was obliged to take cognizance lest his own position be undermined. Küchlüg, the ex-king of the Naiman, had taken refuge among the Kara-Khitay, the sinized

Mongol aristocracy imposed on the Muslim Turkish peoples of the Altaic steppes who had established their centre at Balasaghun, west of Lake Issik-kul. Under the last of their *yeh-lü*, the Gur-Khan Chi-lu-ku (1178–1211), their power had decayed and their vassals, the Uighurs and the Karluks, had renounced their authority and turned their faces towards the rising sun of Chingis Khan. Küchlüg, a treacherous and incompetent prince, overthrew and supplanted his benefactor the Gur-Khan, who died his captive in 1213, but his rule disgusted his subjects; he provoked a rising in Kashgaria, where he persecuted the Muslims, in Khotan he executed the leading *imam* on a charge of disloyalty, and the prince of Ili was put to death for transferring his allegiance to Chingis. The Mongol chief could scarcely ignore the activities of his old enemy, now in possession of a substantial kingdom, but appeals from his oppressed subjects provided an excuse for intervention. Jebe was sent with 20,000 men against Küchlüg; Balasaghun fell without resistance, the Muslims everywhere welcomed the Mongols as liberators; Küchlüg fled to the Pamir country,[17] where he was killed in 1218, and the former realm of the Kara-Khitay was added to the Mongol empire.

The fall of the Kara-Khitay brought the western boundary of Chingis's realm to the dominions of Muhammad Shah, the ambitious and haughty prince of Khwarizm. Towards this kingdom the Mongol chief at first cherished no hostile intent: indeed he despatched an embassy to Muhammad, proposing that commercial contacts between them could be pursued to their mutual advantage. But the shrewd and clever stratagems of Chingis were becoming widely known, and it was suspected that spies and secret agents were often concealed under the guise of harmless merchants. A Mongol mission, ostensibly concerned only with trade, reached the frontier post of Utrar on the Sir-Darya in 1218; the Khwarizmian Governor, convinced that its purpose was merely to report on the military strength of the kingdom, seized its goods and executed its members, who numbered among them a Mongol diplomatic envoy. Chingis furiously demanded reparation, and on being refused, declared war. For the first time the Mongol military machine was set in motion against a Muslim state,[18] and rivers of blood were destined to flow before Islam, after suffering the most grievous hurts, at last tamed and converted these ferocious pagans.

In this terrible war,[19] in which more lives were lost probably than in any similar conflict of such duration (a mere three years), the advantages once again were wholly on the side of the Mongols. The outrage at Utrar, which involved the slaying of an ambassador, enabled Chingis to appear not as an aggressor but as a redresser of a grievous wrong. His new enemy was powerful only in appearance. The Khwarizmian kingdom was a loose and flimsy structure; the Turkish ruling class was disliked and despised by the Persian subject population; the army was recruited from mercenaries, whose loyalty rarely survived a defeat; the people were oppressed by heavy taxation and the devout were disturbed by the quarrel with the Caliph, and the Sultan, vain, frivolous and incompetent, was neither a statesman nor a soldier, and his soaring ambition to reign as the Great Seljuks had reigned, the leading sovereign of Islam, was belied by his clear unfitness for the role. To him must be ascribed much of the blame for the hideous calamities which fell on the urban centres of eastern Iran. The cold and deliberate genocide practised by the Mongols, which has no parallel save that of the ancient Assyrians and the modern Nazis, perhaps arose from the mixed motives of military advantage and superstitious fears. The Mongols were unaccustomed to fighting in settled and thickly populated lands; however skilled they became in siegecraft, the reduction of fortified places was costly and laborious; as nomads roaming the steppes, they despised the inhabitants of cities and felt constrained and imprisoned within their walls, and by terrorizing the people by massacres they might hasten the surrender of the next town and facilitate the rapid conquest of the region. Yet their material interest was never lost sight of. From the thousands of defenceless civilians who perished at their hands, they always selected a number of useful craftsmen, artisans and engineers who were deported into the heart of the empire and spared to work for their masters. However merciless their rage for destruction, they commonly permitted, after a decent interval, the rebuilding of the cities they had burnt and ruined, since they were satisfied that ruins produced no revenue and that a flourishing trade and manufacture was a source of wealth and prosperity to them.

Chingis prepared for this new conflict with his usual cool deliberation. In the spring of 1219, in the upper Irtish valley, an army was assembled, which, including the Uighurs and Karluks who were now numbered among the Mongol auxiliaries, reached the figure of nearly 200,000 men. The Khwarizmian forces were superior, but as Muhammad distrusted their loyalty, he refused to risk pitched battles in open country and dispersed his troops in garrisons in the principal cities of his empire, trusting to Mongol inability to besiege and capture walled strongholds. The Muslims, says Barthold, displayed much heroism, but all discipline and organization was on the Mongol side. Hostilities opened with the siege of Utrar, the scene of the outrage which had precipitated the war. Two of Chingis's sons, Chagatai and Ögedei, were given charge of this operation; another division under Jochi descended the Sir-Darya to besiege Khojend, while Chingis himself, with his younger son Tolui, made for Bukhara, the richest and most populous city of Transoxiana. The Turkish garrison tried to break out, the citizens surrendered (February 1220), the buildings were systematically pillaged, but the burning of mosques and palaces may have been involuntary and no general massacre was perpetuated. The Persian historian Juvaini narrates that Chingis entered the pulpit of the principal mosque and delivered a political sermon or admonition to the terrified crowd, in which he declared he was 'the flail of God' sent to punish them for their sins.[20] From Bukhara he proceeded to Samarkand, where he was joined by Chagatai and Ögedei who had captured Utrar and punished the perfidious governor by pouring molten gold down his throat. Prisoners taken at Bukhara were driven before them in battle formation so as to give the impression of a vast army. In five days (March 1220) Samarkand capitulated; the inhabitants were ordered to evacuate the city, which was more easily plundered in their absence; the Turkish garrison was put to the sword, the artisans to the number of 30,000 were deported to Mongolia and the clergy were spared, but a great deal of indiscriminate killing went on and only one quarter of the place was reoccupied when the survivors were permitted to return.

Terrified by the avalanche of destruction falling on his kingdom, Sultan Muhammad fled westwards in the hope of raising new armies in Persian Irak, despite the dissuasions of his courageous son Jalal ad-Din,[21] who represented to him that such conduct would appear cowardly desertion in the eyes of his suffering people. Chingis gave orders to Jebe and Sübedei, two of his most valiant captains, to pursue the hapless sovereign from town to town and from province to province; the Mongol cavalry chased him through Tus (where Sübedei burnt the tomb of Harun

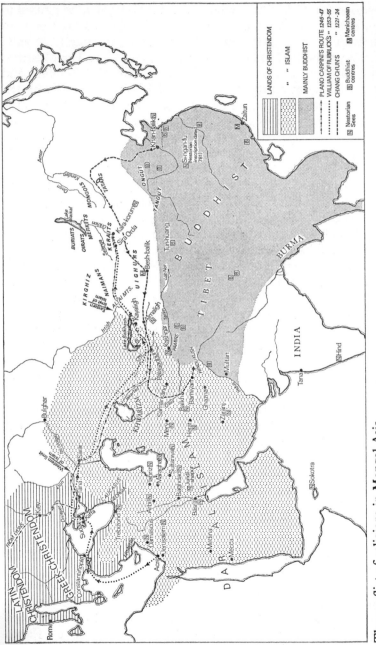

The conflict of religions in Mongol Asia

al-Rashid) and Rayy to Hamadan, where contact was lost, the fugitive managing to reach the shores of the Caspian at Abaskum, near which was a small island where he found (December 1220) asylum and death. The pursuers, doubtless encouraged by this victorious parade through a demoralized and almost defenceless kingdom,[22] continued their advance until they had accomplished a feat never before attempted and rarely imitated since. Riding north-wards into Azerbaijan, whose lush pastures attracted every nomad invader, they thrust their way into the Christian kingdom of Georgia, whose army was broken before Tiflis (February 1221),[23] and after ruining the town of Maragha,[24] they turned back to punish a revolt of Hamadan by the total annihilation of the place and its people. Threading their way through the pass of Derbend,[25] they came out on to the steppes north of the Caucasus, to be con-fronted with a coalition of Alans,[26] Cherkes[27] and Kipchak Turks[28] who sought to bar their approach to the Russian plains. By cunningly pleading Turco-Mongol solidarity, they detached the Kipchaks from this alliance, whose forces they easily routed; the princes of Russia, who laboriously assembled an ill-organized and heterogeneous army, were crushed (May 1222) in the battle of the Kalka,[29] a small river flowing into the Sea of Azov, and after sacking Sudak, a Genoese trading post in the Crimea,[30] they advanced up the Volga to chastise the Muslim Bulghars and the Kangli Turks, and rounding the northern shores of the Caspian, rejoined Chingis and his main army on the steppes beyond the Jaxartes. This astonishing raid, which defeated twenty nations and achieved a complete circuit of the Caspian, produced no immediate political consequences, but set a precedent for the invasion of eastern Europe nearly twenty years later.

Meanwhile Chingis proceeded with the methodical destruction of the Khwarizmian kingdom. Before moving south of the Oxus into Khurasan, he resolved to subdue the homeland of the shahs, the fertile region to the south of the Aral Sea which had for its defen-sive centre the city and fortress of Gurganj.[31] His three sons, Jochi, Chagatai and Ögedei were placed in charge of its siege, and the Mongols, finding a dearth of stones for projectiles, cut down whole groves of mulberry trees, soaked the trunks in water to harden them, and employed them in their siege engines to batter down the walls. The siege was laboriously prolonged for seven months (October 1220–April 1221); the attackers suffered heavy losses,

59

and some blame for this probably attaches to a quarrel between Jochi and Chagatai which forced Chingis to intervene and place them both under the command of Ögedei. When Gurganj finally fell, the Mongols broke the dams and flooded the town, enslaved the women and children, deported the artisans to the number, it is said, of 100,000, and slew the rest. Gurganj was completely ruined, but a new city later arose near its site and received the name of Urgend; the dams were never repaired (perhaps no one could repair them), and the Oxus, having been diverted from its normal course, flowed into the Caspian for 300 years.[32]

Even before Gurganj had fallen, Chingis with his main army had crossed the Oxus and advanced into the rich and populous province of Khurasan. The main forces of the Khwarizmians had been almost destroyed; the defence of the remnant of the kingdom rested on the garrison of the towns, and the fearful massacres which accompanied the progress of the Mongols through eastern Persia were doubtless intended to speed the surrender of these places and save the attackers long and laborious siegework. Not that prompt capitulation always averted the wholesale killing of the civilian population: if the Mongols were provoked by some special circumstances, such as the death in action of one of their leaders, the entire town was likely to suffer fearful retribution. Tirmidh was the first place to be taken and destroyed south of the Oxus, and the chroniclers tell a grim story of how a woman, hoping to be spared, cried out that she had swallowed a pearl, but the merciless butchers merely ripped open her belly and extracted it, and Chingis gave orders that all corpses should be disembowelled lest such treasures should be similarly secreted.[33] Balkh was taken next and spared for the time. Merv fell in February 1221 to Tolui, who butchered 700,000 persons, says the contemporary chronicler Ibn al-Athir,[34] and only eighty craftsmen were spared; Sanjar's tomb was burnt, and a small clan of nomad Turks, who grazed their flocks on the pastures just outside Merv, fled westwards through Irak into Asia Minor, where they were granted asylum by the Seljuk princes there and became the progenitors of the Ottoman Turks.[35] Nishapur was next marked out for vengeance, in particular because the previous year, when Sübedei and Jebe were pursuing the shah, Chingis's son-in-law Tokuchar had been killed by an arrow from its walls. It could therefore expect no mercy and received none. Taken by assault by Tolui in April 1221,

3 Ögedei Khan seated with his two sons Küyük and Kadan

4 Portrait of Ögedei Khan in the Imperial Portrait Gallery, Peking

it was the scene of a carnival of blood scarcely surpassed even in Mongol annals. Tokuchar's widow presided over the butchery; separate piles of heads of men, women and children were built into pyramids, and even the cats and dogs were killed in the streets.[36] Herat, whose citizens opened the gates to the enemy, was strangely spared, but Bamiyan,[37] in the Hindu Kush, where Chingis's favourite grandson was killed, suffered the fate of Merv. Muhammad's son, Jalal ad-Din, had broken through the Mongol lines and reached Ghazna, where he was striving desperately to raise fresh armies, hampered by the general terror inspired by the Mongols and the jealous quarrels of Turks and Ghurids,[38] on whose joint support he depended. He actually succeeded in routing a Mongol detachment at Parwan near Kabul in Afghanistan,[39] an event which raised many false hopes and led to fatal uprisings against Mongol rule in Merv, Herat and elsewhere in the autumn of 1221. This reverse, the only one suffered by the Mongols in the whole campaign, brought Chingis to the scene; he inspected the site, reprimanded his generals for tactical errors, and marched against Jalal, who retired eastwards to the banks of the Indus. Here was fought (November 1221) the battle which concluded the campaign. Jalal and his paladins performed prodigies of valour, but Mongol discipline and organization prevailed; the presence of Chingis was worth several divisions; when defeat was conceded, the young prince, throwing off his armour, rode his horse into the river and reached the further side, under the admiring gaze of Chingis himself.[40] No pursuit on to Indian territory was attempted; a Mongol patrol penetrated as far as Multan, but the heats of India were too much for these sons of the chilly steppes, who turned aside to inflict condign punishment on those rebels who had dared to rise in arms against them on the morrow of Parwan. Herat was levelled to the ground, after a full week had been devoted to the killing of the inhabitants[41] and the few thousand who had survived at Merv were put to the sword. The stench of death hung over the stricken land.[42]

No attempt was made by Chingis to consolidate Mongol rule in Khurasan or to invade Persian Irak, or to prepare for a possible return from India of Jalal ad-Din, who might in the wake of a Mongol retreat attempt to rebuild his father's kingdom. Chingis might feel that the fearful punishment he had inflicted would leave the region prostrate for many a year, and he may also have deemed unwise a longer absence from Mongolia and China, where his lieutenants were still pursuing the war against the Chin. When military operations ceased after the battle of the Indus, he retired to the pastures south of the Hindu Kush, where he received in May 1222 a visit from the Chinese Taoist sage Ch'ang Ch'un, whom he had summoned to his presence to discuss the philosopher's stone and the problem of immortality.[43] Mellowed perhaps by these philosophical conversations, the conqueror returned to Transoxiana in the autumn of 1222 and at Bukhara required some learned doctors to expound to him the faith of Islam. He listened with interest to their exposition, approved the rites and dogmas of the religion of Muhammad, with one exception: he deplored the annual pilgrimage to Mecca, observing that the whole world and not a single building was the house of God.[44] At Samarkand, where he passed the winter of 1222–3, he ordered the imams to pray for him in the mosques in place of the Khwarizmian prince and exempted the 'clergy', that is, the imams and kadis, from all taxation, a concession confirmed by his successors and erected into a general rule for the ministers of all religions. In the spring of 1223 he crossed the Jaxartes and passed a leisurely year or two, hunting animals instead of men in the steppes of western Turkestan where he received Jebe and Sübedei on their completion of the circuit of the Caspian. Only in the spring of 1225 did he set out to return to Mongolia.

After this rest from carnage, the conqueror, before whom all Asia now trembled, found fresh scope for military activity when he returned home after an absence of six years. In China, the Chin were far from subdued, and Mukali, the Mongol general left in command, had died without completing the conquest. The Tangut kingdom of Hsi-Hsia had proved a refractory vassal: when Chingis demanded troops from it for the Khwarizmian war, a Tangut official scornfully observed that if the Mongol leader had not enough soldiers, he had no right to claim the sovereign power.[45] Such an insult must be avenged, and at the close of 1226 Chingis took the field and laid siege to Ning-hsia, the Tangut capital. In the open country, he displayed the same barbarity which had turned eastern Persia into a charnel-house, and the Chinese history mournfully speaks of fields piled with human bones.[46] The last months of Chingis's life (he was now sixty) were darkened by troubles with his eldest son Jochi, who had stayed behind to enjoy his appanage in the Kipchak territory, and the chronicles hint darkly of plots against his father's life. In February 1227 Jochi suddenly died there, at the age of forty or thereabouts, and the succession was doubtless bestowed shortly afterwards on Ögedei, the conqueror's second and favourite son.[47] Chingis did not long survive him. He died in the district of Ch'ung-shui in Kansu province on 25 August 1227;[48] Ning-hsia did not fall till after his death, and in accordance with his wishes, the entire population was put to the sword. His body was conveyed with great funeral pomp to the holy mountain of Burkan Kaldun, at the sources of the Onon and Kerulen rivers in Mongolia, where it was buried at a secret spot, and where in 1229 great sacrifices were held by Ögedei and forty slave-girls and as many horses were despatched to join their master in the next world.[49]

The personal appearance of Chingis is brought but dimly before us by the Persian historian Juzjani, who describes him as 'a man of tall stature, of vigorous build, robust in body, the hair on his face scanty and turned white, with cat's eyes, possessed of great energy, discernment, genius and understanding, awe-inspiring, a butcher, just, resolute, an overthrower of enemies, intrepid, sanguinary and cruel'.[50] This curious catalogue of physical and moral qualities is typical of the mixture of fear and hate and grudging admiration with which the Islamic world regarded the 'accursed one' who had inflicted such dreadful injuries upon it. At a distance of over seven centuries we may judge more objectively this Alexander of barbarism, the nomad who wreaked vengeance on civilization, yet in his best moments rose far above pure destructiveness. I shall first consider his achievement in his double capacity of (1) soldier; (2) administrator.

(1) As the first general of his age, Chingis's ability consisted, not in startling innovations, but in the uncanny power he showed in adapting and improving existing practices. His armies were divided into units of ten, from divisions of 10,000 men to brigades of 1000, companies of 100, and platoons of ten. This decimal system was familiar to the Turks and Mongols, and had hitherto been bound up with the old tribe and clan order; Chingis broke this up, and created new units made up of mixed races and tribes. The army[51] consisted essentially of a cavalry force and a corps of engineers: infantry was hardly ever used, since a nomad fighter without a horse was unthinkable. The heavy cavalry wore armour

63

and was armed with sword and lance: the light cavalry wore no armour and used bow and javelin. The bow was the deadliest and most accurate of Mongol weapons. It was extremely heavy, with a pull of 160 pounds and had a range of from 200 to 300 yards. Each archer carried two or three bows, three quivers, and files for sharpening arrow-heads, which when dipped in redhot brine could pierce armour. The Mongol soldier was well clad to withstand the intense cold of the steppe: in winter he wore a fur cap and coat and heavy leather boots. His food was mostly *yogurt* (curdled milk) or *kumiz* (fermented mare's milk), and a bag of millet meal would last him for days. In addition to his arms, he carried his iron rations, a camp-kettle, and a waterproof pouch with a change of clothing for crossing swamps and rivers. At reviews, the troops' kit was rigorously inspected, and those whose equipment was found deficient were severely punished.

The Mongol battle formation took the form of two ranks of heavy armoured cavalry in front, with three ranks of armourless mounted archers behind. The latter, moving forward through the intervals of the front ranks, poured forth a devastating fire and then withdrew, whereupon the heavy cavalry charged the demoralized enemy off the field. The Mongol horse was small and wiry and perfectly trained and disciplined; it could travel at ten miles an hour, and a short but solidly built stirrup enabled the rider to direct his fire with precision while moving rapidly across country. Chingis, like all outstanding nomad chiefs, understood the value of the medieval equivalent of mechanized warfare, but he alone brought it to the highest pitch of skill. In the days before gunpowder, the walls of fortified places were broken down with stones and other missiles discharged by giant catapults, and various inflammable compounds, usually including naphtha and saltpetre, were poured from tubes or cylinders to set fire to the defences. Under Chingis's orders, his officers sorted out from among their prisoners all artisans, skilled workers and anyone with a pretence to technical knowledge, and drafted them into the engineering corps of the army. Captives whose lives were of no value were employed to fill in moats and put siege-engines and battering rams in position: it did not matter how many of these were killed by arrow fire from the city walls.

Not least among the causes of Chingis's success was his care of maintaining the communications of his expanding empire and his excellent intelligence service. Along the main roads was constructed a series of *yams* or post-houses, each of which was kept provided with food, drink, horses and other supplies.[52] Envoys and messengers arriving at a *yam* showed their passes and were given a meal, rest and fresh mounts to proceed on their journey. Chingis never embarked on a campaign till he had gathered every piece of information he could concerning the size, strength, resources and morale of the enemy. Spies often travelled in merchant caravans, picking up gossip in the bazaars and markets, and relayed what they learnt back to the Khan's camp. Even apparently peaceful trading missions for the Mongols were viewed with alarm and suspicion by foreign princes, and the caravan whose members were killed at Utrar in 1219 may well have contained secret agents sent to spy out the condition of the Khwarizmian defences.

Chingis was an adept at psychological warfare of the most horrific kind. He deliberately set out to create a reputation for ferocious terror, in the expectation (often realized) of frightening whole nations into surrendering without resistance. There is something indescribably revolting in the cold savagery with which the Mongols carried out their massacres. The inhabitants of a doomed town were obliged to assemble in a plain outside the walls, and each Mongol trooper, armed with a battle-axe, was told to kill so many people, ten, twenty or fifty. As proof that orders had been properly obeyed, the killers were sometimes required to cut off an ear from each victim, collect the ears in sacks, and bring them to their officers to be counted.[53] A few days after the massacre, troops were sent back into the ruined city to search for any poor wretches who might be hiding in holes or cellars; these were dragged out and slain. Some modern critics have suggested several reasons for this bloody policy; that the nomads feared and hated walled cities and on taking possession of them were seized with a kind of frenzy of destruction, or that the killings were intended to prevent revolts in the rear as the Mongol army passed on, or that Chingis and his successors, being convinced of their divine mission to conquer the world, treated resistance as an unforgivable crime against God and the Khan. But it is more probable that terror was erected into a system of government to spread fear and panic and demoralize their enemies before a shot had been fired against them.[54]

So impressive were Chingis's victories that his campaigns have been critically studied by modern military planners.[55] Hitler may have owed something to him, for the blitzkrieg and the deep drives into the enemy's defences and the trapping of whole armies, as in the 'Barbarossa' campaign against Russia in 1941, are strongly reminiscent of Mongol strategy and tactics. But in many ways the Mongol was cleverer than the Nazi. Hitler took insufficient pains to acquaint himself with the strength and resources of the enemy and provoked a worldwide coalition against him. Chingis's foes were never able to combine against him, partly because owing to his control of the interior lines of Central Asia, they could make no contact with one another, so that China, for example, could not ally with Persia or Russia.

(2) Chingis not only created an empire: he organized it so well that it went on expanding for fifty years after his death. Clearly he was something more than a talented warrior chief: he was also an outstanding civil administrator. This was a surprising achievement for a man of his background. He was an unlettered nomad, who despised farming and hated towns, and viewed settled, civilized lands only as sources of loot and plunder. The free roaming life of the limitless steppes was the only life he knew or wanted: for peasants and workers he had only contempt, the toil they engaged in was fit only for slaves. The Mongols were, after all, remote from the centres of civilized life, and were almost untouched by cultural or religious influences from the cities of eastern and southern Asia. They had no permanent dwellings, no towns or villages, no writing and no manufactures. With an able warrior to lead them, it was no great task to subdue other nomadic or semi-nomadic tribes (this had been done before, by the Huns and Turks among others), but how could an illiterate, barbarous people conquer and hold ancient civilized states? Chingis was intelligent enough to see the value of things outside his normal experiences; like Peter the Great centuries later he realized how backward his people were, and though caring nothing for the arts of civilized existence, he was intensely interested in the technical 'know-how' of defence, in whatever could improve military efficiency, and in how the lands he conquered could be made to yield higher revenues. His own Mongols could not help him: hence he enlisted the services of advisers and officials from more advanced societies. He was wholly devoid of race prejudice; his

ministers and commanders were recruited from twenty different nations, and there was a general pooling of military and administrative experience which enriched and strengthened his empire.

His first step was to reduce the Mongol language to writing. Like most barbarians, he was impressed by the art of writing, which seemed so permanent, so magical; he marvelled at the facility with which these strange signs could be read and interpreted, and resolved that his own tongue must be written down, so that his laws and decrees could be published in it. Among the prisoners taken by Chingis in his early campaigns was an Uighur named T'a-t'a-t'ong-a,[56] who had been secretary to a local chief; the Khan showed great interest in his documents and seals, and asked him to teach the Mongol princes to write their language in the Uighur script.[57] From this time onwards the Mongol chancery issued all its edicts in the script which the Turks had spread over Central Asia.[58]

Even more useful as a counsellor was Yeh-lü Ch'u-ts'ai,[59] a member, as his title implies, of the imperial family of Liao, who was twenty-five when Peking was taken by the Mongols in 1215 and whose outstanding abilities commended him to the conqueror, who took him into his service and carried him with him on his western campaign of 1219–25. A typical scholar-mandarin, he gained great influence over Chingis and taught him how to organize a civil service; he doubtless reasoned that by serving the Mongols, he might be better able to protect his countrymen from their excesses. Once, when a Chinese province had been subjugated, one of Chingis's generals observed that the Chinese peasants were of small value as fighting-men and might as well be killed off and their fields turned into pastures for the Mongol horses. Ch'u-ts'ai, hearing of this, knew it would be useless to appeal to the Khan's humanity to avert the threatened massacre: Chingis would be impressed only by practical arguments of a material kind. He pointed out, with great skill and eloquence, that if he were allowed to organize the province as had been done in the past, land-tax and customs-dues would produce every year 500,000 ounces of silver, 80,000 pieces of silk, and 400,000 sacks of grain. Chingis thought this an excellent idea: Ch'u-ts'ai was commissioned to set the old administrative and revenue system going; nothing more was heard of the 'farms into pastures' plan, and the population was saved. It was Ch'u-ts'ai who organized the *yam* system, set up training schools for officials, fixed the State budget, improved the tax yield, suppressed brigandage, built grain stores, and revived on a bigger scale the old Chinese device of paper money. In short, he applied the traditional techniques of Chinese government administration to the expanding Mongol empire, and Chingis seems to have given him more or less a free hand.

Two further traits strengthen Chingis's claim to statesmanship: his policy of religious toleration and his encouragement of international trade.

(1) In his day, the Mongols were untouched by any of the higher religions; they were shamanists, as all the steppe people had once been, with a vague belief in a sky-god *Tengri*, 'eternal Heaven'; they had no temples or organized worship; they sacrificed animals, chiefly horses, at stone cairns, and they paid reverent regard to their *shamans*, holy men whose principal function was to keep in touch with the spirits of their departed ancestors and see that no evil from them befell the tribe. Chingis was firmly convinced that his God had made the Mongols his chosen people and given them a divine commission to conquer the earth: Mongol proclamations were issued in the name of *Tengri* and the Khan, their victories were piously ascribed not to themselves but God. Yet Chingis showed no disposition to force his faith on others. On the contrary, he granted full freedom to all faiths; Christians, Muslims, Jews, Buddhists, all acquired perfect liberty to worship as they pleased and to propagate their tenets anywhere in the Mongol realm provided they did not encroach on the freedom of others. Never had the continent of Asia enjoyed so complete a liberty of conscience, never had it been filled with so many ardent missionaries seeking to push their doctrines. Thus the clergy of all the competing religions tended to preach loyalty to the Mongols, a circumstance which helped to perpetuate their rule.

(2) Chingis was fully aware of the value of international trade, both from the revenue it brought to the Mongol treasury and its role in binding together in a close economic network the many different regions won by the Mongol sword. The Mongols in their homeland in pre-conquest days traded but little; mostly buying arms, clothes and metal goods from the Chinese in exchange for furs and skins. But as Chingis's empire spread and he learnt from men like Ch'u-ts'ai how big a revenue customs

duties could bring to the State, everything was done to encourage a brisk commercial traffic: the roads were policed, post-houses established, caravans given armed protection, thieves and robbers put down; the peasants tilling their fields in the fertile oases of Central Asia were guarded against the old curse of peaceful cultivators, raids by nomadic tribesmen. Mongol military power, perhaps we may add Mongol terror, made the highways of Asia safer than they had ever been. Companies of merchants who entered partnership with a prince who provided the capital[60] were given extensive rights and privileges, including exemption from direct taxation, and they journeyed regularly to and fro across the continent from China to Persia and beyond. Such men must have blessed the *Pax Mongolica*, the peace and security the conquerors brought to lands usually torn by war and invasion. When a region was subjugated, Chingis took care to put its economy on a new footing; the ruined cities were rebuilt, and the trading classes encouraged to resume their operation under the protection of the Mongol Army.[61] Profits must have been high, and the influential moneyed men were long among the strongest props of the Mongol Empire.

Chingis aspired to be the lawgiver of his people; at some unknown date subsequent on his assumption of the supreme khanate, he promulgated a code known as the *Yasa*,[62] of which no complete text has come down to us, though we know enough of its contents from the copious extracts given by the chroniclers[63] to get a fair idea of its scope and spirit. It was a curious mixture of enlightenment and superstition: it enacted religious toleration, exempted the clergy of all faiths from taxation, forbade washing or urinating in running water (flowing streams and rivers were held to be 'alive' and sacred and were not to be polluted), and prescribed the death penalty for spying and desertion, theft and adultery, the killing of animals in Muslim fashion, and in the case of a merchant, a third bankruptcy! Copies of the code in Uighur script were traced out on great sheets of parchment, and kept in the treasuries of the Mongol princes, to be taken out and consulted as the need arose. The same princes were permitted to issue *yarliks* or decrees in their own domains, but these were never to conflict with the *Yasa*. From a superstitious belief that it contained the secret of the Mongol's success, the *Yasa* attained a wide currency and was adopted in a modified form as far away as Mamluk Egypt.[64]

As administrator and lawgiver, Chingis rose above any other nomad chief known to history, and his fame rests upon this as much as upon his brilliant gifts as a soldier. For the rivers of blood he shed, no forgiveness is possible: the fearful destruction of civilian life in eastern Iran was far worse than anything Attila did in Europe, and he lives in the Muslim chroniclers as the Evil or Accursed One. Yet this man, so contemptuous of human life, was not destitute of finer qualities: he was cool and sensible in his judgments and loyal and faithful to friends and dependants and those who had once rendered service to him.[65] He had a horror of traitors, and often rewarded those who had stood loyally by his enemies. He was receptive to new ideas, dimly grasped some of the merits of civilization,[66] and his imperial ordinances promoted a mingling of cultures such as had never before been seen in Asia.

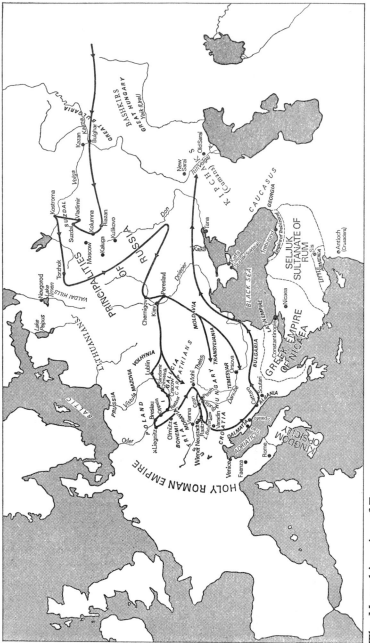

The Mongol invasion of Europe 1237–42

5

The Mongol drive into Europe

According to the custom or tradition of the Mongols, the land under their control belonged to the family from whom they had selected their *khan* rather than to an individual sovereign. They were unfamiliar with the idea of a territorial state or the law of primogeniture; the youngest son commonly inherited the patrimonial domain, and the political leadership was conferred on the nearest male relative of the deceased khan whose qualities commended him to the notables of the *kuriltai* who were charged with the election.

By his first and favourite wife Borte, Chingis left four sons: Jochi, Chagatai, Ögedei and Tolui. Over Jochi's[1] legitimacy hung an uneasy doubt; he was born during his mother's return journey from Merkit captivity; the *Secret History* implies that the Merkit khan *may* have been his father, and his relations with Chingis seem never to have been cordial. He took part as a youth in the Chinese wars; he fought in the western campaign against the Khwarizmians, but at the siege of Gurganj in 1221 he quarrelled with his brothers Chagatai and Ögedei and hampered the operations; their angry father interposed and gave the chief command to Ögedei, but Jochi received none the less an extension of his *yurt* or appanage, which spanned the steppes from the Irtish to the Volga. Thither he retired, after attempting to mollify Chingis with a present of 20,000 grey horses, but relations between the two worsened, and a sinister tale alleges that Jochi was disgusted at the devastation wrought in the lands allotted to him and plotted to kill his father while he was hunting.[2] What is certain is that an open clash between Jochi and Chingis was averted only by the former's sudden death in February 1227 at the age of forty-three. Before his own death six months later Chingis sanctioned the division of Jochi's *yurt* between his sons Orda and Batu, who became the fathers of dynasties, the former of the White, and the latter of the Golden, Horde.

Chagatai,[3] the second son, also served under his father in China and the West; during Chingis's last campaign he was left in command of the troops in Mongolia, and on his father's death he retired to his appanage, which included the Uighur country, the former territory of the Kara-Khitay, and Transoxiana. He enjoyed great prestige, both as the eldest surviving son of the Conqueror and as an authority on the *Yasa*; he was consulted on matters of tribal law and custom, and presided over the *kuriltai* which elected Ögedei as Great Khan in 1229. The Muslim chroniclers complain bitterly of his hostility to Islam, and allege that he cruelly punished Muslims who killed their animals and performed their ablutions according to the sacred law, since these rituals conflicted with the ordinances of the *Yasa*. He dismissed Mahmud Yalavach,[4] the Muslim governor of Transoxiana, after a rebellion in Bukhara in 1239, but was obliged to reinstate him on the demand of Ögedei, who claimed that such appointees were answerable only to him and not to a local khan. He died shortly after Ögedei himself, in 1241 or 1242, and the Chagatai Khanate, which perpetuated his name, survived in Central Asia till the days of Timur.[5]

Ögedei, by his election to the supreme khanate in 1229, became a world figure until his death in 1241. The youngest son Tolui received the patrimonial land in the valleys of the Onon and Kerulen; he acted as regent of the empire in the interval between the death of Chingis and the accession of Ögedei, and he joined with his brother in the renewed offensive against the Chin in 1231. Within a year he was dead at the age of forty or thereabouts,[6] of drink say the chroniclers, who have frequent occasion to note the intemperance of the Mongol princes. By the Kerait princess Sorkaktani, a Nestorian Christian and a niece of the Wang-Khan, he was the father of two Great Khans, Möngke and Kubilai and of Hülegü, the conqueror of Baghdad, and the displacement of

74

the house of Ögedei by the house of Tolui was the major political revolution of Mongol history.

After the death of Chingis, his people remained for two years without a supreme ruler. The interval was occupied with funeral ceremonies and mourning and the slow assemblage of the Mongol nobles at the *kuriltai* held on the banks of the Kerulen, where the khans were traditionally chosen. Military operations were suspended, and Tolui conducted the civil administration until the vacancy of the throne should be filled. The election of Ögedei[7] (September 1229) was only a formality; Chingis had indicated some time before his death his wish that his third son should succeed him, and no *kuriltai* would have dared to repudiate the expressed desire of the Conqueror. The new Great Khan was devoid of his father's volcanic energy; he preferred to enjoy rather than to expand the empire, and he established a more settled court at Karakorum, a camp city near the old centre of the Hiung-nu, which he surrounded with a wall in 1235 and which was destined to shine with a rough splendour for fifty years as the hub of a world monarchy.[8] But the most lethargic Mongol sovereign could not be indifferent to the aims and ambitions of the great Chingis, which were largely unrealized at his death; a superb army must continue to be employed; the nations of the earth must be brought to submission to the living representative of Tengri, and as long as any people or State remained defiant or ignorant of its duty, the Mongol sword could not be sheathed. The reign of Ögedei (1229–41) pushed forward the frontiers of this nomadic imperialism in three directions: (1) against the Chin empire in North China; (2) against the remnant of Khwarizmian power in Persia; and (3) against the western end of the Eurasian steppe in Russia through Poland into Hungary.

(1) When Chingis removed the bulk of the Mongol forces to the west in his massive campaign against the Khwarizm-Shah, the Chin regained heart, mobilized their resources, and recovered some lost ground in Shensi and Honan.[9] When the conqueror returned, he had but a short while to live, but tradition related that he drew a comprehensive strategic plan for the destruction of the Chin resistance and bequeathed it to his heirs to fulfil. As soon as Ögedei had consolidated his position, he resumed in 1231 the war in China, and a formidable army under the command of himself, his brother Tolui, and his brilliant general Sübedei,

75

carrying out a vast encircling movement, entered the province of Honan at three different points. On Tolui's death in 1232, Ögedei ordered Sübedei to press the siege of K'ai-feng, the Chin capital, which fell in May 1233; the Chin emperor Ai-tsung fled from town to town, hotly pursued by the enemy, and finally reached the city of Ts'ai-chou, where despairing of further resistance, he committed suicide in the spring of 1234. After a struggle of twenty years, the Chin empire was no more, and we may suspect that as an alien régime, it commanded only a qualified loyalty from its Chinese subjects. Its Sung rival reposed on stronger foundations, and now stood forth as the only Chinese national state, but its leaders, though militarily courageous, were politically inept and appeared unable to grasp the limitless global ambitions of the Mongols. The fall of the Chin exposed the Sung to attack, yet the latter could only see an opportunity to regain much of North China, which had long been abandoned to the barbarians. Sung contingents had assisted in the war against the Chin, and the Sung government in its haste to take over the former Chin territories, seized the cities of K'ai-feng and Lo-yang without troubling to secure the assent of the Mongols. Such presumption cried out to be punished, and at a *kuriltai* held at Karakorum in 1235, Ögedei proclaimed war against the Sung and entrusted his sons Koten and Kochu with the task of subduing a new and more stubborn enemy.

The struggle thus opened in 1235 was to be brought to a successful conclusion forty-five years later in 1279, in the reign of Kubilai and this long interval of time is a measure of the difficulty the Mongols encountered in crushing the national resistance of the Chinese people. The Sung were a much more formidable foe than the Chin, who had no real roots in China, whereas the southern dynasty could claim to be the heirs of the Han and the T'ang and the guardians of Confucian culture against the unlettered savages who dominated the north. The Sung defended their heritage fiercely until the Mongols themselves, like other invaders, developed an appreciation of Chinese civilization and could thus be deemed not unworthy to exercise power over the Middle Kingdom. The process began under Chingis and was continued under Ögedei, who retained in office his father's shrewd adviser Ch'u-ts'ai. When Ögedei boasted of the military might of the empire, Ch'u-ts'ai boldly answered, 'The Empire was won on horseback, but it won't be governed on horse-back!'[10] and secured permission to apply the traditional methods of Chinese administration to the territories taken from the Chin. A chancery was organized in separate bureaux and staffed with trained Chinese officials, and schools were opened for the instruction not only of natives but also of Mongols who might wish for a career in the civil service.[11] At the capture of K'ai-feng, Ch'u-ts'ai was at hand to prevent its destruction and rescue its priceless literary and artistic treasures. The exertions of this tamer of barbarism may well have mitigated Chinese hatred of the Mongols and multiplied the number of those who in time withdrew their allegiance from the Sung and rallied to a régime which grew progressively sinized and which under Kubilai could almost pass for a Chinese dynasty.

A consequence of the destruction of the Chin was the Mongol occupation of Korea, that remote peninsula which during the greater part of its history has obeyed the masters of North China.[12] In 1218, while chasing the Ch'i-tan over the Yalu river, the Mongols encroached on Korean territory, but a serious invasion was attempted only as part of the last great campaign against the Chin. The country was transformed in 1231 into a vassal state, but in the following year it rebelled against the *darughas*[13] or governors whom Ögedei had left in charge; the Mongols were massacred, but punishment was swift and condign, and in 1236 the kingdom was reoccupied and its king sought refuge on an island off the coast. The conquest of Korea added little to Mongol power, but it served to familiarize the Mongols with the existence of Japan, though the subjugation of that island empire was not attempted till the time of Kubilai.

(2) Since the return of Chingis from his Western campaign, the Iranian world had lapsed into anarchy. The cities of Khurasan had been ruined; Transoxiana, less seriously damaged, was partially recovering, but a gash of destruction lay across eastern Persia, whose once flourishing cultural life had been stricken a grievous blow. But the southern provinces of Fars and Kirman had escaped the invader and made timely submission; the caliph still ruled, or at least reigned, in Baghdad; Irak Ajami, the Persian Irak,[14] was governed still by its native princes or atabegs, and in Asia Minor the Seljuk sultans fought with the Greeks of Nicaea and the Latins of Constantinople. When Jalal ad-Din, the

legitimate Khwarizm-Shah, deeming that the Mongol storm had passed, returned from his Indian exile, in 1224, he was received with relief and hope by some of his Muslim subjects, who recalled with pride his valour and gallantry which contrasted so sharply with the pusillanimity of his father and who might have endorsed a statesmanlike effort to rally the forces of Islam and reconstruct the Khwarizmian State. But that brilliant paladin was totally destitute of political skill or even common sense. He was adept only at making war; he took no precautions against the almost inevitable return of the Mongols, and far from attempting to build up a military coalition against them, he attacked the Christian kingdoms south of the Caucasus and quarrelled with his fellow Muslim princes, the caliph, the Ayyubid sultan of Damascus, and the Seljuk sultan of Rum. Handing over Irak Ajami as a fief to his brother Ghiyath, he concentrated a newly gathered army in the north-west of his former dominions, seized Azerbaijan and captured Tabriz in 1225, invaded Georgia and sacked Tiflis in 1226. Fighting his way through the Armenian highlands, he clashed with the Syrian Ayyubids at Akhlat, on the western shores of Lake Van, and provoked against him an alliance of the Ayyubids and the Seljuks. When he threatened to violate the frontiers of the Sultanate of Rum, Kaikubad marched against him and routed the aggressor at Arzinjan, in the upper western Euphrates, in 1230. At this moment Ögedei decided to resume the war in the west, and in the winter of 1230–1 a new Mongol army of 30,000 men under the command of Chormagan approached along the great road from Khurasan. Terrified at the renewal of this deadly menace, Jalal fled southwards into the district of Diyar Bakr,[15] where in obscure circumstances he was killed (August 1231) by a Kurdish peasant.[16] What was left of his kingdom was submerged in the Mongol deluge, and until the days of Baybars, nearly thirty years later, Islam in Western Asia was bereft of a leader.

When the Mongols returned to Persia, they made straight for the great grazing lands of Azerbaijan, and the adjacent plains or swamp of Mughan and Arran, which in later years were to be the centre of the power of the Il-khans. From these extensive camping-grounds, they could threaten alike the Muslim principalities of Irak, Syria and Anatolia and the Christian kingdoms of the Caucasus. They were now operating on the frontier between the two faiths, in relation to which they maintained the impartiality of indifference, but the chroniclers of the churches of the East complain that the Muslims of Persia urged on the Mongols to persecute the Christians. Yet the ravages committed in Georgia and Armenia[17] in 1235-6 by the armies of Chormagan may well have been intended to keep open communications with the northern steppes, from which an offensive into Europe was to be launched in 1236-7. The unity of the Georgian kingdom was shattered; the nobles were encouraged to rise against the crown; the crown was disputed by two claimants, both of the name of David, a confusion which naturally facilitated a Mongol occupation. Further south, Ani, the ancient capital of Armenia, was sacked and its population massacred in 1239, and these melancholy events assumed the appearance of an anti-Christian campaign. The more perceptive of the Christian princes realized that to escape further ill-treatment, a humble submission to the new masters of the world was requisite. A Georgian embassy reached Karakorum in 1240 to complain to Ögedei of the injustices of his generals, and Simeon, a Nestorian ecclesiastic, on appealing to the Khan against the violations of religious freedom as prescribed in the *Yasa*, was sent back to Armenia in 1241 with warnings to the local Mongol commanders to protect the churches against persecution and spoliation.[18]

King Hayton of Little Armenia in Cilicia embraced a wider vision: an alliance of the Eastern Christians with the Mongols against Islam. This bold plan appeared more plausible when Chormagan was replaced in 1241 by the *noyan* Baiju or Baichu,[19] who resolved to expand the domain of the Khan into Asia Minor by the destruction of the Seljuk principality of Rum or Iconium. Mongol aggression was thus switched again to a Muslim power; Baiju's armies moved westwards; the great fortress and market of Erzurum[20] fell in 1242; the Sultan Kai-Khusraw suffered an ignominious defeat at Köse-Dagh (June 1243), and was forced to sue for peace and profess himself the vassal of the Great Khan. The Mongol lines of communication were, however, dangerously extended; Baiju refrained from pressing westwards to the Aegean; most of the Seljuk territories remained inviolate, and they successfully shielded the lands of Byzantium, now divided between the Greeks of Nicaea and the Frankish crusaders who since 1204 had been in possession of the imperial city of Constantinople.

The policy of Hayton was wise and prudent; harsh experience

79

had shown that prompt and unqualified submission to Mongol overlordship could alone purchase for a nation immunity from bloody disaster. But the hopes and plans of the Armenian king went far beyond this. Reports from Karakorum revealed the growing influence of the Nestorian clergy at the court of the Great Khan; the acts of such Mongol leaders as Chagatai could be interpreted as motivated by strong hostility to Islam,[21] and the conversion of the nomad world empire to the Christian faith, a mirage which now began to float before many eyes, might conceivably destroy the power of the Muslims and evangelize the whole of Asia. The fall of the Khwarizmian kingdom had been a severe blow to Islam and opened up Central Asia to western penetration, and the Christians of Europe and the Near East might now make direct contact with the Turkish Christian peoples of Farther Asia. A Christian-Mongol alliance against Islam seemed not impossible of realization. Yet at this very moment the Mongol drive through Persia into Irak and Anatolia, which threatened to engulf Baghdad and Cairo, was halted, and a new and terrifying offensive was launched from the western end of the Eurasian steppe which carried the conquerors of the world deep into Europe and overturned so many Christian kingdoms that the religion of Christ seemed likely to perish before that of Muhammad.

(3) When Chingis bestowed on his eldest son the lands of the West, the boundaries of Jochi's appanage were ill-defined; of his two sons, the elder Orda was assigned the region of western Siberia and the younger Batu received the area beyond the Volga, 'as far as the soil has been trodden by the hooves of Mongol horses'. But this *yurt* was potential, not actual; the raid of Jebe and Sübedei into Russia had no lasting effects, despite the annihilating Mongol victory on the Kalka in 1223, and Batu must first conquer the territory over which he was to rule. That territory would embrace the steppes of Russia north of the Black Sea, their detached extension in the Alföld of Hungary, and those kingdoms of the West of which the Mongols' ignorance of European geography gave them but a dim concept. To secure for Batu this noble inheritance became a matter of common concern to the entire Mongol leadership. At a *kuriltai* summoned by Ögedei in 1235, as soon as the final conquest of the Chin had been achieved, the western campaign was planned, the armies were mobilized, provisions col-

lected, lines of communication secured, and each adult member of the imperial family assigned his task and office. To Batu was given the nominal command; his brothers Orda, Berke, Sinkur and Siban served under him; Ögedei's sons Küyük and Kadan were allotted their stations, as were Tolui's son Möngke, and Chagatai's son Baidar and grandson Buri. The army, in which thus served two future Great Khans, numbered 150,000 men; in matters of grand strategy the princes probably deferred to the professional skill and experience of the veteran Sübedei, whose presence was almost a guarantee of victory, and in the spring of 1236 the vast host marched out on a campaign which was to carry it from Siberia to the Adriatic.

The first enemy it encountered (and every nation which did not instantly submit was an enemy) was the Bulghar kingdom of the middle Volga.[22] The Bulghars, a nomadic people of Turkish speech, had established themselves in a profitable and strategic position athwart a main route of international commerce; they sold furs and slaves to the markets of Transoxiana, and received in exchange arms, manufactured goods, and the Muslim religion.[23] They lived in tents and bred cattle, but the profits of trade lifted them slightly above barbarism; they took to farming, and struck silver coins in imitation of Samanid dirhams, and their fortified stronghold, built near the confluence of the Volga and the Kama a few miles south of modern Kazan, grew into the city of Bulghar, adorned with palaces, mosques and public baths.[24] Yet their prosperity might be offset by social and racial disunity; Finns and Slavs and Alans chafed under the yoke of the Bulghar ruling class, and the first stroke of the Mongols shattered the state. Bulghar was taken and sacked by Sübedei;[25] the kingdom was reduced to vassalage, and its fall was speedily followed by the subjugation of the Bashkirs, who dwelt on the slopes of the Urals and whose land, being the original home of the Magyars, was styled in the geography of the age Great Hungary.[26]

While Sübedei crushed the Bulghars, Möngke, commanding the Mongol left flank, was despatched against the Kipchaks of the lower Volga north of the Caspian Sea, a pagan Turkish people known to the Byzantines and Hungarians as Cumans and the Russians as Polovtsians.[27] Divided into several tribes, they formed a numerous confederacy, and the title of Kipchak khanate was later given to the Golden Horde which Batu founded with its base in the territories of this people. Bachman, their valiant chief, gave the Mongols much trouble; he evaded their pursuit, hid in the forests lining the banks of the Volga, was chased up and down the river by Möngke at the head of a flotilla of 200 boats, and finally run to earth on an island. A high wind caused the waters to subside, the Mongols forded the river and seized Bachman. Ordered to prostrate himself, the Kipchak proudly replied, 'I have been myself a king and do not fear death. I am not a camel that I should kneel,' and on Möngke's orders was put to death by being cleft in two.[28] His people submitted to the conquerors, but a section of the Kipchaks continued to resist, until they were subdued by Berke in 1238, whereupon the remnant of 40,000 'tents' under their leader Kutan migrated over river and mountain to the plains of Hungary, where they turned Christian and were granted asylum, an act of generosity ultimately fatal to the Hungarian kingdom.

Before the close of the year 1237 the invaders, leaving behind them the ruins of Bulghar, crossed the Volga into Europe.[29] In the thousand years of her history, Russia has been several times assaulted from the west, but the Swedes, the French and the Germans on each occasion encountered a valiant nation and a powerful centralized state and were ignominiously expelled. On the single occasion when the attack was delivered from the east, Russia suffered and succumbed, and her failure to withstand the savage fury of the Mongols, who inflicted on her a permanent injury, may be attributed mainly to the extraordinary fragmentation of political power which dissipated her strength and energies through a dozen mutually quarrelling principalities and never permitted, even in the face of acutest danger, a concentration of military force. The lessons of the battle of the Kalka fourteen years before were never learnt, and the new and more formidable invasion found the Russian princes as divided and disorganized as ever. The principality of Riazan stood first in the path of the Mongols; two brothers Yuri and Roman governed respectively the city of Riazan and that of Kolomna; each was attacked and annihilated separately. Riazan was taken by assault in December 1237; Yuri and all his people perished; the same fate befell Roman in Kolomna, and in the striking phrase of a chronicler, 'No eye remained open to weep for the dead'.[30] Advancing rapidly into central Russia, Batu struck at the princedom of

Vladimir or Suzdal, whose ruler enjoyed the title and status of Grand Duke; the two cities were taken and destroyed in February 1238, the ducal family was killed, and many of the inhabitants were burnt in the churches in which they had taken refuge. At this point the Mongol chiefs held a *kuriltai* and decided to divide their forces; one army defeated and killed Grand Duke Vladimir on the banks of the Siti river in March 1238, and Batu himself led another northwards over the Valdai Hills towards Novgorod and the Baltic.[31] The approach of the dreaded enemy from Asia excited alarm throughout northern Europe; the rich commercial city of Novgorod hastened to set its defences in order, and the fishing fleets that normally crossed the North Sea to England stayed at home, resulting in a glut of herrings on the English market.[32] But here the irresistible march of the Mongols was checked, not by man but by nature. Batu's advance towards Lake Ilmen was delayed by the resistance of Torzhok, which withstood a siege of two weeks, and when it was resumed the spring thaws had melted the snows, swollen the rivers, and turned the whole countryside round Novgorod into a swampy morass. Sixty miles from the city, the Mongols, fearing to be caught in the rising floods, resolved to retire for the summer to the pastures of the south; on the way back the town of Kozel'sk, south of Kaluga, held out against them for seven weeks, but by the end of the campaigning season the hosts of Batu were encamped on the steppes of the Don. Their losses, both of men and horses, had doubtless been severe; fresh recruits were conscripted, fresh remounts were seized from the Cumans and others; but a prolonged period of rest and re-equipment was required, and the whole of 1239 was suffered to pass without further military operations.[33]

When hostilities were reopened, Batu directed his offensive against the middle Dnieper, the cultural centre of old Kievan Russia. The towns of Chernigov and Pereyaslavl were destroyed, and the capture of the great city of Kiev seems to have been entrusted to Möngke. The usual summons to surrender was ignored; the envoys who brought it were killed, and Mongol vengeance was inevitable. The chroniclers speak of the 'clouds of Tartars' approaching the town, and assert that the noise of carts, the bellowing of camels and cattle, the neighing of horses, and the savage war-cries of the attackers, raised so awful a clamour

that conversation within the walls was drowned out.[34] After ferocious fighting, the Mongols breached the defences; a crowd of
terrified refugees who had rushed into the cathedral perished when
the building collapsed under their weight, and the rest were put
to the sword when the enemy took possession of the place on
6 December 1240. Kiev was reduced to ashes; its Byzantine
churches were ruined, its wealth of artistic treasures destroyed,
and the very bones of saint and prince were torn from their tombs
and burnt. Some of the surviving Russian chiefs fled westwards to
Poland and Hungary, and in Mongol eyes this fact justified the
invasion of those kingdoms, the Hungarians in addition being
chided for granting asylum to the fugitive Cumans.[35] But in truth
Mongol desire for pasture for their horses necessitated the
occupation of the *puszta*, the rich Hungarian prairie, which they
might then make a base for the conquest of Western Europe, just
as the plain of Azerbaijan was the starting-point for the conquest
of Irak and northern Persia.

The campaign against Hungary, so meticulously planned and
so brilliantly executed, was a marvel of the military art, and
betrays the master hand of Sübedei, a genius of war not inferior
to Chingis himself. Since the Mongol soldiers were natives of a
cold climate and were well equipped to fight in snow, Sübedei
preferred a winter campaign, when communication was facilitated
by the frozen rivers. The absence of maps and charts, which
instruct a modern commander, was supplied by the careful
collection of information from spies and deserters, who revealed
the state of the roads, the distances to the next towns, the presence
of enemy detachments, and the level of morale in the defenders'
camp. The armies that Sübedei led into Europe were not enormous, but their discipline and organization were as usual superb,
and far superior to that of the feudal chivalry of the West. As in
almost every land they traversed, the Mongols found aid in the
errors and quarrels of their opponents. The political chaos of
Russia was reproduced in Poland, divided into four mutually
antagonistic princedoms,[36] and in Hungary the efforts of Bela IV
to strengthen the Crown of St Stephen were thwarted by the
resistance of a swarm of powerful magnates lay and ecclesiastic,
who preferred that the monarchy should perish rather than that
they should sacrifice a portion of their feudal privileges, and the
unity of the kingdom was further undermined by the entry of the

Cumans, barbarous nomads detested by the native peasantry and townsfolk. [37] Yet when allowance is made for these circumstances, the wonder must remain that the Mongols achieved such dazzling success in lands so far from their base and whose geography and resources were entirely unfamiliar to them.

Early in 1241 the Mongols entered Poland [38] from Volhynia and attacked Lublin. Sübedei's motive was doubtless to secure his right flank for the invasion of Hungary. Crossing the Vistula on the ice, they sacked Sandomir; a detachment under Baidar (the Peta of the Polish chroniclers) and Kadan, [39] swept aside a Polish force under Boleshlav and Chmielnik (18 March 1241); the defeated prince escaped into Moravia, and Cracow, deserted by its inhabitants, was occupied and burnt on Palm Sunday. The bridges across the Oder were down, but the Mongols passed the river at Ratibor on an improvised fleet of boats, and struck north-wards towards Breslau, the capital of Silesia. The citadel resisted their assault, or as pious contemporaries put it, the prayers of a Dominican prior produced a light from heaven which dazzled the foe. Bypassing Breslau, they moved on to Liegnitz where Duke Henry of Silesia, with some help from the grand master of the Teutonic Order, had collected a small army of 20,000 Poles and Germans to bar their advance into the territory of the Holy Roman Empire. On a plain outside the town, where later arose the village of Wahlstadt, or 'place of battle', the chivalry of Europe was annihilated (9 April 1241) by the pagan nomads of Asia; Duke Henry galloped off the field, was overtaken and slain, and nine sacks of ears collected by the victors attested to the heavy losses of the defeated. The citadel of Liegnitz, like that of Breslau, held out, notwithstanding that the besiegers held up the head of Henry on a spear to intimidate the defenders, but Moravia was devastated, a score of small towns and monasteries were levelled to the ground, and those who evaded the brutal savagery of the invaders hid in woods and caverns. [40] Satisfied that organized resistance was at an end, the armies of Baidar and Kadan moved southwards over the Carpathians to join the main force of Batu and Sübedei in Hungary.

That doomed kingdom was penetrated from at least four different directions. [41] Baidar crossed the Carpathians from the north, [42] Batu entered from Galicia, Küyük struck from Moldavia into Transylvania, and the German Saxon district, while the great

Sübedei, moving further south towards the Danube as far as Orsova, entered via the Mehedia Pass the region later known as Temesvar. From these gigantic pincers the Hungarians could scarcely escape, even had their position not been weakened by a popular rising against the Cumans, whom rumour accused of inviting the Mongols into the country; Kutan and his chiefs were killed, and his people fought their way across Hungary towards the Danube and sought asylum in Bulgaria. As the main threat seemed to be from the north, Bela concentrated his forces at Pesth, sent his family to Austria, and marched to the heath of Mohi, near the vine-clad slopes of Tokay, through which ran the river Sayo, a tributary of the Theiss. The King was an incompetent commander; his army was riddled with jealousies and discontents, and while Batu engaged it at a bridge, Bela's camp was suddenly attacked (11 April 1241) by Sübedei, who undetected had crossed the river upstream in the night. The surprise was complete: the Hungarians were ridden down by the Mongol cavalry; Bela escaped, but nearly all his generals, including two archbishops, were killed, his valiant brother Coloman died of his wounds, and the casualties are alleged to have amounted to 65,000 men.[43] Pesth was captured and burnt shortly afterwards, but the Mongols, true to their common practice, suspended operations during the summer and encamped on the Hungarian plain while they forced the peasantry to sow and reap the harvest for them and the artisans to restock their armoury.

The double catastrophe of Liegnitz and Mohi, fought within two or three days of one another, stunned Europe, and the swift ruin of two great Christian kingdoms might seem to presage the total destruction of the Latin Catholic world. The defence of Christendom properly rested on the Emperor Frederick II, its secular head, but that strange unbelieving prince, the sworn enemy of pope and clergy, was resident in his Sicilian kingdom, had confided the government of Germany to his son Conrad, and was more anxious perhaps to defeat the Papacy than the Mongols. His activity was confined to the issue from Faenza in July 1241 of a circular letter to the kings of Europe announcing the fall of Kiev, the invasion of Hungary and the growing threat to the German lands (in this same month a Mongol patrol made a raid into Austria), and begging that each should contribute a quota of men and arms to the common defence.[44] Nor could Christendom expect much from its spiritual chief. Pope Gregory IX had time, in response to frantic appeals from Bela,[45] only to publish one appeal for co-operation before his death in August 1241; his successor Celestine IV died in a few weeks, and Innocent IV was not elected till June 1243, by which time the enemy had evacuated Europe. The Mongols had the same effect here as everywhere: they were treated as something more than human, a dreadful visitation from hell;[46] the frantic reports of refugees intensified instead of diminishing the fear and paralysis which gripped every land they approached,[47] their tricks and stratagems appeared inexhaustible.[48]

With the approach of winter, the Mongols stirred anew into murderous activity, nor had their enemies used the respite to still their quarrels and strengthen their defences. On Christmas Day Batu crossed the Danube on the ice, and thirty catapults battered down the walls of Gran or Strigonia, which was then the civil and ecclesiastical capital of the kingdom.[49] Kadan was despatched in pursuit of Bela, who fled to the south-west and escaped through Croatia into Dalmatia, now crowded with refugees, and after halting briefly at Spalato, finally took ship for the island city of Trau or Trogir.[50] After taking Buda, then an insignificant place, and being repulsed from St Martin's monastery near Raab, Kadan passed along the shores of Lake Balaton and followed his quarry through Croatia; he did not venture to attack Spalato or Trau, but destroyed Cattaro and penetrated Albania to within a few miles of Scutari, the most southerly limit of the Mongol operations in Europe.

The ultimate intentions of the Mongol leaders are obscure. They *may* have considered Hungary, the western extremity of the Eurasian steppe, as the terminus of their endeavour, and planned no further advance,[51] but had they undertaken the invasion of Germany and Italy, it is difficult to imagine their being repelled by the forces of a divided and disorganized Europe. Yet their prodigiously lengthened lines of communication must have rendered it difficult to supply their armies, and they could draw little sustenance from a ruined land. By the time that Hungary lay prostrate at their feet, dissensions among the Mongol princes were placing their conquests in jeopardy. The dominance, perhaps the arrogance, of Batu provoked resentment; he had a violent quarrel with Chagatai's grandson Buri, in which Küyük was

87

involved;[52] complaints and counter-complaints were lodged in Karakorum, and Ögedei recalled both subordinates. Möngke, though remaining on good terms with Batu, for unknown reasons also left the army and returned to Mongolia. These vexatious disputes must have seriously disturbed Batu when he learnt early in 1242 that Ögedei had died at Karakorum on 11 December 1241. A struggle for the succession portended, and if the throne should pass to Küyük, Batu's position would be gravely threatened. He resolved to break off the campaign, abandon Hungary, and reassemble his armies at a point where their presence might exert some influence on the election of the new Great Khan. By a last refinement of cruelty, he published a decree that all captives in Mongol hands were free to return home, but they were scarcely on the road when they were overtaken and slain. In the spring and summer of 1242 the various contingents were collected from all over Hungary and Dalmatia; the conquerors repassed the Carpathians into Moldavia and Wallachia, and moving slowly across the steppes north of the Black Sea, reached their old encampments on the lower Volga in the winter of 1242–3. The terror was past, though the memory long remained, and Europe was saved, not indeed by her own exertions but by an event in remote Mongolia.

At a distance of more than seven centuries, the historian is still struck with wonder at this extraordinary campaign. Whether one considers the geographical scope of the fighting, which embraced the greater part of eastern Europe, the planning and co-ordination of movement of so many army corps, the clockwork precision whereby the enemy was surrounded, defeated and pursued, the brilliant manner in which difficult problems of supply were solved, or the skill with which Asian armies were handled in an unfamiliar European terrain, one cannot fail to admit that the Mongol leaders were masters of the art of war such as the world scarcely saw before or has seen since. The time has long passed when the Mongol triumphs were attributed to the sheer weight of numbers bearing down their opponents, for numbers are useless without intelligent organization, and it is not proved that the Mongol armies were more numerous than those of the Christian kingdoms. Two further observations may be made: (1) The reaction of Europe to the Mongol invasion proves that the most alarming danger is incapable of compelling bitter rivals to sink their differences and unite if each party is persuaded that it can extract advantage from the discomfiture of the others. While the Mongols were pressing through Russia, the Swedes landed at the mouth of the Neva, in an attempt to bar Novgorod from the sea, and had to be driven off by Alexander Nevsky, whose uncle had perished at the battle of the Siti.[53] When King Bela was in desperate straits after the disaster of Mohi, Duke Frederick of Austria, from whom he begged assistance, took advantage of his plight to seize some of the western lands of the Hungarian crown. The Emperor pleaded the enmity of the Pope as an excuse for his supine inaction in face of the Mongol approach to Germany and Italy. The Pope was rumoured to be encouraging the Mongols to attack his two main enemies, Frederick II and the Nicaean emperor John Vatazes, who was threatening the Latin Empire of Constantinople.[54] Had the Mongol offensive not been abruptly broken off in 1242, it is most unlikely that the powers of Europe would have combined in a common defensive effort; Latin Christendom would have suffered the fate of China and Persia, and the wholesale destruction of life and culture would have rendered impossible the subsequent Renaissance of art and learning. (2) The halting of a powerful attack is often due, less to the valour and unity of those attacked than to dissensions within the camp of the aggressors. The salvation of Europe was effected, not so much by the death of Ögedei as by the widening breach between the family of Ögedei and that of Batu. Now that Ögedei was gone and Küyük might take his place, Batu realized that never again would he be able to count on the co-operation of all the Mongol princes in the drive against Europe. His policy now was to consolidate his hold on the Russian or Kipchak steppes, and a new camp city of Sarai was founded on the lower Volga as the centre of the *ulus* which came to be known as the Golden Horde.[55]

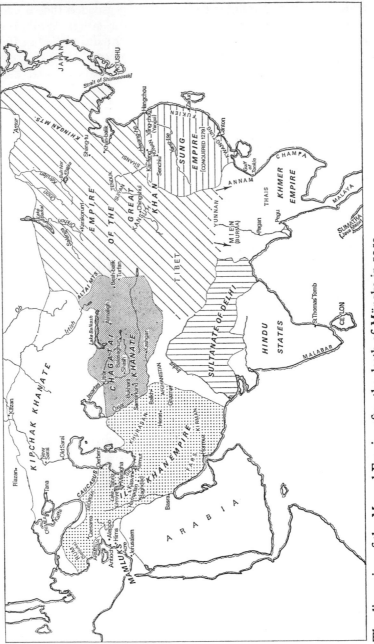

The disruption of the Mongol Empire after the death of Möngke in 1259

6

The Christian response

The trail of death and horror across eastern Europe in the fateful years 1237–42 convinced Christendom of one thing, that the ferocious 'Tartars' were not the people of Prester John who could be relied on to co-operate with the West in the destruction of Islam. With impartial savagery, the Mongols had rained their blows on Muslim and Christian alike; they were clearly godless pagans who had been sent for the chastisement of sinful men, yet it might be the will of God that they should be brought to the light of the gospel and made the instrument for the conversion of the heathen world. As the shock of the invasion subsided with the withdrawal of Batu's forces to the Volga, Europe had time to take stock and consider what measures, if any, could be usefully employed to deal with a renewal of the scourge. The throne of the Great Khan was for the moment vacant; but once it were filled, a second and perhaps even more formidable assault might be expected. At this juncture, Innocent IV, one of the most states-manlike of the popes, ascended St Peter's chair in the summer of 1243; he presided over a Church which had been re-invigorated by the foundation of the Franciscan and Dominican orders and was animated by a missionary zeal seldom seen before and never sur-passed till the days of the Jesuits. To Innocent, the greatest dangers facing the Church were the implacable enmity to the Papacy of the Emperor Frederick and the Mongol menace which threatened the military conquest of all the Christian kingdoms. To cope with these crises he summoned to meet in June 1245 at Lyons in France (for most of Italy was under the Emperor's control) a General Council of the Church, on whose agenda these two items stood first.

Even before the formal opening of the Council, the Pope had decided on heroic measures, none less than a diplomatic mission to the Mongol leaders themselves, which should protest at the atrocities perpetrated in eastern Europe and at the same time strongly urge them to accept Christian baptism. To this end, Innocent selected as leader of the mission John of Plano Carpini,[1] a stout, elderly friar of sixty or more, an early companion of St Francis, who had spent some years in Germany, Poland and Bohemia and proved himself a man of worth and energy. Furnished with papal letters addressed to 'the King and People of the Tartars' (no king was named, for the election of a new Great Khan had not yet taken place), Carpini with two or three companions left Lyons on Easter Day (16 April 1245), travelled to Cologne and thence across Germany.[2] At Breslau they were joined by another friar, Benedict the Pole,[3] and entered the country devastated by the Mongols three or four years earlier. They were now in contact with people who had experience of the dreadful 'Tartars' and could give them helpful advice and information: Duke Conrad at Cracow supplied them with a number of beaver furs which would be useful in winning the co-operation of Mongol officials they might encounter. Moving into Russia, they were received by the Grand Duke Basil, who evaded a papal request they made to him to join the Roman Church and sent them on to Kiev, where they arrived half-dead by sledge over the snow early in 1246. The scars of the Mongol injuries of 1240–1 were clearly visible: the bones of the victims still whitened the ground. They were now at the limit of civilized Europe, and on 23 February, three weeks after leaving Kiev, they reached the first Mongol outposts, and 'the Tartars rushed in upon us hideously armed, inquiring what manner of men we were'. Satisfied with their credentials, the frontier guards led them through and they rode along the banks of the Dnieper to the camp of Batu's nephew Khurumsi, who commanded in that region, and in whose presence they were obliged to kneel and explain the object of their journey. Proceeding down the Dnieper on the ice, they crossed the frozen Sea of Azov, passed over the Don, and on 4 April reached Batu's capital of

Sarai almost a year after their departure from Lyons. Here they were forced to conform to Mongol usages, to pass between two fires to be purged of evil thoughts and intentions[4] and to bow to a golden image of Chingis Khan. Batu received them in audience in a fine linen tent looted from King Bela; a Russian interpreter translated the Pope's letter into Mongol, and orders were given that guides and horses should be provided for the journey to Karakorum, where if they hurried they would arrive in time for the great *kuriltai* at which the new sovereign of the Empire was to be chosen.

Since the death of Ögedei in December 1241 the Empire had been without a head. In accordance with Mongol practice, the Regency was assumed by his widow Töregene,[5] who was ambitious of seating her son Küyük on the imperial throne. She enjoyed the support of Chagatai, the last surviving son of the Conqueror, but he died in 1242. Küyük was not generally popular among the Mongol princes, who may have been aware that Ögedei himself had wished his grandson Siremun[6] to be his successor, while Batu, who enjoyed high standing as the son of Chingis's eldest son, was his declared enemy. Töregene employed her four years' regency in removing possible critics and opponents from office and building up a party devoted to Küyük's cause. Ch'u-ts'ai, the sage adviser of Chingis and Ögedei, was replaced by Abd al-Rahman, a Muslim merchant who undertook to double the tax-yield of North China; grieved at the abandonment of his prudent administrative methods, the disgraced minister died in 1244 at the age of fifty-five. Mas'ud Yalavach, the governor of Trans-oxiana, escaped proscription by a timely flight into the domains of Batu, and the governor of eastern Persia, a Uighur named Korguz, was not only dismissed but executed. The Regent was much influenced by a female favourite named Fatima, a Persian slave captured at the sack of Tus in 1220, whose servile status, foreign ways and political interference were widely resented. Yet Töregene achieved her heart's desire, and after much shrewd manoeuvring she summoned a grand *kuriltai* to meet at Sira-ordu, or yellow camp, near Lake Koku-nor, a few miles from Karakorum, in the spring of 1246, a magnificent display of Mongol imperialism. The vast plain where the election was held was covered with the tents, not only of the Mongol princes, notables and officials but also of delegations from all over the earth. Christian Russia was represented by the Grand Duke Yaroslavl, Seljuk Rum by Sultan Kilij-Arslan IV, Armenia by the Constable Sempad, Egypt by the Sultan's brother, the Caliph of Baghdad by an accredited envoy, Korea by a royal prince, and the Christian kingdom of Georgia by two rival claimants to the throne. Our knowledge of this memorable occasion is due to the humblest of the participants. The Carpini mission had left Sarai on 8 April, to face a formidable journey across the boundless steppes.[7] Insistent on observing the Lenten fast even in these strange and dreary lands, they subsisted on boiled millet and salt and melted snow from a kettle; notwithstanding hunger and fatigue and the rapid pace of their movements (they travelled 3,000 miles from Batu's camp in a little over a hundred days), they crossed the Urals, passed through the old Kara-Khitay and Naiman territories in June, and reached Sira-ordu on 22 July.[8] Preparations for the *kuriltai* were far advanced; a day had been fixed, but a heavy hailstorm on 15 August impelled the shamans to postpone the ceremony till the 24th. On that day, the electoral college formally and unanimously chose Küyük, who was lifted on a piece of felt[9] and then led to a golden throne, in which he was placed to receive a homage of nine prostrations from the vassal princes and foreign ambassadors of half the nations of the globe. From a respectful distance, the unnoticed friars among the crowds watched the enthronement of the new master of a world monarchy. He is about forty or forty-five years of age[10] (they reported), of medium height, grave and serious in manner, and never seen to laugh or joke. The imperial election was followed by a week of feasting and drunken revelry, and Carpini and his companions must have rejoiced in the meals of roast meat and wine after the meagre fare of their travels. The fulfilment of their mission presented obstacles: unlike more experienced suppliants at the Mongol court, they had brought no presents, were dismissed with scorn for this breach of etiquette, and not admitted to Küyük's presence till November. The interpreters read the papal letters;[11] the Khan was displeased that the Pope should urge him to receive baptism and criticize the Mongol massacres in Poland and Hungary, and he dictated a curt and uncompromising reply,[12] which remarkably reflects Mongol notions of political theory and public law, partly borrowed from the Chinese. To the Pope's complaint of the ill-treatment of Christian nations, he answers, perhaps with honest bewilderment: 'I do not understand these words ot yours. The Eternal Heaven (*Tengri*) has slain and annihilated these peoples, because they have adhered neither to Chingis Khan nor to the Khagan, both of whom have been sent to make known God's command.' As to the request to be baptized: 'Thou, who art the great Pope, together with all the princes, come in person to serve us. At that time I shall make known all the commands of the Yasa.' The missive ends on a note of menace: 'If you do not observe God's command, and if you ignore my command, I shall know you as my enemy. Likewise I shall make you understand. If you do otherwise, God knows what I know.'

From which it was clear that the Mongol leadership considered itself charged by God with the task of world conquest.[13] Every nation was required to submit or be destroyed. The Khan was the representative on earth of Tengri, the sky god, and refusal to acknowledge his supremacy was blasphemy and sacrilege.[14] The *Yasa* was the divine code by which all must live. The Mongol Empire was not one State among others: it was the supreme universal monarchy, and all lands not within its frontiers were subordinate and inferior and potential vassals. Embassies from foreign kingdoms were treated as acts of formal submission and presents were received as tribute, as was the Chinese practice down to the end of the eighteenth century.[15] To enter into normal diplomatic relations with Karakorum was impossible. The Mongols were particularly suspicious of potentates like pope or caliph, who seemed to claim a wide jurisdiction rivalling that of the Great Khan. They themselves alone possessed authority from God to govern the world and enforce peace; their victories were God's victories, and they never boasted of their military might but merely observed, 'God knows what will happen.'

If Carpini was disconcerted by the arrogant reply of the Khan, his experience was less alarming than the mission of Ascelin or Anselm, a Dominican of Lombardy,[16] who had been sent by Innocent IV at the same time to the Mongols of Persia, apparently with instructions to deliver the papal letters to the commander of the first Mongol army they met. Travelling through Asia Minor, they reached in August 1247 the camp of Baiju, the governor of Persia, at the castle of Sitiens or Sisian, in Armenia,[17] who was incensed at their refusal to prostrate themselves before him and still more when they incautiously observed that the Pope possessed the highest dignity in the world. 'Do you not know (they were asked) that the Khan is the Son of Heaven?' and Baiju would have had them flayed alive but for the intervention of his wife. After a long delay, they were sent back with replies drafted in Mongol and translated first into Persian and then into Latin which bear a close resemblance to Küyük's response to the Pope. 'By order of the divine Khan, Baiju sends you this reply, know O Pope that your envoys have come and brought your letters. They spoke in a haughty tone, whether by your order we know not. You complain we have killed many people, but see the command of God and of him who is master of the earth. Whoever obeys us remains in possession of his land, but whoever resists is destroyed. We send you this order, Pope, so that if you wish to keep your land, you must come to us in person and thence go on to him who is master of all the earth. If you don't, we know not what will happen, only God knows.'[18]

From these perilous missions, the Europeans returned with a clearer picture of Mongol strength and methods, if not intentions, and the masters of Asia were impelled to enter into less warlike relations with the sovereigns of Christendom. Ascelin was sent back with two Mongol envoys, probably Nestorian Christians, whose secret interviews with papal officials in Italy released a flood of rumours over Europe.[19] Carpini and his brethren made part of the return journey with the ambassadors of the Sultan of Egypt; they separated at the Persian frontier, endured a dreadful winter of snow and blizzards on the open steppe, and regained Batu's camp in the spring of 1247. Reaching Kiev on 25 May, they were welcomed 'as if we had come back from the dead', and crossing the more familiar regions of Poland and Germany, re-entered Lyons on 18 November, after an absence of two years and a half. Carpini had kept notes of the journey, which he worked up into a full report immediately on his return, and the demand for information about the 'Tartars' was partially satisfied by a series of public readings from this report which he gave in the ensuing winter.[20] The intrepid friars deserved their success: as 'the men who came back from the Tartars' they were deemed to have been under the special protection of God, and their marvellous journey, the first European exploration into the heart of Asia of which we have record, justified the bold initiative of the Pope and substituted precise knowledge for fearful speculation.[21]

For Carpini had seen at close quarters the mighty military machine which had already subdued half Europe and Asia; he explained its workings and revealed its secrets, and recommended to his countrymen the counter-measures he deemed appropriate.[22] Without minimizing the danger of a second assault on Europe, he shrewdly noted that the rift between Küyük and Batu might well prevent it.[23] And though he could not announce the discovery of Prester John or any powerful Christian king in Asia, he could hopefully report the growth of Christian influence at the Mongol court and the likelihood of the conversion of the Great Khan.

In every age barbarian potentates have been found susceptible to the attractions of the higher religions, whose sacred books and impressive ceremonies appealed to shrewd but uneducated minds. Loyalty to the national tradition and to the command and example of Chingis might restrain the khans from abandoning their ancestral shamanism and the worship of Tengri, but under cover of the universal tolerance enjoined by the Conqueror they might examine the beliefs and participate in the rituals and services of the Buddhists, the Muslims and the Christians, without committing themselves unreservedly to the acceptance of any of these faiths. The rise of Christian or partly Christian Turkish peoples like the Naimans and the Uighurs to positions of authority and influence in the Mongol world empire presented the Nestorian clergy with an opportunity to resume the evangelization of eastern Asia and to capture the Mongol leadership, particularly through Christian women who had found their way into the harems of the khans. The mother of Küyük was a Naiman or Kerait Christian, and the Great Khan, who owed his throne to her efforts, might well feel a special interest and curiosity in her religion. The Carpini mission was informed by the Nestorian priests they encountered at the *kuriltai* that he was about to be baptized;[24] two years later the Mongol envoys who met Louis IX of France in Cyprus assured the devout king that Küyük had received baptism on the Feast of the Epiphany in 1248,[25] and his conversion is asserted, not only by a Christian chronicler like Bar Hebraeus[26] but by the Muslim historians of Mongol Persia,[27] who could have no inducement to magnify an event so inimical to the interests of Islam. That Küyük was highly sympathetic to his mother's faith is certain; that he was baptized is probable; that he deemed himself

97

seriously a Christian and renounced Tengri is more than doubtful. The news, though received with some scepticism,[28] excited widespread hopes among Christians in east and west;[29] it led to fresh missions to Asia, notably that led by William of Rubruck at the instance of Louis IX, and it encouraged the efforts of King Hayton of Armenia to construct a Christian Mongol 'front' against Islam.

Whatever might be the real beliefs of Küyük, his reign was too short to allow of the implementation of either a civil or religious policy. His domestic administration was signalized by a sweeping change of personnel: Abd al-Rahman, charged with extortion and malversion in China, was tried and executed, and replaced by Mahmud Yalavach, Chinkai was restored to office, the more supple Eljigidei superseded the inflexible Baiju as commander in Western Asia, his mother's favourite Fatima, convicted of causing by witchcraft the death of his brother Koten, was wrapped in felt and thrown into the river, and Chagatai's grandson was deposed from his khanate in favour of a younger son. The affairs of vassal kingdoms were settled by arbitrary decree: Kilij-Arslan IV was adjudged Sultan of Rum in place of his elder brother Kai-Kawus II, and the succession disputes in Georgia were decided by dividing the kingdom in two and giving half to each claimant. As his principal duty Küyük undertook to bring the remaining kingdoms of the earth under the sway of God and the Khan; his banner of nine yak-tails was raised outside his tent as a declaration of war against the Sung of China and other lands which had not yet submitted, and the princes of the blood were required each to furnish two men out of ten of the new armies. As the tone of his reply to the Pope implied, Küyük, whether or no a nominal Christian, was resolved to resume the war against Europe, but no action could be initiated on this front until his relationship with Batu had been clarified.

From the vast throng of relatives, vassals and dependants who had attended Küyük's inauguration, Batu was conspicuously absent. He pleaded ill-health, but the new Khan, harsh and suspicious, remembered the quarrels during the Hungarian campaign and feared that Batu, even if he had no pretensions to the supreme power, might hope to be kingmaker and displace the house of Ögedei from the throne. Küyük was not widely popular; he felt the insecurity of his position, and had already put to death his uncle, a younger brother of Chingis, on an accusation of treason. To test the loyalty of Batu, he demanded that the latter should meet him at an agreed spot in the Ili valley, Küyük's personal domain. Not daring to refuse, Batu set out from Sarai, but on the road between Ili and Lake Issik-kul received a message from Tolui's widow Sorkaktani[30] warning him to proceed no further, as Küyük planned to arrest and execute him. Küyük himself travelled west to a point a week's march from Besh-balik, where he fell ill and died (April 1248) of gout and alcoholism, at the age of forty-two, after a reign of less than two years.[31] Batu was saved; Europe was spared a fresh attack and the vacancy of the throne once more halted the Mongol march of world conquest.

The early death of Küyük was fatal to the house of Ögedei. In accordance with customary usage, his widow Oghul-Ghaimish assumed the Regency until the convocation of an electoral *kuriltai*, but neither her skill nor her position was equal to that of Töregene after Ögedei's death six years earlier. The family of Ögedei had no obvious candidate for the throne; their enemy Batu enjoyed renown and influence as the senior prince of the Empire, and his alliance with Sorkaktani, who was determined to press the claims of her eldest son Möngke, ensured an almost irresistible pressure against them. Oghul-Ghaimish might hope to persuade the electors to choose Küyük's nephew Siremun, whom Ögedei himself was believed to have favoured; she established herself in her late husband's *ulus* in Central Asia, adjacent to the domain of Chagatai, whose family were prepared to support her, and here in 1250, acting as supreme governor of the realm, she received a mission sent by King Louis of France and led by Friar Andrew of Longjumeau, and in characteristic Mongol fashion affected to treat the royal presents as tribute and haughtily required the king to make a more abject submission if he wished to escape the conquest and destruction of his realm.[32] But her day of authority was short. Batu summoned a *kuriltai* to meet at Alakmak, north of Lake Issik-kul; the representatives of the Ögedei and Chagatai families refused to attend, on the ground that such an assembly could meet only on the sacred soil of Mongolia, and they refused to ratify the election of Möngke, which was made in their absence. Batu ordered his brother Berke to convoke a second meeting, this time in the Onon-Kerulen area of the Mongol homeland; the opposition remained recalcitrant, failed to send delegates, were overruled, and Möngke proclaimed Great Khan on 1 July 1251.[33]

When the heirs of Ögedei realized the full extent of their political defeat, they took clumsy and ineffective steps to nullify the coup by which they had been ejected from power in favour of the house of Tolui. Surrounded by armed escorts, they arrived at Karakorum, ostensibly to do homage to the new khan, in reality to surprise, seize and dethrone him. The plot was detected; Möngke was forewarned, the conspirators were arrested and disarmed; and a full inquiry was followed by a series of State trials. Kadak and Chinkai, the old and trusted advisers of Ögedei, were charged with master-minding the plot, found guilty and executed, but the accused princes were arraigned before special courts, at their head being Küyük's widow, the former Regent Oghul-Ghaimish, who was the object of Möngke's particular detestation.[34] Convicted, she was sewn up in a sack and drowned; Siremun, who was probably intended to be Möngke's supplanter, was saved for a while by the intervention of Kubilai, who got him transferred to the army in China, but on the khan's orders was ultimately put to death there, while Chagatai's grandson Buri was handed over to the vengeance of Batu, whom he had grievously offended during the campaign in Europe.[35] Kadan the son and Kaidu the grandson of Ögedei submitted in time and were spared, on condition that they retired to the ancestral *ulus* in the Emil valley, an act of clemency later regretted no doubt by Kubilai, since Kaidu became a competitor for the succession after the death of Möngke. The ramifications of the plot apparently extended into Persia; Eljigidei, whom Küyük had appointed to supersede Baiju, was executed, and his sons, who were charged with him, were killed by having stones thrust into their mouths. These severities consolidated the throne of Möngke, whose power was cemented by his alliance with Batu, who was rewarded with a position of virtual independence and reigned as a kind of co-emperor over the western regions of the empire.

Since the return of Batu to the Volga and the relinquishment of his western conquests, his attention had been concentrated on the political changes at Karakorum. He did not himself aspire to the great khanate, but his ambition was satisfied with the role of kingmaker and a position of independent authority. An extensive region obeyed his mandates: the Kipchak steppes were the core of his *ulus*, in the west his rule extended as far as Bulgaria, in the east to Khwarizm, and the Crimea, and the northern Caucasus were included in his area of jurisdiction. Neighbouring vassals, such as the Seljuks and the Georgians, sought his protection, though he was not their nominal suzerain, and over the quarrelling princes of Russia his power was so absolute that he might almost be styled the first of the Tsars. Hungary might be abandoned with little regret, though no doubt it was hoped to reoccupy it after a short interval, but the Mongols never contemplated the slightest weakening of their hold on Russia. Immediately on his return from Hungary, Batu despatched his brother Sinkur to crush a rebellion of the Bashkirs, Bulghars and Finns beyond the upper Kama;[36] though he stationed no garrisons in northern Russia, he forced Novgorod to pay tribute; from 1254 a series of censuses determined how much the Russians should provide in taxes and soldiers, and the contrasting fates of the two principal Russian princes read an instructive lesson to all vassals of the Mongols. Daniel of Galicia, a supple and cautious ruler, strove to placate the master; he put his troops into Mongol uniform, visited Batu's camp as a suppliant, and by drinking *kumiz* with the khan, proclaimed his adhesion to the laws and customs of the conquerors. Michael of Chernigov, a tougher and less resilient man, accepted the demand that he should walk between the purifying fires, but he refused a humiliating prostration on the ground before an image of Chingis and was executed for his defiance.[37] The bitter quarrel between Batu and Küyük might encourage some faint hopes among the Russians of recovering their independence; the princes of the east, Yaroslav and his son Alexander Nevsky, looked to the Great Khan to lighten the yoke of his enemy on them,[38] while those of the west, especially Daniel, cherished some expectation of military help from the Latins. The election of Möngke and the virtual division of the empire between him and Batu extinguished the possibility of playing off Sarai against Karakorum; the affairs of Russia were now dealt with exclusively by Batu, or rather by his son Sartak, and when Daniel, urged by Carpini to accept the papal supremacy, submitted to Rome and was recognized as king by Innocent IV, he commented bitterly that he had received a crown when he expected an army.[39]

The name of Batu still had the power to terrorize Europe, and the efforts of Pope Innocent and King Louis to tame these ferocious barbarians had been sufficiently discouraging. Yet evidence was accumulating of the rising strength of the Nestorian Christians at the Mongol court. Sempad, the constable of Armenia, had been received with civility by Küyük in 1247, as the delegate of his brother Hayton, who had long professed himself the loyal and humble vassal of the Khan. From Samarkand, on his way back, Sempad despatched (April 1248) a letter to his brother-in-law Henry of Cyprus, in which he spoke with intemperate zeal of 'Tartary' being ripe for conversion and noted that Batu's son Sartak had received Christian baptism. The death of Küyük in 1248 and the arrogant response of Oghul-Ghaimish to Andrew of Longjumeau in 1250 had dampened the ardour of the French king, but the disastrous outcome of his Crusade in Egypt, in which he himself fell a prisoner into Muslim hands, and perhaps the prompting or example of Hayton of Armenia, induced him to make a renewed attempt to seek Mongol co-operation against the Saracens, especially by contacting Sartak and through him influencing the leadership at Karakorum. For this purpose Louis selected William of Rubruck, a Flemish Franciscan, who was commissioned to undertake, not an official diplomatic mission, but a journey of inquiry as a simple preacher of the faith: such a precaution would avoid another humiliating rebuff and information might be gathered which would enable the Christian princes to gauge Mongol intentions and determine what degree of support, if any, might be looked for in a future crusade against Islam. Friar William was cast in the same heroic mould as Carpini; of intrepid courage, shrewd intelligence and acute observation, he compiled a report of his journey, simple, direct and vivid, which ranks high in the literature of travel and has left us an unforgettable picture of Mongol Asia in the mid-thirteenth century.[40]

He set out in 1253, with three companions, from Acre in Palestine, where Louis IX, released from Saracen captivity, was then holding court, and proceeding by sea to Constantinople, he reached Sudak or Soldaia on 21 May, and as he moved out on to the plains north of the Crimea it 'seemed as if I were stepping into another world'.[41] Distressed by the boorishness and exactions of the Mongol officials and robbed by their guides, they crossed the Don and reached the camp of Sartak on 31 July. Introduced by a Nestorian priest, they were well received; Sartak asked their blessing, assured them that King Louis was 'the greatest lord among the Franks', and examined their Bible, crucifix, vestments and royal letter. Ordered to go on to Batu, they crossed the Volga,[42] ascertained that the Caspian was an inland sea, sailed down the river to the khan's *ordu*, the sight of which filled them with fear, for it 'seemed like a great city stretching out a long way and crowded round on every side'. Batu gave audience to them seated on a golden couch, with one of his wives next to him; he questioned them, but made little comment on their answers, offered them some *kumiz*, and sent them on to Möngke. Provided with warm clothing, they left on 14 September, crossed the Ural river, suffering much from cold and hunger, rode past Lake Balkash and through the Uighur country, where they met many Nestorian clergy, spent twelve days at Kayaligh (in modern Kazakhstan),[43] and by Christmas had reached Möngke's *ordu* north of the Altai. On 4 January 1254, they were brought into the presence of the Great Khan, who was sitting on a couch inside a tent covered with cloth of gold; they found Möngke 'a flat-nosed man of medium height, about forty-five years old', and when they explained they had been sent by Batu, he exclaimed: 'Just as the sun spreads its rays in all directions, so my power and the power of Batu is spread everywhere.'[44] Clearly he had strongly Christian sympathies: there were many Nestorian priests about the court, and a church on the *ordu*, in which Möngke sometimes attended services along with his Christian wife, but although an Armenian monk assured Rubruck that the Khan would receive baptism on the feast of the Epiphany, two days later, nothing of the sort took place and instead he observed Möngke practising an ancient form of divination by the shoulder-blades of sheep.

As spring approached, the court prepared to move northwards to Karakorum. The friars accompanied it and reached the Mongol capital on Palm Sunday. Rubruck was not impressed: the place was no bigger than St Denis, the village outside Paris, it was divided into two sections, a Muslim and a Chinese, and the tolerance of the khans was evinced by its twelve temples, two mosques, and one church.[45] It swarmed with European captives and foreign envoys: among the former Rubruck distinguished William Buchier, a master goldsmith from Paris, Paquette, a woman of Metz married to a Russian, and an Englishman named Basil, all of whom had been captured in Hungary in 1241; among the latter were representatives of the Caliph, the Sultan of Rum, and the 'Sultan of India'. Men of all races and creeds jostled in this centre of world empire. Yet though the friars might hope, through the good offices of Bolgai, Möngke's Nestorian minister or secretary of state, to preach the faith to the master of that empire, the nearest they got was to participate in a theological debate before him, in which the Christians, the Muslims and the Buddhists[46] set out their respective systems. In private converse at Pentecost, Möngke assured them that the Mongols believed in one God but that there were several roads to heaven, as there were five fingers on one hand, but he encouraged no discussion about Christianity and contented himself with asking them to take back with them a letter to King Louis. Its tone was only a shade less arrogant than Küyük's reply to Pope Innocent: 'It is the decree of the Eternal Heaven which we make known to you. When you have heard and believed, if you wish to obey us, send your envoys to us; in this way we shall know for sure whether you wish to be at peace or war with us. When by the power of the Eternal Heaven the whole world from the rising of the sun to the going down thereof shall be at one in joy and peace, then it will be made clear what we are going to do; if you are unwilling and say, "Our country is far away, our mountains are mighty, our sea is vast", and in this confidence you bring an army against us—we know what we can do. He who has made difficult things easy and far off things near, He knows.'[47] With this dusty answer, the friars departed, retracing their weary steps back to Batu, who had Möngke's letter translated for him; they made a dreadful crossing of the Caucasus in the depth of winter, passed through the territory of the Sultan of Rum, who received them at Konia at Easter 1255, moved into Little Armenia, sailed to Cyprus, and then to Tripoli in Syria, which they reached in August, the journey having taken two years and a half.

The achievement of this laborious and dangerous expedition was more noteworthy than its results, which were disappointing. Yet there is a remarkable difference between the mission of Carpini and that of Rubruck eight years later. The former was a papal diplomatic embassy, consisting of an appeal and a protest: the latter was a purely religious mission, whose members sought permission to bring the Christian faith to the notice of the Mongol leaders, one of whom they had reason to believe was baptized. Carpini acted under the powerful impact of the frightful Mongol devastation of Eastern Europe, then quite recent; he inquired discreetly into the sources of Mongol military power, and returned with practical advice on how to repel a second invasion. When Rubruck was despatched to Mongolia, the memory of the suffering of Russia, Poland and Hungary twelve years before was beginning to fade; as Batu did not return, the confidence of Europe revived, and King Louis's friars, though sceptical of conversions reported among the khans,[48] were apprehensive of danger less from the Mongols than from the Muslims, and Rubruck's report concludes with an optimistic estimate of the chances of a new Crusade for the recovery of the Holy Land. The change of attitude was due probably to the impression Rubruck brought back from Möngke's court, not that the Mongols were about to turn Christian, but that they were planning a tremendous offensive against Islam which might shatter the power of the remaining Muslim States and so restore the whole Christian position in Western Asia.[49]

A few months after giving audience to Rubruck, Möngke received the King of Armenia, who was vigorously pursuing his policy of a Mongol alliance in the hope that an offensive against Islam would redound to the advantage of Asian Christianity. At the summons of Batu, Hayton left Sis[50] early in 1254, travelled in disguise through the territories of the Sultan of Rum, who (says the chronicler[51]) hated the King on account of the succour he had received from the Tatars, crossed the Caucasus to the *ordu* of Batu and Sartak,[52] who sent him 'by a very long road' beyond the Caspian. Shaping his course by a more southerly route than Carpini and Rubruck, he crossed the Irtish and passed by the Naiman country into Mongolia, where on 13 September the faithful vassal was welcomed by the Great Khan, who gave him a diploma (*yarlik*) of safe conduct and a letter of enfranchisement for the Christian churches everywhere. Repledging his loyalty, Hayton spent fifty days at court, and returned via the Dzungarian desert, the Ala-tau and the Ili valley. At Talas early in 1255 he heard of the approach of Hülegü, Möngke's brother, who had been commissioned to subdue the Muslim kingdoms of the West, and passing the Oxus, he made his way back through Khurasan and Azerbaijan to Armenia. The brief narrative of his journey is enlivened by curious details of natural history such as the wild horses and wild camels still to be found in these regions,[53] by references to the Buddha[54] and the yellow-robed Buddhist monks, and by fantasies of a race of hairy dogs with human wives.[55]

During their sojourns in Karakorum, both Rubruck and Hayton heard of the plans and observed the preparations for the next stage of Mongol world conquest which was intended to render the reign of Möngke illustrious. The succession disputes were temporarily stilled; the coup of 1251 had signalized the victory of the house of Tolui, and the new Great Khan, having crushed the conspiracy against him, announced in a solemn *kuriltai* that expeditions would be mounted in east and west, against the Sung in China and against the Assassins and the Caliphate 'as far as the borders of Egypt'. So grandiose a scheme of world domination was perhaps never conceived. Möngke himself proposed to take charge of the Chinese war, but the Western expedition was confided to his younger brother Hülegü,[56] who thereby became the conqueror of Baghdad and the founder of the Il-khan dynasty in Persia. The march of Hülegü from the Oxus almost to the Nile is one of the great epochs of history; it promised to revolutionize the political and religious relationships of western Asia, yet it ended at last in stultification when the old dynastic feuds broke out afresh and stopped the hands of the conquerors.[57]

The decision to re-establish Mongol power in Persia was a wise one, for since the time of Chingis's devastating sweep through Transoxiana and Khurasan in 1219–24 the provinces of eastern Iran had languished in anarchy. The first Mongol commander after Chingis, Chormagan, had destroyed the remnants of the Khwarizmian kingdom, and his successor Baiju, who took over in 1242, had moved west and crushed the power of the Seljuks of Rum at Köse-Dagh in 1243. But the Mongol forces were limited and concentrated in Azerbaijan and the pastures of the Araxes valley; the princes of Georgia, the kings of Armenia, the *atabegs* of Mosul, and the petty dynasts of Fars and Kirman, retained their thrones at the price of admitting themselves to be the vassals of the Great Khan; the Abbasid caliphs still reigned in Baghdad, and the Isma'ilis continued to terrorize the Muslim world from their castles in the Elburz mountains. The regions under direct Mongol rule, Khurasan and Irak Ajami, had scarcely recovered from the ruin and massacres of Chingis's day, and their misery was deepened by the fiscal exactions of the Mongol officials, whose tyranny might have proceeded more from ignorance than brutality. As the years passed, the level of barbarism fell and that of civilization rose; more competent or educated governors employed experienced native administrators, and the peasant, trader and artisan were relieved of the worst oppression. Korguz, an Uighur Turk from Besh-balik,[58] appointed governor of Khurasan by Ögedei, punished corruption and dishonesty, brought the old Persian bureaucratic machine back into operation, rebuilt the ruined city of Tus,[59] and though himself a Buddhist,[60] protected the Muslim majority of the population, whose faith he himself ultimately adopted. A reformer makes many enemies; those whose abuses he punished falsely accused him of misgovernment, and under the regency of Töregene he was put to death. His successor Arghun Agha,[61] an Oirat Mongol who had served in Ögedei's chancery, fortunately walked in his steps; he stopped the ruinous embezzlement of the public funds, and persuaded Möngke to restore in Persia by means of a new census the efficient and equitable system of taxation which Mas'ud Yalavach had long administered in Transoxiana. Yet the separation of military and civil powers characteristic of the Mongol régime in these lands for twenty years was productive of much mischief and confusion, and the appointment of Hülegü with supreme authority over his extensive viceroyalty implied the substitution of firm and unitary governments under native officials.

In this pursuit of unity, the survival of independent powers could no longer be permitted. Möngke resolved to destroy both the Assassins and the Caliph, since too many men bestowed on them a loyalty and veneration to which the Great Khan alone was entitled. That both these doomed powers were Muslim created in Christian circles the impression that the Mongols had decreed the overthrow of Islam,[62] yet the motive in each case was political and not religious. The friendly spirit manifested by generals and governors towards the Christians usually masked secular aims and was sometimes no more than the tolerant indifference to all faiths required by the *Yasa* of Chingis. When the monk Simeon arrived in Persia armed with orders from Ögedei, the local officials overnight became gracious and even deferential to priests and monks of all churches. Baiju was more hostile, perhaps simply because of Ascelin's tactlessness, but Eljigidei,[63] sent by Küyük in 1247 as a kind of *missus dominicus*, assured Louis IX that the Mongols would take all Christians under their protection and hinted that a new Crusade against Egypt could be run parallel to a Mongol attack on Baghdad. Yet, notwithstanding the more courteous tone of the Mongol embassy to Cyprus in 1248, the court of Kara-korum regarded every foreign king who sent envoys to it as a suppliant or vassal, and the responses of Oghul-Ghaimish and Möngke to Louis IX are couched in the language of the most arrogant imperialism. The Mongol leadership was far from being consistently anti-Muslim; it had employed Muslim minis-ters and advisers from early days, and the khans, anxious for the blessings of the ministers of every cult, were as willing to frequent mosques as churches.[64]

None the less, the character and composition of Hülegü's western expedition was such as to raise the hopes and spirits of Christians who had languished for six centuries under Muslim domination. Though Hülegü himself was a pagan with Buddhist leanings, his principal wife Dokuz Khatun, a Ke024 princess and niece of the Wang-Khan,[65] was an ardent Nestorian Christian; a woman of ability and intelligence, she was highly respected by Möngke as well as her husband;[66] her heart and purse were ever open to favour her co-religionists, and a movable chapel, in which mass was celebrated daily, stood at the entrance to her *ordu*. The ablest of Hülegü's captains, the *noyan* Ked-Buka or Kitbuka,[67] was a Christian Naiman, and as the campaign developed, more and more contingents of Christian troops (Turks, Georgians, Alans, Armenians) swelled the khan's army. The Nestorians, so long exiles and wanderers in Central Asia, were returning to the lands of their origin; some may have viewed the war against the Assassins, the Caliph and the Mamluks as a crusade against the enemies of Christ, but the Mongol chiefs were intent solely on removing the impious rivals of God and the Khan.

The campaign was planned with usual Mongol thoroughness.[68] Möngke assigned to his brother two out of every ten fighting men in the Mongol armed forces; a thousand 'teams'[69] of Chinese engineers were recruited to work the siege engines and the naphtha flame-throwers; agents were despatched far and wide along the intended route of the expedition to requisition meadows and grazing-lands, to collect adequate stores of flour and wines, to round up herds of mares for the provision of sufficient *kumiz*, to clear stones and thickets from the roads, to build or repair bridges, and to hold boats in readiness on the rivers. Ked-Buka led the van of the army out of Karakorum in the spring of 1253; after receiving his final instructions from Möngke, Hülegü followed in October, moved by slow stages across the Central Asian steppes, and encamped in the pastures outside Samarkand in the autumn of 1255. Contingents from other Mongol princes, including Batu, joined him; at Kish he was welcomed by Arghun, the governor of Persia, and on New Year's Day 1256 the mighty army made the passage of the Oxus, on the Persian side of which its master received the homage of the rival sultans of Rum, Shams al-Din of Herat, and a crowd of amirs and atabegs. Not since Chingis had been here nearly forty years before in pursuit of the Khwariz-mian Shah had there been so formidable and terrifying a display of Mongol power. The Assassins,[70] who were the first marked for destruction, trembled behind the walls of their castles; their last grand master, Rukn ad-Din, a frightened young man, strove to parley and gain time; ordered by Hülegü instantly to dismantle his fortifications, he shuffled and evaded; Ked-Buka commenced siege operations; Rukn ad-Din surrendered (November 1256), and was told to order the capitulation of Alamut and other strongholds. One by one the 'eagles' nests' were dislodged and destroyed, and their inmates pitilessly slaughtered even to the children in their cradles; some spasmodic resistance was crushed as much by fear as by force, and the fanatical sect which had terrorized the Muslim world for nearly two centuries was exter-minated. The grand master begged to be allowed to go to the Great Khan; Hülegü granted his prayer, but when Rukn ad-Din reached Karakorum, Möngke refused to see him and ordered him away. On the road back, he was slain by his guards by being kicked to pulp and finished off with a sword. Thus (says the historian piously) was the world cleansed which had been polluted with their evil.[71]

The orthodox Muslims might applaud the ruin of the heretics, even if accomplished by the hand of pagans, but their rejoicing speedily turned to alarm and horror as the Mongol arms were next turned against Baghdad, the metropolis of Islam and the seat of the Abbasid Caliphate. Whatever his private religious opinions, Hülegü had no hostility towards the Muslim faith, but the con-tinued existence of a sovereign like the Caliph, who claimed a vague authority over millions, was an affront to Tengri and the Great Khan, who brooked no rival on earth. After smoking out the last nests of Assassins in the Elburz hills, Hülegü moved in March 1257 to Hamadan, where he took into his service the celebrated astronomer Nasir ad-Din Tusi,[72] reproached Baiju for neglecting to extend Mongol power farther in Persia and Irak, and issued an imperious summons to the Caliph, complaining that he had failed to furnish troops for the war against the Assassins, reminding him of the many kingdoms that had succumbed to Mongol attack, and demanding that he should dismantle the fortifications of his capital and present himself in person at the camp of the Khan. The recipient of this arrogant message was perhaps the least worthy of the thirty-seven commanders of the faithful who had reigned at Baghdad; weak, vain, incompetent and cowardly, Mustas'im had never displayed a trace of statesmanship or nobility, and his foolish confidence in his political and military strength was perhaps deliberately fostered by a treacherous vizier of Shi'ite sympathies who might hope with Mongol help to replace the Abbasids with a descendant of Ali.[73] He returned a haughty answer: the house of Abbas would stand firm till the Day of Resurrection, all who had attacked Baghdad in the past had perished, Muslims from east and west were the servants of his court and would defend him, he possessed thousands of troops 'who would dry up the waves of the sea', and he advised Hülegü, 'O young man scarcely entered upon your career', to retire to Khurasan.[74] The Mongol envoys were mobbed in the streets of Baghdad, and Hülegü concentrated his forces against the doomed city. Baiju was ordered to proceed from Rum via Mosul to encompass it on the western side, Ked-Buka advanced from Luristan, the contingents from the Golden Horde, commanded by three nephews of Batu, approached from Kurdistan, and Hülegü himself led the main body from Hulwan. The Caliph's army, amounting to 20,000 men, checked the first onslaught, but the Mongols broke the dykes and flooded the enemy camp; thousands were drowned, and the survivors escaped back into the city, where their stories doubtless disheartened the defenders. In January 1258 the investment of the great metropolis was completed; a general assault was ordered, a week's bombardment shattered the tower flanking one of the gates and allowed the attackers to break in, the whole eastern wall was captured, retreat down the Tigris was cut off, and when Hülegü had roughly refused to treat with several deputations sent out to him, Mustas'im lost hope and resolved to surrender. On 10 February, accompanied by his sons, ministers and notables, he came out;

Hülegü told him to order resistance to cease, which being done, the Mongols swarmed into the city and plundered and murdered for a week.[75] The unhappy Caliph was forced to disgorge his treasures and to listen to mocking reproaches for not having used them to put up a stronger defence;[76] his palace, the grand mosque, the tombs of the Abbasids, and other public buildings were burnt, much of the cultural accumulation of five centuries was destroyed, and a blow was struck at Arabic civilization from which it never recovered. Ten days after his surrender, Mustas'im was taken to a village outside Baghdad and there executed, apparently by being rolled in a carpet and kicked to death by horses.[77] Nearly all the male members of his house met a similar fate. Of the other cities of his dominions, Wasit resisted and its population was massacred, Kufa and Basra submitted and were spared; Irak bowed beneath the Mongol yoke, and the way was prepared for advance westwards towards Syria, the Mediterranean and Egypt.

The Mongols always displayed a shrewd cunning in exploiting the feuds and quarrels of their enemies. By proclaiming war against the hitherto invincible Assassins, they engaged the sympathy of Sunnite Islam; by destroying the head and centre of Sunnite Islam, they won the gratitude of the Shi'ite factions and the eastern Christians. Shi'ite notables like Nasir ad-Din Tusi were patronized and employed as Mongol agents; the Alids were encouraged to believe that they would profit by the fall of the Abbasids, and a Mongol guard, stationed at the tomb or shrine of Ali at Najaf near Kufa,[78] might seem to proclaim the reverent regard of the conquerors for the first of the Imams. For the churches of the East the ruin of Baghdad was clearly a divine retribution for five centuries of oppression, and in Hülegü they discerned a protector and potential convert. On his way to Baghdad, he had received at Tabriz the chiefs of Georgia, who agreed to furnish substantial bodies of troops for the campaign, and these doughty mountaineers, who had long considered the orthodox Muslims the enemies of their faith and nation, are alleged to have displayed peculiar relish in the work of killing and destruction when the city fell.[79] The Christian inhabitants of Baghdad, who presumably were mostly Nestorians, were gathered in a church under their patriarch and not one suffered injury while the Muslim citizens were dying in their thousands in the streets and houses. 'During the time of Baghdad's supremacy,' cried the Armenian

THE CHRISTIAN RESPONSE

chronicler, 'like an insatiable bloodsucker she had swallowed up the whole world. Now she has been punished for all the blood she has spilled and the evil she has wrought, the measure of her iniquity being filled.'[80]

Never indeed had the fortunes of Islam stood at a lower level. It no longer had a recognized head or centre of unity; the ferocious pagans were in occupation of its plundered and ravaged metropolis, and no Muslim prince reigned east of the Tigris save by their permission and as their slave. The future was bleak: Hülegü's commission was to subdue 'all the lands of the West', and even the holy cities of Mecca and Medina might not be safe from the brutal and sacrilegious enemy. As the Mongol armies rolled forward, the Christians of every sect raised their heads and prepared to avenge themselves on their Muslim rivals and oppressors; the example of the Georgians was followed by that of the Armenians, whose king might feel justified in having some years before humbly placed his kingdom and person at the disposal of the Great Khan; the Frankish Crusaders, clinging precariously to a narrow strip of Syrian coast, both hoped and feared that the Mongols might drive the Muslims from Jerusalem and restore the holy places to Christian possession; and the Nestorian clergy, rejoicing in the benign protection of Dokuz Khatun[81] and Hülegü's Christian general Ked-Buka, envisaged the early triumph of the Cross in the old homelands of Christianity and the permanent subjection of the Muslim remnant. In the eyes of the eastern Christians, the next stage of Mongol advance assumed the character of a Crusade, and they eagerly awaited the destruction of the few remaining centres of Muslim power and resistance.

When Hülegü occupied Baghdad, he was master of the greatest and richest city the Mongols had ever captured. Before the stench of corpses drove him out into the purer air of the countryside, he ordered the bazaars to reopen and the bodies to be cleared from the streets, assigned one of the Caliph's palaces to the Nestorian patriarch, and collected the mass of treasures, part of which was despatched to Möngke in Karakorum and the rest conveyed to a building constructed especially to house it on an island in Lake Urmiya.[82] He retired to Hamadan and then to Azerbaijan, where he received a crowd of trembling suppliants, sultans, amirs and atabegs,[83] and reorganized and refitted his army, which perhaps reached the formidable figure of 400,000 men. King Hayton

112

contributed a force of 16,000 Armenians, and his son-in-law Bohemund VI of Antioch and Tripoli the only contingent of Western troops who ever fought under the banner of the khan. Muslim Syria, the new target of attack, was divided into six principalities, governed by Ayyubid princes, descendants of the house of Saladin, the senior being Nasir Yusuf, who ruled from Aleppo or Halab and who cherished the hope of restoring Ayyubid power in Egypt, where the Mamluk slave soldiery had seized control in 1250. In the autumn of 1259 Hülegü launched the offensive; marching from Azerbaijan, he moved into the province of Jazirah, or northern Irak, and laid siege to Maijyfarikin, the ancient Martyropolis, whose amir Kamil Muhammad, a fanatical Muslim, was marked out for vengeance for having crucified a Jacobite priest who was travelling through the land with a Mongol passport. The Georgians and Armenians took a prominent part in the blockade, which produced a terrible famine and ultimate capitulation. [84] Kamil Muhammad met a dreadful end: pieces of flesh were cut off his body and thrust into his mouth, and so (says the chronicler, soberly) he died, while his head stuck on a lance, was paraded around the cities of Syria as a grim warning. Crossing the Tigris, the Khan moved through Nasibin, Harran and Edessa, passed over the Euphrates by the bridge of boats at Manbij, and brought up twenty catapults to smash down the walls of Aleppo, from which Sultan Nasir had fled to Damascus. The city fell in January 1260, and was punished for its resistance by the usual methodical massacre, prolonged for six days; [85] King Hayton gratefully accepted part of the booty, and Bohemund recovered several castles and districts he had lost to the Muslims. Panic spread through Syria; Nasir abandoned Damascus and took the road to Egypt, and the great city surrendered itself without a fight into the hands of Ked-Buka. Three Christian chiefs, Ked-Buka, King Hayton and Count Bohemund made a triumphal entry; Muslims were forced to bow to the cross as it was carried in procession through the streets, and one of the city mosques was turned into a Christian church. [86] True to the policy of allowing escaping foes no rest, Ked-Buka set off in pursuit of Nasir; his patrols passed through Samaria and reached Gaza; [87] the Sultan was betrayed and captured and sent to Hülegü, who now issued the usual imperious summons to the Mamluks of Egypt to surrender or perish. [88] 'You have heard [he said] how we have conquered a vast empire and have purified the earth of the disorders which tainted it. It is for you to fly and for us to pursue, and whither will you fly, and by what road shall you escape us? Our horses are swift, our arrows sharp, our swords like thunderbolts, our hearts as hard as the mountains, our soldiers as numerous as the sand. Fortresses will not detain us, nor arms stop us: Your prayers to heaven will not avail against us. We mean well by our warning. At present you are the only enemy against whom we have to march.' But by the time the message was delivered, a distant and unexpected event had transformed the situation. At his camp near Aleppo Hülegü received with grief the news that the previous August his brother Möngke had died in China. The campaign in the West was not yet over, and the imperial throne was vacant.

The death of Ögedei in 1241 had saved Christian Europe: the death of Möngke in 1259 was to save Muslim Asia. Like Batu on the earlier occasion, Hülegü had no ambition to take the supreme power himself; as Möngke's children were young and untried, he favoured the succession of his younger brother Kubilai, who had already distinguished himself in the Chinese campaigns, but another of the sons of Tolui, Arik-Böke, who was in control of the Mongolian homeland, hastily summoned a *kuriltai* in Kara-korum and had himself elected Great Khan. An armed conflict broke out between the rival claimants; Arik-Böke intervened in the affairs of the Chagatai khanate;[89] Hülegü might fear a similar interference in his own domain, and he deemed it prudent to concentrate the bulk of his forces in Azerbaijan, leaving behind in Syria only a light screen of troops under the command of Ked-Buka.[90] This weakening of the Mongol position soon became known in Cairo; the Mamluk Sultan Kutuz reminded his generals that the defence of Islam rested on them alone; the Mongol envoys were executed and their heads displayed on the city gates; a *levée en masse* was decreed against the pagan enemies of the faith, the killers of the Caliph, and the army marched out of Egypt and took the road to Palestine. A request was sent to the Franks for permission to pass through their territory. The barons met at Acre in an atmosphere of doubt and uncertainty.[91] Their Saracen foes were hard pressed: the long foretold Mongol-Christian alliance, so ardently embraced by King Hayton, might deal the deathblow to Islam. On the other hand, the Mongols were treacherous and blood-thirsty pagans; the fearful devastation of

eastern Europe less than twenty years before had not been forgotten; these arrogant imperialists required slaves not allies, and
submission could be bought at a heavy price. Count Bohemund's
association with them was strongly disapproved and was punished
by papal excommunication; a local conflict between a Mongol
patrol and a Frankish baron Julian of Sidon had resulted in the
death of Ked-Buka's nephew and the ravaging of Sidon town and
harbour,[92] and the Crusaders in the end rejected the policy of the
eastern Christians and agreed to allow Kutuz passage for his
troops. Ked-Buka moved his depleted force to meet them. At Ain
Jalut[93] near Nazareth on 3 September 1260 the superior Mamluk
army inflicted a crushing defeat; Ked-Buka was killed, and the
spell the great Chingis had cast upon the world was broken
for ever.[94]

The battle of Ain Jalut was a turning-point in history. The
Mongol advance in the West ground to a halt and was never
seriously renewed; Egypt was saved and rose in consequence to
the status of a Muslim Great Power and the repository of what
was left of the old Arabic civilization; the Muslims in the wake
of their victory opened a great counter-offensive against the
Mongols and their Christian allies, and the dream of a Christian
restoration in the Near East was dispelled for ever. Five days after
the battle Kutuz entered Damascus; within a month the Mongols
had lost Aleppo, and the Mamluks were soon seriously con-
sidering the restoration of the Abbasid Caliphate in Baghdad.[95]
Here their zeal outran their capacity; though the Mamluks annexed
Syria, the Mongols retained a firm grip on Irak, and Baybars, the
brilliant soldier who seized the throne on the morrow of Ain Jalut
by the simple expedient of murdering Sultan Kutuz, was content
to install a relative of the last Abbasid as puppet Caliph in Cairo,
whose main function was to legitimize Mamluk rule and convince
the Muslim faithful that Egypt was now the heart of Islam.[96]

The defeat of Ked-Buka is less surprising than the failure of
Hülegü to avenge that defeat, which inflicted so severe a blow to
the prestige of the masters of the world, to whom victory appeared
natural and automatic. A Mongol detachment did indeed pene-
trate Syria and pillage Aleppo for the second time, but it was
repulsed by the Mamluks near Hims (December 1260) and driven
back across the Euphrates. In fact, Hülegü dared not commit the
bulk of his army in Syria in view of an external situation menacing

to his position. Having declared himself for Kubilai, he might well fear a victory of Arik-Böke, and this contest was not decided in favour of the former until 1262. Alghu, a protégé of Arik-Böke, was a growing potential threat beyond the Oxus to Hülegü's domination of Persia. And most serious of all, Batu had died in 1255 and been succeeded, after the brief reign of his son Sartak, by his brother Berke, who had adopted the Muslim faith and been outraged by Hülegü's treatment of the Caliph.[97] The boundaries of their respective realms were ill-defined; Berke developed territorial claims in the Caucasus against his cousin;[98] he might fear the reduction of his khanate to vassal status if Hülegü subdued both Syria and Egypt, and after Ain Jalut it was common prudence on his part to enter into alliance with the Mamluks. The rulers of Egypt and the Golden Horde were indeed separated by lands and seas, but the recovery of Constantinople by the Greeks under Michael Palaeologus in July 1261 enabled them to communicate through that city, which lay athwart the sea route connecting Alexandria with the Crimean ports.[99] Embassies were exchanged;[100] the new Abbasid puppet Caliph in Cairo blessed the alliance; the names of Berke and Baybars were jointly pronounced in the *khutba* in the mosques of Egypt, and Hülegü was threatened by a vast encircling movement extending from Chagatai through the Kipchak khanate to the Mamluk realm, which now included Syria as well as the Nile valley. The victory of Kubilai over Arik-Böke in 1262 brought him no profit, since Kubilai was far away and preoccupied with the war against the Sung.

The death of Möngke ended the unity of the Mongol Empire. The succession was for the first time decided by armed conflict, but though Kubilai won out against Arik-Böke and reigned as the fifth Great Khan, his direct authority and even his interest was confined to China. The long and stubborn struggle against the Sung was not decided until 1279, and Kubilai then expended much effort, men and money in a last striking and disastrous manifestation of Mongol imperialism, the vain attempt to conquer Japan. Of the affairs of the Western regions he could take no cognizance, and the khanates of Chagatai, the Golden Horde and Persia went their several ways as virtually independent States, in which the Mongol ruling class was gradually submerged in the subject population of Turks and Iranians. A vast imperial realm comprising nearly all Asia and much of Europe could not be governed by one man from one centre; Karakorum which for a few years was a world capital, shrank back into the obscurity of the Mongolian steppe, and in the absence of a single authority capable of enforcing the *Yasa* of Chingis, each local khan sought to perpetuate his power by respecting the laws and religions of the majority of his subjects.

In these circumstances, the hopes so long entertained by King Hayton and the Nestorians of a Christian restoration in Asia remained unfulfilled. The skirmish at Ain Jalut had raised everywhere the spirit of the Muslims, so recently depressed by the horrors of the sack of Baghdad, and their optimism was strengthened when the quarrel between Hülegü and Berke issued in open war in 1262.[101] Already Berke had demanded the return of the troops he had contributed to Hülegü's expedition; commercial relations were severed, and the growing amity of Kipchak and Mamluks at length provoked Hülegü into marching northwards through the pass of Derbend against his recalcitrant kinsman. On the banks of the Terek he was surprised by an enemy force under the command of Berke's nephew Nogai; many thousands were drowned when the ice of the river gave way beneath them; Hülegü was obliged to retreat back into Azerbaijan, and Berke called on Allah to curse him who had caused Mongols to perish by the swords of other Mongols.[102] The Mamluks were encouraged to press the Muslim *revanche* against the Latins and Armenians, whom they considered in part responsible for the injuries inflicted on Islam; Antioch fell to Baybars in 1268, Armenia was ravaged, King Hayton abdicated in despair in 1269, the Crusading outposts in Syria were taken one by one, and with the surrender of Acre in 1291 the Frankish kingdom of Jerusalem, created nearly two centuries before by Godfrey of Bouillon, was finally snuffed out. When Hülegü died at Maragha in 1265, followed in a few months by his Christian wife, the Christians of the East mourned the passing of the new Constantine and the new Helena; his son and grandson shared his religious sympathies and sought the alliance of the Popes and the Christian princes of Europe, but the Mamluk-Kipchak union remained firm and undefeated, and Islam rose to new strength in Western Asia.

Although some faint hopes continued to be cherished of the conversion of the 'Tartars' and even Polo expected that Kubilai might consent to be baptized, the issue was really decided on the morrow of Ain Jalut. Only the most sanguine missionary could hereafter envisage the Mongol leaders adopting a policy so inimical to their interests. For Christianity disposed of no political or military power of consequence in Asia, and a few Turkish tribes and small Christian kingdoms like Georgia and Armenia were hopelessly outbalanced by the massive urban populations of Persia and China, who adhered to Islam or Buddhism and whose goodwill their Mongol rulers were anxious to purchase. The Nestorian Church had a noble record of evangelical endeavour, and the Latin missionaries who followed them into the depths of Asia in the thirteenth and fourteenth centuries displayed equal courage and intrepidity, but if the harvest was plenteous, the labourers were few, and when the unity of the Mongol Empire, which had facilitated communication throughout the continent, was once destroyed after the death of Möngke, the small Christian colonies were cut off from their sources and withered and died in isolation. That the Il-khans of Persia should have turned Muslim and Kubilai and his heirs in China have favoured Buddhism should occasion no surprise, though it may seem strange that the Golden Horde did not go Christian and adopt Byzantine-Slav culture. But Russia was a marginal land so far as the Horde was concerned, and the heart of the khanate (the lower Volga) was in a Turkish-speaking region, already partly islamized before the Mongol invasion. Even so, Sartak was apparently a Christian (his conversion is better attested than that of Küyük and Möngke), and the adherence of the ruling house to Islam was delayed here longer than elsewhere in the Mongol West.[103]

7

Nomad imperialism: Mongol rule in China and Persia

Because of the gigantic scale of their conquests, the Mongols were the first and only nomadic people to face in its acutest form the problem of ruling, with no previous experience, ancient sedentary societies whose population derived sustenance and wealth from the cultivation of the soil. The ancient story of Cain and Abel recalls the age-old conflict between the shepherd and the husbandman; the horseman of the steppes had always despised the peasant of the field, and early raids and invasions had been destructive and transitory. Even the vast though ephemeral Turkish conquests of the sixth century scarcely extended beyond the limits of the steppe, and the inroads of the Seljuk Turks into the Persian and Arab lands in the eleventh century were softened by the common religion professed by invader and invaded. But the Mongols, pagan and uncultured, ranged far beyond the Eurasian regions dominated by the mounted stockmen; they broke into and reduced to subjection the civilized realms of China and Persia, the half-civilized plains of Russia, and the commercial oases of Central Asia. The battles of peace are proverbially the most difficult to win; when the Mongols had stamped out the last sparks of resistance, they were obliged to consider how best they might perpetuate their rule, exploit the wealth and conciliate the natives of the lands they had occupied. Their response to this challenge varied in form and effectiveness, and if not all their leaders were as skilled and successful as Kubilai in China, their achievement in general was on a higher level than might have been expected from men whose horizon was limited by the primitive customs of tribal society.

The transition from conquest to consolidation was made soon after the death of Möngke in 1259, which ended the heroic age of Mongol expansion. The battle of Ain Jalut in 1260 excluded the conquerors of the world for ever from Egypt and Africa; the Golden Horde never seriously renewed the assault on Europe, and if Kubilai destroyed the power of the Sung by 1279, his attempts at overseas conquests in the Far East foundered on Mongol ignorance of naval warfare. The unity of the Empire was dissolved; the dissolution was followed by internecine conflict; the Golden Horde fought the Il-khans of Persia, and Kubilai, the fifth and last of the Great Khans, reached that position only after a civil war which decided more than which of two claimants should occupy the imperial throne.

Towards the close of his short reign, the Great Khan Möngke, leaving his youngest brother Arik-Böke[1] in command in Karakorum, took charge of the campaign in China, where his other brother Kubilai acted in a subordinate capacity. In the summer of 1259 Möngke died of dysentery at the town of Hochwan, in the province of Szechwan;[2] Kubilai summoned a *kuriltai* at Chang-tu in Jehol in June 1260, at which he was proclaimed Great Khan, but Arik-Böke, rightly asserting that such an assembly convoked outside the Mongol homeland was invalid, and encouraged by Möngke's Nestorian minister Bolgai, was himself raised to supreme power by a rival *kuriltai* at Karakorum. The struggle for the succession distracted the empire for four years; Kaidu,[3] the head of the house of Ögedei, and Alghu, of the house of Chagatai, embraced the cause of Arik-Böke, but the superior generalship of Kubilai and the loyal backing of the army in China decided the issue; Arik-Böke surrendered and was pardoned in 1264, and though Kaidu's hostility was unabated and indeed outlived Kubilai himself, the latter's throne was never henceforth seriously shaken. As the rivals represented totally different policies, the conflict was politically decisive. Arik-Böke spoke for traditional Mongol conservatism, which abhorred the corruption of the people of Chingis by the insidious lure of civilized luxury. Kubilai saw no future for the empire except in a partnership between the Mongol ruling class and their sophisticated and far more numerous subjects. With the defeat of Arik-Böke, Karakorum was abandoned as the imperial capital, and Kubilai, fixing himself at Peking in 1260, enlarged it in 1267 into a magnificent winter residence which received the name of T'ai-tu, or 'great court', but which the Turks knew as Khan-Balik, 'the Khan's city', the Kanbalu or Cambulac of Marco Polo and the Latins.[4]

Almost the whole of Kubilai's long life was spent in China. As a boy, he was present at his grandfather's last campaign; by Möngke he was appointed to command the war against the Sung, and on vindicating his claim to the imperial throne, it seemed natural that he should transfer the centre of empire to a Chinese city within the Great Wall and that he should aspire to reign as Son of Heaven rather than as a Mongol khan. He exercised a nominal suzerainty over the whole vast domain which had been subdued by Mongol arms; the Golden Horde acknowledged his supremacy, and the successors of Hülegü in Persia by assuming the title of Il-khans, or subordinates,[5] proclaimed their vassal status, Kubilai's seal was impressed on their State documents, and his representative, a kind of high commissioner, resided at Tabriz.[6] From long experience, he acquired an appreciation of Chinese culture, and if a knowledge of the difficult script and language eluded him,[7] he admired the refinements of urban life, the beauty of Chinese architecture, and the ordered and pacific stability of Chinese society. Always a proud Mongol, he never forgot that he was the grandson of the divine Chingis who should not rest till the whole globe had been brought under the sway of Tengri and the khan; but in him the harsh and barbarous militarism of the Mongols was blended uneasily with the smooth and sophisticated civilization of the Middle Kingdom. After the defeat of Arik-Böke, Kubilai devoted himself to the affairs of China, and his policy and acts are an instructive lesson in the problems facing an intelligent barbarian who rules an ancient and literate society.

The primary objective of Kubilai was to restore the unity of the Chinese realm, a unity destroyed at the fall of the T'ang. The succession of barbarians who had reigned in the north concluded with the Mongols, but China south of the Yang-tse still obeyed the mandates of the Sung, who could plausibly claim to be defenders of native life against the men of the steppe. In the struggle against the Sung, Kubilai could rely, not only on his superb army officered by brilliant generals trained in the school of Chingis and Sübedei, but on the age-long rivalry between north and south, two Chinas which despised each other and seldom remembered their common past and culture.[8] Bayan, his most distinguished general, and A-chu, a grandson of Sübedei's, conducted a war of sieges in the Yang-tse valley; the reduction of the twin cities of Siang-yang and Fancheng was prolonged during five years,[9] but the fall of the Sung capital Hangchow in 1276 announced the impending collapse of southern resistance. In the closing stages of the war, the Sung were betrayed by a perfidious minister, but the more loyal defenders of the dynasty retired to the provinces of Fukien and Kwangtung, and when operations on the mainland could no longer be sustained, sought refuge, with the last Sung emperor, a boy of nine, on the fleet which patrolled the coast around Canton. The ships were attacked and dispersed; the child-emperor was drowned, along with hundreds of his followers, and Kubilai, 'the most powerful man since Adam', reigned undisputed over the most numerous nation on earth. The conquest of the Sung, by placing at his disposal the richest provinces of China and the most flourishing ports, more than doubled his power and resources; the landed gentry were placated by the assurance that their proprietary rights would be respected, and the navy he inherited was employed to reduce to submission the islands and distant kingdoms which had once paid tribute to the Son of Heaven.[10]

Of these kingdoms, the nearest and most powerful was that of Japan, whose civilization was indeed derived from China, but whose national pride and vigour had been buttressed by six centuries of political independence. When the islanders refused the usual summons to surrender, Kubilai prepared an expeditionary force which sailed from Korea (a docile vassal) in 1274 and disembarked on the island of Kyushu, in the strait of Shimonoseki, but the men, consisting mostly of Chinese and Koreans, were driven out by the local *daimyo*. A second armada was despatched in 1281 from the southern ports of Zaitun and Quinsay, consisting of 45,000 Mongols and 120,000 Sino-Koreans, but the fleet was wrecked by a violent summer typhoon and the invaders perished in the sea or by Japanese swords.[11] To the south, the Mongols penetrated the jungles or patrolled the seas of Indo-China and a host of petty kings were reduced to varying degrees of subservience.[12] A naval assault on Champa, whose prince had declined a personal visit to Khan-Balik, resulted in the capture of its capital in 1283; an invasion of Tonkin was halted at Hanoi in 1285; the king of Annam submitted in 1288; the two Thai states acknowledged the suzerainty of the Great Khan in 1294; but Burma had to endure the ravages of a Mongol army and the sacking of her capital Pagan before she was brought in 1297, after the death of Kubilai, to an acceptable condition of thraldom. Nor were the islands of the Indonesian archipelago safe from the ubiquitous conquerors; an army under the command of Chinese generals was landed in 1292 in Java, but after taking the capital, the intruders were expelled by the valour of Raden Vijaya, the hero and founder of the Hindu kingdom of Majapahit. Some idea of the fantastic range of the Mongol conquests may be acquired by reflecting that they extended from Dalmatia to Java. In seventy years the Mongols had traversed the greater part of the globe, but their military progress was accompanied by a growing humanity, and the campaigns of Kubilai's day are on the whole free from the atrocious massacres of non-combatants which stained indelibly the name and fame of Chingis and his immediate successors.

The Chinese may perhaps have applauded the triumphs of Kubilai's arms as the achievements of the emperor of China rather than of the khan of Mongolia. They were not unused to barbarian rule; invaders who had shown a respectful appreciation of Chinese culture were commonly enrolled among the official dynasties, and the house of Kubilai reigned under the title of Yüan, whose annals were compiled in the days of their Ming supplanters. Indeed, during ninety years (1279–1368) the Mongols alone exercised sovereign power in China and discharged the mandate of Heaven; their writ ran from the Great Wall to the Gulf of Tonkin, and after the fall of the Sung, the south was no longer a place of refuge for scholars, monks and officials fleeing from the barbarians of the north. It would not be easy to generalize about their impact on Chinese society. The upper classes, whose standards were formed by the Confucian principles of harmony, order and good taste, were doubtless disgusted and shamed by the offensive presence of uncouth nomads who were destitute of manners and letters, but the merchants profited by the *Pax Mongolica*, and to the peasants it was of no consequence whether they paid their taxes to a Chinese official or a Mongol *darugha*. The resentment of the educated at Mongol rule no doubt explains the policy of racial segregation practised by the conquerors: the Chinese were forbidden to learn the Mongol language, marry a Mongol, or carry arms, and Kubilai and his successors reigned over a disarmed nation and safeguarded the purity of their people, who might else have been sucked into the vast Chinese quicksand.[13] The Mongols were no more than a police force, an army of occupation, but the administration of an imperial realm required the services of a trained, honest and efficient bureaucracy, and Kubilai dared not fill the highest posts with the scholar-mandarins, nourished on the Confucian classics,[14] whose hatred of their new masters might tempt them to betray the régime. The barbarian chief invariably suspects the loyalty of the officials of the conquered people; the case of Theodoric and Boethius is only one of many instances which might be cited in illustration; but as the government cannot be conducted without the professional expertise which the newcomers neither possess nor are capable of acquiring, they are driven either to suffer the machinery of the administration to run down completely or to employ outsiders on whose fidelity they can depend. This second expedient was resorted to by Kubilai. He recruited capable and intelligent foreigners as advisers, members of government bureaux, and even as governors of provinces;[15] Marco Polo acted for three years as governor of the city of Yangiu, or Yangchow, near Nanking;[16] Ahmed Fanakati, a native of Banakat near Tashkent,[17] acquired an unenviable notoriety for his brutal extortions as minister of finance during a period of twenty years,[18] and more honourable service was given by two other Muslims from Transoxiana, Shams ad-Din[19] and his son Nasr ad-Din, who held successively the governorship of Yunnan and distinguished themselves by the measures of flood-control and water-conservancy they undertook by the construction of hydraulic works.[20]

Whatever might be the quality of Kubilai's officials and the disadvantage that many of them were ignorant of the Chinese language, the impressions of contemporary observers are evidence of a high degree of prosperity when domestic peace was restored after the overthrow of the Sung. The Mongol *yam* or postal service was grafted on the traditional Chinese system of communication and speeded the transport of news and goods throughout the empire;[21] the completion of the imperial grand canal (for travel in China was more commonly by water than by road) ensured the regular delivery to the capital of food and other commodities from the distant interior;[22] the public granaries were repaired and restocked as a precaution against famine in years of bad harvests; the provincial viceroys were commanded to make regular distribution of rice and millet to the aged and infirm, and Marco Polo assures us that the poor of Khan-Balik were fed and clothed at the expense of the Great Khan.[23] The ports and harbours and rivers of China were filled with a flourishing commerce; 200,000 boats a year descended the Yang-tse; the wealthy merchants, organized in guilds, transacted their business with paper money, less risky than cash;[24] of the leading entrepôts, Khan-Balik dealt mainly in silk, Yangchow in rice, Hangchow or Quinsay in sugar, and Zaiton in pearls and precious stones.[25] The Chinese market was closely linked to the markets of India and Malaya; Chinese merchant fleets sailed regularly to Java, Ceylon and South India, and as the two countries were governed by members of the same imperial family, China and Persia enjoyed a mutually advantageous trade, and silks and porcelain were unloaded at the rising port of Ormuz, on the shores of the Persian Gulf and the westward limit of Chinese maritime activity. For the first time in history, China was linked to Europe by international trade routes which ran from the Crimea through Sarai and Utrar to Peking, from Trebizond through Tabriz and the cities of Persia to Kashgar and Kansu, and through Almaligh and Besh-balik in Central Asia to the western provinces of the empire, a peaceful and profitable intercourse which may be considered some offset to the dreadful effusion of blood that had been necessary to establish the Mongol global domination.[26]

Between the competing religions of his empire, Kubilai picked his way with caution and prudence. His personal preference was for Buddhism; he received with reverent ceremony some relics of the Founder despatched to China by the king of Ceylon;[27] he sent to Turfan to obtain copies of the Buddhist scriptures;[28] Phags-pa, a Tibetan lama, advised him on matters of ecclesiastical policy and more practically, composed a new alphabet for the Mongol language,[29] and a pious Buddhist historian Ssanang Setzen bestows on the Khan honorific Buddhist titles as a tribute to his services to the faith.[30] The lamas betrayed him into swerving from the tolerance enjoined by the *Yasa* by commanding the destruction of the books of the Taoists, and the Confucians murmured at the favour shown to these clerics, who are accused of extortion and debauchery and arrogantly riding about on horseback displaying their passports in letters of gold.[31] In the scales of imperial favour, the Buddhists were nicely balanced by the Christians. Kubilai followed the path of Küyük, Möngke and Hülegü. Churches were opened in the capital and mass was occasionally attended by members of the court, and though we may reasonably doubt the assertion of Marco Polo that Kubilai requested his father and uncle to obtain for him some holy oil from the lamp which burned in the church of the Resurrection in Jerusalem and professed his belief in the divinity of Christ,[32] the appointment of Christians to high-ranking office is sufficiently attested. Of these, a Nestorian named Isa, who possessed, like many of his co-religionists, some skill in medicine and astronomy, was nominated successively Director of the astronomical bureau, Commissioner for the Christian cult, and finally Minister of State.[33] A guard of 30,000 Christian Alans of the Greek rite were stationed at Khan-Balik, and when some of them were treacherously slain at the siege of Chen-ch'ao in 1275, the revenues of the town were applied by the Khan to the relief of their dependants.[34] The remarkable biography of Mar Yahballaha by Rabban bar Sauma[35] revealed the presence of considerable Nestorian communities on either side of the Great Wall, especially among the Öngut, a Turkish people located in Sui-yuan and governed by a family of hereditary princes whose names in a Chinese transcription are those of slightly disguised Christian saints.[36]

In this competition of creeds, no surprise will be felt at the ultimate predominance of Buddhism, which had been known in China since early Christian times and notwithstanding its persecution by the T'ang, had established itself as a third religious force along with the Taoists and the Confucians. In Tibet it was already the national faith in its Tantric form;[37] the archaeology of Central Asia reveals its hold on many Turkish tribes of the Altai and the Tarim; it was encroaching on the domain of Hinduism and paganism in south-east Asia, and the numerous Buddhist temples and *stupas* in Il-khan Persia cannot be ascribed solely to Mongol encouragement. The personal sympathies of Kubilai may have been equally divided between Buddhism and Christianity, but he probably calculated that by favouring the former he acquired more merit in the eyes of the Chinese, to whom the Christian religion, both in its Latin and Nestorian forms, appeared a foreign importation which attracted few native converts. Kubilai pursued the traditional Mongol policy of toleration for all creeds, whose priests, imams and bonzes continued to be exempt from taxation, and he allowed but two partial exceptions, by suppressing the literature of the Taoists and banning the propaganda of the Muslims.[38] Islam was creeping through the heart of Asia, and though it never imposed itself on China, it gained a lodgment in the western provinces, especially in Yunnan, a success which, despite Kubilai's coldness towards it is to be attributed chiefly to the freedom conferred on all cults by the law of the *Yasa*.[39]

At the end of a long reign of over thirty years, Kubilai may well have felt himself as much a Chinese as a Mongol emperor. He had reunited the Chinese empire, which enjoyed internal peace after the fall of the Sung; he had made its influence felt all over eastern Asia and had brought back under its sway regions which had escaped into freedom in the confusion that followed the overthrow of the T'ang, and his lavish encouragement of the arts and sciences, within the limits always marked out by despotism, was expressive of a genuine admiration for Chinese culture.[40] Yet none of this reconciled the Chinese to barbarian rule. Their exclusion from the army and the higher ranks of the civil service rankled; they resented the power, the wealth and often the insolence of foreigners placed in command over them, and they secretly despised and detested rulers who could scarcely speak or understand their language. Such hostility towards their Mongol sovereigns was stronger in the south, whose traditional dislike of the north had been the strongest prop of the prolonged resistance of the Sung; to mollify the old governing classes, Kubilai and his successors confirmed and extended their social privileges and sacrificed the peasantry to the avarice of the landlords, thereby weakening their régime by depriving it of the sympathy and support of the mass of the population. The valour of the Mongol warriors decayed in an atmosphere of peace; the Mongols in China were themselves divided between those who followed the example of their prince and aped the manners and customs of the Chinese and those who, proud of the traditions of the steppes, maintained a haughty disdain for the luxuries and corruptions (as they deemed them) of civilized urban life. So long as Kubilai lived, such discords were masked, but under the faltering rule of his feebler heirs they broke into the open, and the Mongol government in China collapsed little more than seventy years after his death.

At the opposite end of Asia, Mongol power had been bloodily imposed on the civilized land of Persia. With no easily defensible natural frontiers in the east, Persia had been struck again and again by hordes of nomads from across the Oxus; the Parthians and the Ephthalites had spread over a large portion of the Iranian plateau, and in the decay of the Caliphate, Turkish tribes from the Ghaznavids to the Seljuks had brought a new racial element into an Aryan realm and had effectively turcicized the rich pastures of Azerbaijan. But none of these intruders committed more destruction than the Mongols, and the ruin begun by Chingis was completed by Hülegü. If the southern regions of Fars and Kirman were protected by their remoteness and hot climate, and the provinces of Gilan and Tabaristan bordering on the Caspian Sea by mountains, forests and swamps, the central highlands were mercilessly ravaged, their cities razed, and their inhabitants, especially of Khurasan, in places almost exterminated. The educated class of Persia was decimated; scholars, teachers and officials perished in their thousands in the massacres; the cultural and educational life of the nation was disrupted, and the peasants were often harried from field and farm by mounted horsemen who despised tillage and sought only grazing land for their stock. It might seem impossible that Persia should ever rise again after these prostrating blows. Yet human societies have an infinite capacity for recovery, given even a brief period of rest and peace, and the most brutal and ignorant conqueror cannot wish to reign over a wrecked and unproductive land. The story of China was repeated in Persia, with certain noteworthy variations; once their rule was firm and unchallenged, the Mongol princes looked around for trained and experienced administrators to rebuild the shattered economy and augment the revenues of the state. The fascination which an advanced culture has for untutored minds exercised as powerful an effect in Persia as in China, and under the patronage of the Il-khans, Persian art and letters rose to a new height of brilliance and sophistication.[41]

When Hülegü was despatched by Möngke to subdue the nations of western Asia, no precise boundaries were allotted to his *ulus* and he was, of course, in theory extending the realm of the Great

Khan and not creating a kingdom of his own. Had the scheme of conquest fully matured, his family might have ruled over Egypt, Ethiopia and the Sudan as well as Persia and Irak, but the sudden and unexpected death of Möngke and the fatal setback at Ain Jalut circumscribed his activities and confined them, as it were by accident, to the Iranian plateau and the adjacent regions. Even here, after the loss of Syria, he was threatened by the alliance of his Muslim cousin Berke with the Mamluks, a union cemented by common interests, a common faith and a common racial background, and by the enmity of Alghu, the son of Baidar, the khan of Chagatai, who, embracing the cause of Arik-Böke, wished to prevent Hülegü sending assistance to Kubilai. The battle of the Terek confirmed the power and independence of Berke, bitterly wounded the pride of Hülegü, and determined him to concentrate his political and military forces on the plains and pastures of Azerbaijan and confirmed his choice of capital at Maragha,[42] a fruitful and well-watered spot near Lake Urmiya, from which he might watch the movements of the Kipchak enemy. Yet the worsening of his position and the failure of his early hopes did not induce him to conciliate his Persian subjects, save perhaps by appointing the historian Juvaini, a member of an old and distinguished bureaucratic family, governor of Baghdad, and his brother as director of finances; disdaining to conceal his contempt for Muslims, he showered favours on Christians and Buddhists alike, and churches and pagodas arose in the principal cities of Persia, seemingly indicative of the degradation of Islam after the destruction of the Caliphate.

Hülegü died at Maragha in February 1265, at the age of forty-eight.[43] The Muslims rejoiced that God had removed the enemy of the faith from the world, while the Christians lamented the passing of the new Constantine and Helena, for their generous patroness Dokuz Khatun survived her husband by only a few months.[44] At his funeral on the island of Shahu, in Lake Urmiya, a Mongol prince for the last time was accompanied to eternity by a retinue of slaves and young women, who were slaughtered at his tomb. His eldest son Abaka succeeded less to a throne than to a viceroyalty, since he sought and obtained from Kubilai a *yarlik* empowering him to exercise jurisdiction in the name of the Great Khan. The policy of Abaka, domestic and foreign, did not depart materially from that of his father. He followed the path of the

Buddhists and impartially bestowed his favours on the Christians of every sect; he married a Christian wife, the natural daughter of the Byzantine emperor Michael Palaeologus; he was the protector of Mar Denha, the patriarch of the Nestorians, and when the latter died in 1281 and was succeeded by the Turkish Öngut pilgrim Mark as Mar Yahballaha, Abaka in person placed on his shoulders the mantle of investiture, seated him on his throne and gave him a *paiza* or golden tablet confirming his authority.[45] Obliged to fight his fellow Mongols as well as the Mamluks he was freed from one enemy by the death of Berke in 1266 while on the march to the invasion of Azerbaijan, but the Chagatai Khan Barak, who first opposed and then allied with Kubilai's rival Kaidu, crossed the Oxus in 1269 and seized part of Khurasan and Afghanistan, doubtless in the hope of breaking Abaka's communications with the Great Khan. Barak's invasion was repelled near Herat in 1270, and Abaka, taking the offensive, moved into Transoxiana and sacked Bukhara in 1273. The distraction of this eastern war encouraged Mamluk aggression from Syria; Baybars, cast in the role of valorous champion of the faith, struck at all enemies of Islam within reach; he conquered Antioch from the Crusaders in 1268, ravaged Christian Armenia, intrigued with the *parwana* or regent of the Seljuk sultanate of Rum to withdraw that kingdom from Mongol obedience, and invading Asia Minor, routed the Mongol occupation forces at Albistan (April 1277) and captured Caesarea in Cappadocia. Abaka fought the Mamluks with diplomacy as well as arms. The Western Powers were distressed by the loss of Antioch; St Louis, the last of the crusaders, died at Tunis in 1270, but Edward of England had fought with skill in Palestine, and Abaka despatched missions to Europe to renew the old project of a Christian-Mongol alliance against Islam, two Il-khan envoys presenting themselves to Pope Gregory X at the Second Council of Lyons in 1274.[46]

The wheel had come full circle. Less than thirty years before, the Papacy had made its first tentative approaches to the masters of the world, only to be snubbed and humiliated and told that nothing short of slavish submission would suffice. In those halcyon days the heirs of Chingis had no need of allies, only of clients; convinced that the whole world must soon fall under their dominion, they frankly warned the emissaries of foreign powers that only timely surrender would avert disaster. But when

Hülegü's great drive into Western Asia ran up against the resistance of Mamluk Egypt and Ain Jalut shattered the legend of Mongol invincibility, the chastened Mongol leadership changed its tone and consented to negotiate on equal terms with those it had hitherto despised. By this time, however, the reluctance was on the other side. The Christian nations, recalling the long and sombre record of Mongol aggression and treachery, were deeply suspicious of such overtures, which were unaccompanied by any decisive commitment to the Christian faith. Though the Crusading spirit was far from dead, the Popes had long been concerned less with saving the Christian outposts in Palestine than with crushing the dangerous power of the Hohenstaufen in Italy; the most energetic Western prince of the time, Charles of Anjou, was aiming primarily at restoring the Latin Empire in Constantinople, and the commercial republics of Venice and Genoa and the Spanish kingdom of Aragon seeking economic advantage through Mediterranean trade, were unwilling to offend Mamluk Egypt, through which the luxuries of the East, the silks of China and spices of the Indies, were channelled into Europe. The restored Greek Empire had small interest in the fate of Palestine; Michael Palaeologus was courted both by the Mamluks and the Golden Horde, who could communicate only through his territory, and maintained a nice balance of diplomacy by marrying one daughter to Berke's nephew Nogai and another to Hülegü's son Abaka, and the Genoese, who had acquired valuable trading stations at Kaffa and elsewhere in the Crimea, conducted most of the profitable slave trade between Kipchak and Egypt and wished on that account to maintain friendly relations with Cairo.[47]

Abaka thus discovered that the only ally on whom he could rely was that old and trusted client of the Mongols, the kingdom of Little Armenia, whose aged sovereign Hayton abdicated in 1269 in favour of his son Leo. When Baybars died in 1277 and Syria rebelled against his successor Kilawan, Abaka deemed the moment favourable; in 1280 a Mongol army once more marched westwards and plundered Aleppo, but a second incursion the following year, led by the khan's inexperienced young brother Möngke-Temür, came to grief near Hims, where the Il-khan army, though reinforced by contingents of Armenians and Georgians, was put to flight (October 1281) by the Mamluks.[48] The mosques of Damascus and Cairo resounded with thanks to

Allah; the last remaining Frankish strongholds on the Levantine coast were left to their fate, and the Mongols were for ever deprived of access to the Mediterranean. Five months after the battle, Abaka fell into a delirium brought on by excessive drinking and died (April 1282) at the same age as his father. His rule was strong but severe, and in the full Mongol tradition; though he continued Hülegü's policy of employing native administrators like the Juvainis, he made no concessions to the national or religious sentiments of the people; his fondness for the Buddhists was more resented by the Persian Muslims than his partiality for the Nestorian Christians, since in the eyes of Islam the former were pagan idolators without title to the tolerance accorded the people of the Book. Though he failed to eject the Mamluks from Syria, he maintained Mongol control over Irak and Seljuk Rum; his loyal deference to his suzerain the Great Khan opened Persia to commercial and cultural intercourse with China, and his new capital of Tabriz attracted the merchants and missionaries of the West and rose to be a populous station and market on the principal route of international trade connecting Europe to Central and Eastern Asia.[49]

Abaka had willed the succession to his son Arghun, but the latter's claims were disputed by his uncle Taghudar or Tegüder, who though brought up by a Nestorian mother and baptized Nicholas in honour of the reigning Pope,[50] had as a youth espoused the faith of Muhammad. By an adroit mixture of force and cunning, he snatched the throne from his nephew, and immediately proclaimed his adherence to Islam, assumed the Muslim name of Ahmad and the title of Sultan. This dramatic revolution was attended by risks and advantages. On the one hand, the new ruler might hope to win the gratitude and loyalty of his Muslim subjects, set the Il-khan régime on firmer foundations and blunt the hostility of the Mamluks, who would no longer be able to pose as champions of Islam against the heathen tyrants who had killed the Caliph. On the other hand, the Mongol ruling class shared on the whole the anti-Muslim prejudices of Hülegü and Abaka, and its fidelity and that of the army would be strained by so startling a reversal of policy, and an opportunity given to Arghun to step forward as the spokesman and candidate of the Mongol party and defender of the *Yasa*. The fate of Ahmad depended largely on the outcome of his foreign policy. He despatched an embassy to Cairo to announce his conversion to Islam and urge a perpetual peace, but Kilawan returned a cautious reply, being doubtless dubious of the stability of Ahmad's throne and suspecting that the Mongol notables would not easily consent to sheathe the sword.[51] Civil war, in fact, broke out; Arghun marched from his province of Khurasan into Irak Ajami, and though his revolt was at first checked, Ahmad's generals mutinied, his rival pronounced sentence of death on his uncle and mounted the throne (August 1284).

The reign of Arghun (1284–91) marked a return to the pro-Buddhist and pro-Christian attitudes of his father and grandfather, and the Muslims, once more excluded from power and favour, complained of a repression harsher than that of Abaka. The new sovereign was a man of limited ability; he formed an exaggerated notion of the wealth of his realm, and was unable to comprehend why a larger revenue did not flow into the treasury. The Mongol grandees were the principal culprits; a conquered country, in their opinion, existed only to be mulcted, and the terror of their name unlawfully extorted vast sums from peasants, artisans and merchants. The task of the *sahib-divan*, or director of the finances, was an unenviable one; if he pleased the Khan by stopping the plunder of the state, he aroused the hatred of the plunderers, and if he acquiesced in the malpractices which diminished the revenues, he disgusted the prince and endangered his life. Only one of the viziers of the Il-khans died peacefully in his bed. The ablest and least fortunate was a Jewish physician who was raised to office by Arghun in 1288 under the title of Sa'd al-Dawla, 'felicity of the State'; a shrewd administrator, skilled in the Mongol and Turkish languages, he checked the embezzlement of the public funds, suppressed illegal requisitions, subordinated the Mongol military régime to a regular civil government, and ensured that Muslim citizens should be judged by Koranic law and not by Mongol custom. Yet none of these reforms shielded him from popular wrath. The Mongol generals and nobles detested his interference; the purists complained that he placed his relatives and friends in lucrative offices, and pious Muslims, who hated being subject to a Jew, accused him of a deep-laid plot against Islam which involved the transformation of the Ka'ba at Mecca into a Buddhist temple![52]

The repudiation of Ahmad's policy of islamization might have involved the Il-khans in a new clash with Egypt, had not Kilawan been distracted by troubles with the supporters of the family of Baybars, which he had displaced. An attack by Nogai, the general of the Golden Horde, through the pass of Derbend in 1288 was repelled without difficulty; the King of Georgia, who was involved in the treason of Buka, a powerful Turkish general, was put to death, but the frontiers in general were quiet, and Arghun resumed the plan of regaining Syria by agreement with the Christian kingdoms of the West. His son by a Christian Nestorian wife, a niece of Dokuz Khatun, was baptized Nicholas in 1289, in honour of Pope Nicholas IV; in 1285 he wrote to Honorius IV suggesting a joint attack on the Mamluks, who would be defeated 'by the aid of God, the Pope and the Great Khan',[53] and the famous embassy of Rabban Sauma in 1287–8, which took the Turkish ecclesiastic from Constantinople to Rome, Paris and Bordeaux,[54] brought only letters and exhortations to Arghun and not the armies he sought to assist him in driving the common enemy from Syria. In a last appeal to the West, carried by the hand of a Genoese Buscarelli di Gisolf, the Khan announced his intention of attacking Damascus early in 1291 and then of capturing Jerusalem, which would be handed over to the Franks, adding that he would supply 30,000 horses to a Western army disembarking in Syria.[55] The scheme aborted, like all schemes of Mongol-Christian co-operation against Islam. On 3 March 1291, the Mamluks stormed Acre, the last remaining outpost of the Crusaders: six days later Arghun died after a long illness, during which the unpopular Sa'd al-Dawla had been seized by courtiers, hurried from the palace and beheaded.

The religious conflict continued to disturb the state and unsettle the succession. Arghun's son Ghazan, then twenty years old and governor of Khurasan, was a Buddhist, and as such more obnoxious to the Muslims than a Christian; the Mongol generals passed him over and raised his uncle Gaikhatu, a younger son of Abaka's, to the throne. Dissolute and wasteful, Gaikhatu was addicted to drink and boys, but his extravagance had elements of generosity and his indolence sometimes concealed humanity, and some credit is due to a Mongol prince who never in his reign ordered an execution. He speedily dissipated the resources of the state, and his financial advisers, anticipating bankruptcy, listened to the counsel of the *noyan* Prince Pulad or Bolod, the representative or high commissioner of the Great Khan at Tabriz,[56] that they should imitate the Chinese example by issuing paper money. This novelty was sprung upon a surprised nation in September 1294 without forethought or preparation; gold and silver were withdrawn from circulation; the new and strange currency or *ch'ao*,[57] not being covered by Treasury resources, was refused by traders; the shops and markets closed, commercial dealings ceased, food could not be purchased, and Tabriz resounded with riots and disturbances; Ghazan was reluctant to allow the blocks for printing the notes to be brought into his province of Khurasan, and maintained the old system, but elsewhere the state finances collapsed. Amid rising discontent, a conspiracy was formed against Gaikhatu; at its head was placed his cousin Baidu, whom he had grossly insulted at a drinking-bout; the rebels routed the loyalist troops near Hamadan, and the Khan was seized and strangled (April 1295) in his camp at Mughan. In his religious policy, in so far as he had one, he seems to have held the balance evenly between Christians and Muslims, but Baidu, who replaced him on the throne, was notably cold towards Islam, allowed churches on his *ordu* and wore a cross round his neck. By this date, thirty years after the death of Hülegü, a new generation of Mongols had grown up more susceptible to the influence of the faith of most Persians; conversions to Islam were increasing among the conquerors, and the monarchy of the Il-khans could best be strengthened by a union of throne and people. The death of Kubilai in 1294 broke the links with China; his successors were never accepted as Great Khans; their names ceased to be stamped on the coins of Persia or Kipchak, and after Baidu no Il-khan sought confirmation of his title from distant Khan-Balik.[58] Nawruz, a shrewd Muslim general, advised Ghazan, if he wished to obtain the throne of his father Arghun, to renounce Buddha and accept Allah; in June 1295 the young prince proclaimed his conversion and assumed the name of Mahmud; his example was followed by many of his officers; the imams embraced his cause against Baidu, whose brief reign ended with his capture and execution in October 1295. Ghazan received the homage of the nation, and since his day no non-Muslim has reigned over Persia.

The decade of Ghazan's rule (1295–1304) was a watershed in the history of the Il-khans. On the one hand, the new sovereign was a true Mongol, deeply versed in the history of his people, reverent to the memory of Chingis, and respectful to Kubilai's

135

successor Timur as the head of the house of Tolui, still conceiving of his *ulus* not as a separate state but as a branch of the world empire united under the law of the *Yasa*. On the other hand, by formally adopting Islam, he had renounced the traditional Mongol policy of an aloof toleration and identified himself and his house with one particular faith and taken a distinct step towards transforming the Il-khanate into a national Persian kingdom in which the Mongol ruling class must ultimately be submerged in the mass of Iranian-speaking Muslims. The fanatical bigotry of Nawruz hurried the State faster in this direction than the young khan designed. For two years this ambitious general acted as a kind of vice-khan, and his decrees were obeyed as obsequiously as if they emanated from Ghazan himself. The Buddhist bonzes were commanded to embrace Islam; their images and pagodas were demolished, and a religion which had strangely drifted into Persia in the wake of Turkish and Mongol invaders and which perhaps had never attracted more than a small fraction of the people was suppressed with little protest or resistance. The Jews and Christians, who enjoyed a more ancient tenure, could not be so easily put down, but they were ordered to wear a special dress or girdle by which they might be distinguished from Muslims, and mobs were encouraged to harass and persecute these unpopular minorities. Christian icons and altar vessels were broken or burnt or paraded through jeering crowds in the streets of Tabriz; the venerable Mar Yahballaha was arrested, thrown into prison and beaten with clubs, and in 1297 a serious outbreak in Maragha led to the sacking of the Nestorian cathedral and the patriarch's palace, and cost the lives of several priests.[59] Though Ghazan's break with his pagan past was confirmed by a decree enforcing on his fellow Mongol converts the wearing of the turban, the use of which divided believers from unbelievers,[60] he had no wish to reign as the king of a sect; though he professed himself an orthodox Sunnite, he extended a friendly hand to the Shi'a and the followers of Ali were gratified by a royal visit of pilgrimage to the venerated shrine of Husain at Karbala. The growing religious disorders as well as his dislike of an over-mighty subject at length put a term to the rule of Nawruz. In March 1297 Ghazan struck with merciless swiftness; the general's subordinates at court were arrested and executed; their chief fled to Herat, but the Kart prince was unwilling to engage in armed contest with the Khan; Nawruz was given up, and was put to death in savage Mongol fashion by being cleft in two.[61]

The government of Ghazan, the most gifted of the Il-khans, was capable but severe. In the punishment of evil-doers, he was no respecter of persons, and in one month, it is recorded, five princes of the blood and thirty-eight amirs perished by the executioner's axe. His incessant reforming activity invigorated the State, but he could have achieved nothing but for the advice and co-operation of the trained officials, the best of whom, like the historian Rashid, maintained an ancient and honourable tradition of disinterested public service. The indolent and thoughtless sanction which Gaikhatu had given to the device of paper money had bankrupted the finances and damaged the commercial repute of the kingdom; Ghazan liquidated this unhappy adventure, gold and silver coins returned to circulation, business revived, and a new cadastral survey produced a fairer assessment of the land tax. The robbery of the state and the oppression of the poor was severely repressed; the peasants were protected against extortionate landlords, the officials of the post were forbidden to requisition food supplies along their routes, the funds of the *wakfs* or religious foundations were drawn on for the support of the aged and infirm, and a new legal code boldly attempted to harmonize the Mongol *Yasa* with the Muslim *shari'a*. The historian Rashid, who adorned this reign and whose scholarly labours were encouraged by the Khan himself, exclaims that under this excellent prince the Mongols who had hitherto destroyed, now set themselves to build; the city of Tabriz expanded into a fine large capital, decked with mosques, markets, baths and *madrasas*, and the lands left derelict and untilled since the early massacres of Chingis, especially in Khurasan and Irak Ajami, were colonized and reclaimed by industrious peasants who were promised as an inducement exemption from taxes and imposts during their first year's labour.[62]

The external policy of Ghazan was less successful. His acceptance of Islam in no way reduced the hostility of the Mamluks, whose régime in Egypt had now after fifty years been consecrated by time and military victory and who vigilantly guarded the frontiers of Syria against Il-khan aggression. War between the two Powers followed the traditional pattern. Ghazan marched from the Euphrates and captured Aleppo in 1299; in the following year his name was recited in the *khutba* in the Omayyad mosque of Damascus, and he assured King Hayton II of Armenia that he was prepared to occupy the holy places in Palestine and hand them over to the Christian princes if they would send an army to receive possession of them. But crusading zeal in Europe had grown cold; after the fall of Acre in 1291 no more Frankish soldiers fought in Palestine, and Il-khan embassies to the West met with a negative response. The conflict between Mongol and Mamluk continued without participation by a third party, and was sharpened in Ghazan's case by personal animosity. Intensely proud of his Mongol heritage and descent from Chingis, he openly scorned the sultans of mean birth who governed Egypt and whose fathers had been unknown common slaves. Yet although he maintained the traditional Mongol protection over Christian Armenia and intervened frequently to re-assert his house's mastery over Seljuk Rum, he was unable to press forward to a decision and release the Mamluk grip on Syria. The Mongol armies, though heavily diluted with non-Mongol elements, had not wholly lost their original ferocity; if they no longer slaughtered non-combatants on the old terrifying scale, they pillaged and plundered with no regard for decency and humanity; the peasants and townsfolk of Syria dreaded their merciless rapine and longed for the return of their Mamluk deliverers. After Ghazan had notified the Pope, the last major Mongol incursion into Syria took place in the spring of 1303; its commander Kutluk-Shah was decisively beaten at Marj al-Suffar near Damascus;[63] Cairo received the victors as heroes, and the Mongol prisoners marched in procession through the streets, with the heads of their companions who had fallen on the field slung round their necks. Ghazan, already a sick man, and suffering from an affection of the eyes, was depressed by this disaster, but the state of his health precluded him from taking the field to avenge it, and he died near Kasvin (May 1304) at the early age of thirty-three. The aims with which his great-grandfather Hülegü had set out fifty years before remained unrealized; the Nile and the Mediterranean were for ever shut out of the Mongol range; Armenia was left exposed to Mamluk vengeance, the Franks had vanished from the Asian mainland, and the Seljuk sultanate in Anatolia disintegrated into a cluster of small princedoms from which emerged in time the mighty power of the Ottoman Turks.

The deaths of Kubilai in China in 1294 and of Ghazan in Persia in 1304 mark the end of the era of Mongol imperialism. Kubilai's failure to conquer Japan and Ghazan's failure to conquer Syria were final and decisive, and the march of Mongol conquest was never resumed. A policy of consolidation was pursued in these two urbanized societies which the heirs of Chingis had taken over, and such success as it attained was due chiefly to the talents and skill of these sovereigns, who won acceptance rather than popularity from their subjects. But a despotic government depends on the will and ability of the despot; a succession of capable princes can never be guaranteed, a foreign despot is commonly less acceptable than a native, and China and Persia, where the traditional form of rule was a bureaucratic absolutism, were perhaps less favoured in this respect than Mamluk Egypt, where the throne passed not in an hereditary line but to the strongest and often the ablest of the military commanders. Thus in China and Persia Mongol rule disappeared in less than a century, while the slave Sultans of Egypt prolonged their government above 250 years.

8

The anti-Mongol reaction

From the death of Kubilai in China in 1294 and of Ghazan in Persia in 1304, the historian traces the disintegration and ultimate collapse of Mongol rule in these ancient urbanized and settled lands. A series of energetic reformers might have stopped the rot, but such men are rare, and experience teaches that even resolute autocrats are often helpless against the powerful resistance of vested interests which profit from abuses, and that if a break-through is achieved by a Ghazan, the gap will most likely be plugged under his successors. In any case, barbarian conquerors rarely placate their subjects: if they do not accept the national religion, they are hated as heretics or unbelievers; if they employ foreigners to govern the country, they deprive themselves of the skill and experience of native administrators; if they seek the favour of the propertied classes, they must cease to protect the masses against exploitation; if they maintain peace, the martial virtues of their people will decay and their weapons rust from want of use; if they strive to reign as kings of all races and classes, they risk being repudiated as renegades by their fellow-barbarians, who still enjoy a monopoly of military power and lord it over a nation of slaves.

In Persia, where Mongol rule perished much earlier than in China, such problems were scarcely recognized, much less tackled, by any of the Il-khans save Ghazan, whose reign of ten years was adequate only to reveal the dangers which strew the path of the reformer. By accepting Islam he lowered the barrier which separated the bulk of the Iranian people from the ruling house, but at the same time he antagonized the religious minorities, Christians, Jews, Zoroastrians and Buddhists, who had hitherto profited from the tolerant indifference of their pagan masters, and irritated those Mongols loyal to their traditional tribalism, who bitterly resented the supersession of the sacred *Yasa* of Chingis by the Muslim *shariʿa*. Unlike their partners in China, the Il-khans had made use of the Persian bureaucracy, but these officials, trained in a tradition of absolute monarchy going back to Sassanian times, seemed to many jaundiced Mongol eyes to aim at trans-forming the khan into a shah, a change which the conversion of the dynasty to Islam might well hasten, and from Ghazan's reign onwards a tension is discernible between the Mongol warrior aristocracy and the native Persian administrators and civil servants. To rebuild the shattered economy of the state required, firstly, the wholesale reconstruction of towns and irrigation canals, but this could not be accomplished without forced labour and imposed a new and crushing burden on the rural population, and secondly, a recasting of the entire fiscal system, which had become a byword for tyranny and extortion. In addition to the ancient and common Muslim imposts of *kharaj* (land-tax), *ushr* (tithe) and *jizya* (poll-tax levied on non-Muslims), the Mongols had imposed the *tamgha*, a tax apparently of 10 per cent on all trading deals and commercial transactions (including prostitution!), and the *kubchur*, an ancient Mongol levy on pastureland but now a virtual poll-tax on the peasants farmed out to collectors who often exacted, to their own profit, ten or twenty times the legal amount.[1] Instructed by his Persian advisers such as the historian Rashid ad-Din, Ghazan was not unaware of these evils and the plight of the small cultivators, but his attempts to remedy the situation were but partially successful and his warning to the *amirs* or military chiefs not to plunder the peasantry—'If you insult the peasant, take his oxen and seed, and trample his crops into the ground, what will you do in future?'[2]—fell on deaf ears and perhaps had no effect except to strain the loyalty of the Mongol ruling class to the house of Hülegü.

In an agrarian society, where the owners of large estates oppress a numerous and helpless peasantry, the protection of the cultiva-tors must devolve on a strong centralized government, which is willing and competent to curb its mightiest subjects. If the king fails in this duty, the rural victims of tyranny are driven to armed rebellion, and the monarchies of Asia have been repeatedly subverted by peasant risings. The Persians, a more submissive race than the Chinese, were perhaps long restrained by a despair of success and a consciousness of the powers arrayed against them. Among their masters, they reckoned Mongol-Turkish warriors of savage manners expressive of nomadic contempt for the tiller of the soil and possessed of a virtual monopoly of the military power of the State,[3] wealthy merchants and officials who had purchased or inherited fertile fields and were resolved to exact the utmost profit from them, and increasingly *kadis* and other Muslim religious dignitaries, who were rewarded according to Mongol policy by grants of land and exemption from taxation.[4] In the large cities a number of nobles resided who formed a kind of urban patriciate and invested money in the merchant caravans that followed the great highways of international trade and who reinvested their profits in land. Thus a large and expanding landed class, composed of several social strata, impropriated the best land of Persia and reduced the cultivators to the status of serfs. The peasants were afflicted by additional evils peculiar to a government of nomads. In their constant migrations from summer to winter quarters and back, the pastoral chiefs ravaged the sown fields and the crops and plundered the barns and granaries; the Mongol army, no longer supported by the booty of conquest, was paid in cash or kind or in drafts upon named localities, whose unhappy inhabitants were called on to honour these demands regardless of their resources to do so; the widespread use of slave labour in the countryside depressed the wages of the free farmers; the growing power of the great landowners encroached on the rights of the village communities, who by ancient custom distributed the arable land among the households and fixed the seasons of sowing, ploughing and harvesting; the arrival of the *darugha* or tax commissioner in the village was more dreaded than a horde of locusts, and the demands for food and fodder for passing troops and for horses and other draught animals for the post service reduced more and more peasants to beggary. 'Wherever a *darugha* decided to stay,' says the historian Rashid, 'the inhabitants were immediately subjected to constraint, since his slaves and military servants lowered themselves into neighbouring courtyards from the flat roofs and stole whatever their eyes fell on. They shot their arrows at pigeons and chickens and often hit children. Whatever they found that was eatable or drinkable or could be fed to their cattle, no matter to whom it belonged, they stole for themselves. . . . Every year under various pretexts officials took away several thousand cows, bedding, cauldrons, pots and utensils belonging to the inhabitants. They stabled saddle animals and beasts of burden in the gardens, and in one day would ruin a garden which was the product of ten years' work.'[5]

Unlike the countryside, huge tracts of which remained derelict and unsown since the devastations of Chingis's time, the towns of Persia, with the exception of those in Khurasan,[6] had made a fair recovery by the end of the thirteenth century. The oppressive *tamgha* hindered the revival of urban trade, but the cities or caravan-stations on the main routes of international commerce rose to flourishing life and native business was enriched and augmented by the contributions of the Indians, the Latins (principally the Italians) of the West, and perhaps the Chinese, whose fleets in the thirteenth and fourteenth centuries ranged widely over the Indian Ocean. The metropolis of Tabriz boasted some 300,000 inhabitants by 1300, and the new capital of Sultaniya founded by Öljeitü in 1304, doubtless captured some of the trade which linked the Mediterranean and the Black Sea coasts with Central Asia and the Far East. The town merchants and nobles were organized in trading companies, and from their ranks were drawn the principal city officials, the *ra'is* or mayor, the *kadi*, the *khatib* or imam of the mosque, and the *muhtasib* or police chief; the craftsmen and artisans formed guilds, but true civic liberty was unknown in the medieval Orient, and the *darugha* and the *malik* or local large landowner combined to smother such tendencies to self-government as might rise to the surface.[7] The rich merchant and landowner, the *ikta*-holder and high-ranking official, formed together a concentration of power and property before which the mass of the nation was helpless, yet the references in contemporary chroniclers to 'Mazdak' plots among the populace (from a sixth-century social-revolutionary agitator)[8] would seem to indicate a growing degree of social unrest and discontent which may have contributed to undermine the shaky fabric of the Il-khan state.

In an hereditary absolute monarchy, much depends on the health and longevity of the members of the ruling family, whose position is undermined if children or weaklings stand in immediate succession to the throne. The descendants of the great Chingis did not all inherit his physical vigour, their lives were too often shortened by chronic alcoholism, and of the Il-khans few attained the age of forty and none of fifty years. Ghazan, the ablest of his house, died at thirty-two and was succeeded by his brother, also a convert to Islam, whose Persian-Muslim name Khuda-banda, 'servant of God', was added to his Mongol patronymic Öljeitü, the fortunate or blessed. A prince of good intentions, he lacked the strength and ability of his predecessor, whose policies he endeavoured to continue. He retained Rashid ad-Din in office, exchanged embassies with other Mongol rulers in the hope perhaps of restoring the unity of the empire, resumed the war against the Mamluks, and with vanishing prospects of success, despatched envoys to the Christian West to urge yet again that an army should be landed on the Syrian coast which with Mongol help would drive the 'Saracens' from the holy places. A generous patron, like his brother, of artists and men of letters, he followed the progress of his vizier's great history,[9] and the architects who designed the new city of Sultaniya and adorned it with beautiful domed mosques and octagonal towers must have blessed the lavish generosity of the young Khan, whose tomb, attractive even in its battered ruin, alone survives of the many buildings of this short-lived capital.[10]

In his military campaigns, Öljeitü subdued the Caspian province of Gilan, whose swamps and forests had long protected its independence, destroyed the autonomous principality of Herat in punishment for the disloyalty of its *malik*, Fakhr ad-Din Kart, and encouraged by the defection of some Syrian *amirs*, crossed the Euphrates in 1312 and laid siege to Rahbat, a fortified place of some strength. After a month's indecisive fighting, the Mongols suffered heavy casualties and withdrew back beyond the river, a clash of trifling importance had it not marked the end of a forty years' struggle by Hülegü and his successors to subdue Syria and carry the Mongol frontier to the Levan ne coast. This final failure confined the power of the Il-khans to an raea out of which emerged later a national Persian kingdom, withdrew Mongol protection from the Christian Armenians, henceforth exposed to the full fury of Mamluk revenge, and abandoned the heart of Anatolia to the licence of Turkish anarchy, which was ultimately mastered by the

Ottomans. The Christian kingdoms of the West beheld with indifference the ruin of their cause in the East; the Armenian chronicler Hayton might draft at Poitiers a new plan for a Mongol-Frankish attack on Egypt,[11] but crusading ardour had faded, and the Mongol envoys received by Edward II at Langley or Northampton in 1307[12] were the last of a long line of intermediaries between Europe and Asia whose mission failed but whose contacts promoted a Western interest in the Far East which never died.

Öljeitü's last years were disturbed by a bitter feud between his two viziers, Rashid ad-Din and Ali Shah, a feud he endeavoured to quell by dividing the khanate into two administrative units, Rashid being responsible for the south and Ali for the north. In 1316 he died at the age of thirty-six, and his son Abu Sa'id, the first Il-khan to be known only by his Muslim name, was enthroned at Sultaniya in his thirteenth year. This inexperienced youth found himself enmeshed in a web of intrigue; Rashid was dismissed from office; the powerful Commander-in-chief, Amir Choban, who told him he was as necessary for the State as salt for food, urged the fallen minister to seek reinstatement; his enemies redoubled their efforts to destroy him, and in July 1318 the greatest statesman and scholar of the age, then in his seventy-third year, absurdly accused of having poisoned Öljeitü, was condemned for treason, cut in two in Mongol fashion, and his head paraded through the streets of Tabriz to cries of: 'This is the head of the Jew who blasphemed God; may God's curse be upon him!'[13] Abu Sa'id lived to regret this judicial murder and to exclaim pathetically that since Rashid's death he had enjoyed no peace.

The fall of Rashid left Choban virtually master of the State, a kind of mayor of the palace, and the young khan, being destitute neither of intelligence nor ability, resented his tutelage. The power of Choban was undermined by a violent passion which Abu Sa'id conceived for his commander's married daughter, by the treason of his son Temur-Tash who proclaimed himself an independent prince in Asia Minor, and by the jealousy of his fellow-generals. When the khan marched against him in 1327, Choban's troops deserted him; he fled to Herat, but the Kart prince, remembering his brother's fate, surrendered him to Abu Sa'id and to execution. His son fled to Cairo, but the Mamluk sultan was unwilling to reopen hostilities with the Il-khans, to please whom he executed his unwelcome guest. Had Temur-Tash

145

survived the death of Abu Sa'id and the dissolution of the Il-khan State, he might have founded a new Mongol principality in Anatolia, repressed the licence of the Turkish *amirs*, and checked or prevented the rise of the Ottoman Turks.[14]

The last years of Abu Sa'id's reign were passed in comparative peace, broken only by some incursions from the Kipchak steppes by Özbeg, the khan of the Golden Horde. In the autumn of 1335 Abu Sa'id marched against him, but fell ill and died, possibly by poison administered by a jealous harem beauty. He left no son, and the line of Hülegü was extinguished in the male line. A crowd of competitors for the vacant throne started up, but of some history has scarcely condescended to record their names, much less their actions, and an interval of more than thirty years was filled with confused political struggles until the emergence in 1369 of the celebrated Timur or Tamerlane, who set out in that year from Samarkand on the conquest of Western Asia. In this interval Mongol Persia perished, or rather, men of Mongol race and descent ceased to govern the people of Iran. The Mongols inflicted dreadful injuries on Persia, yet their record, though indescribably bloody, was not entirely negative. Under their harsh stimulus, a national consciousness emerged; Persian replaced Arabic as the language of Muslim culture east of the Tigris; the arts and astronomical sciences were promoted; the country was thrown open to influences both from China and from Europe, and the first genuine universal history was compiled under their aegis. The Mongols left few permanent traces as a result of an occupation of only eighty years: some fragments of tower or minaret, some pottery and bronzes, some miniature paintings betraying Chinese features or inspiration, and some words scattered through the rich vocabulary of Persian speech.[15] The Persians who had in their time bowed beneath the yoke of Greeks and Parthians, Arabs and Turks, endured under the Il-khans a crueller and more ferocious tyranny, from whose ruins grew ultimately a compact national state.

The annals of Mongol China are dominated by the gigantic figure of Kubilai, on whose death the strength of the dynasty appeared to be exhausted, for of his nine successors, none have deserved the careful notice of history. His place was filled by a grandson, Temür Khan;[16] the choice was sanctioned by the judgment of the general Bayan,[17] the renowned, humane and influential captain who had conquered the Sung and who died soon after the accession of his protégé, but of the personality and actions of this prince there is little record. The Chinese annalists commend him for building a palace or temple in honour of Confucius and praise his clemency and wisdom,[18] but the only external event of his twelve years' reign was an invasion by Kaidu, the old enemy of his house, in 1301, whose death shortly afterwards closed the long family quarrel between the descendants of Ögedei and those of Tolui and nominally reunited the empire. Temür Khan received at some unknown date the Franciscan missionary John of Monte Corvino,[19] who left Europe in 1291 carrying with him from Pope Nicholas III letters addressed to 'the Emperor of the Tartars' and after a long journey via India presented them at the court of Khan-Balik and was graciously accorded permission to preach the gospel and build churches.[20] After an uneventful reign of twelve years, Temür died in 1307 at the age of forty-two; his nephew Kaishan or Külük, who succeeded him, had fought with distinction against Kaidu, and had the satisfaction of receiving in 1308 the submission of Kaidu's son Chapar. Yet there was still a rival claimant to the throne in the person of Ananda, another grandson of Kubilai's, a zealous Muslim who knew the Koran by heart, and who, had he succeeded, might have striven to impose the faith of Islam on the Middle Kingdom. Ananda was defeated and slain; Kaishan maintained the family favour towards the Christians; John of Monte Corvino, elevated by Clement V at Avignon to the newly-created archbishopric of Khan-Balik in 1308, enjoyed the imperial friendship and patronage, but our credulity is strained by a Franciscan claim to have converted the Khan, whose body was buried in the convent church and when the friars were driven from China, disinterred and transported across Asia to Sarai.[21] The Chinese more plausibly assert and criticize Kaishan's partiality for the lamas. But he ruled but four years, and dying in 1311 at the age of thirty-one, was followed by his brother Buyantu, whose original name Ayur Balibatra is clearly Sanskrit and was doubtless bestowed by the lamas who looked to India or Tibet as their spiritual home.

The reign of Buyantu or Bui-Yantuk (1311–20) marked a slight shift in Mongol policy towards the native Chinese. He revived, after a long interval, in 1313 the traditional examinations in the Confucian classics for the higher posts in the civil service, which were once more thrown open to members of the mandarin class. His son Shutepala or Suddepala, whose Mongol name was Gegen, who succeeded him in 1320 as a youth of seventeen or eighteen, pursued this policy of concession to native sentiment, but if the traditionalists applauded his resumption of the rites of ancestor-worship, they were displeased by his excessive predilection for the Buddhists; he constructed a great Buddhist temple west of Khan-Balik, and put to death some of the official censors who reproved his actions. The Mongol party, we may suspect, was even more antagonized, and put forward a rival khan, and in 1323 a palace revolution destroyed Baiju, the commander of the imperial guard, and the young emperor, who thus became the first Mongol sovereign to perish by assassination. He left no heir, and the throne was taken by his cousin Yesün Temür, a great-grandson of Kubilai's, the annals of whose brief reign (1323–8) are filled only with dry details of floods and earthquakes and similar natural calamities from which China has always suffered. In the next five years three princes sat on the throne; Kushala, a son of Kaishan's, died in 1329, within a year of succeeding Yesün Temür; a younger brother of Kushala's, Tuor Togh Temür, the first of his house to perform the time-honoured sacrifices at the Altar of Heaven, lived only till 1332, and Irinchinbal, his nephew, was a child of seven at his accession and died in two months. Toghan Temür, an elder brother of this lad, was then placed on the throne; his reign of thirty-five years (1333–68) was the longest since Kubilai's, but he was the last of his line, and the accumulated Chinese resentments at barbarian rule at length burst out in the national uprising of the Ming.

Through the dry official records of the dynasty we may glimpse a little of the social tensions which finally ruined it. The peasantry, the beasts of burden in so many ancient societies, were loaded with extraordinary and intolerable imposts by the unthinking and unfeeling men of the steppe.[22] In North China many farms were turned into pasture for the Mongol horses and the cultivators were ruthlessly dispossessed. The vast public works erected by Kubilai and his successors to the greater glory of the Yüan dynasty were built by forced labour and countrymen conscripted into government service; the fleet was manned by press-ganged peasants; on the military settlements dotted around the empire to provide focuses of Mongol powers servile thousands were employed, almost as prisoners, in producing food; the Buddhist and other temples, whose construction was financed or sponsored by the State, were organized economically as large self-supporting estates worked by peasant labour; senior officers of the army and bureaucracy were rewarded with grants of land farmed by tenant-serfs who paid to the owners less what the law allowed than what avarice could extort. When the Mongols had acquired some insight into the workings of Chinese society, they deprived the gentry class, from which the native officials were drawn, of their political power by restricting the higher grades of the civil service to foreigners, but compensated them by relinquishing to them almost complete control over the rural population. Oppressed by two aristocracies, Chinese and Mongol, deprived of the protection of the State, which wished to offend neither, the peasantry sank into debt and servility; the bolder or more desperate fled to the hills and forests of the coastal provinces of Fukien and Kwangtung, and those who remained were soon inflamed by adroit agitators to rise and revenge themselves on their tyrants.

The deceptive picture of prosperity which Mongol China presents is partly due to the vigour and enterprise of the merchant class, also a privileged section of the community, who were exempt from direct taxation and free to travel throughout the vast extent of Mongol Asia as subjects and often agents of the Great Khan. They were mostly foreigners, Persian-speaking Muslims[23] or Italian-speaking Christians,[24] and as the roads were now relatively safe and all Asia was open to commercial activity, their profits were doubtless large, but a high proportion of their wealth flowed out of China and the growing scarcity of coined money probably explains the lavish issue of paper notes which led to an inflationary crisis in the fourteenth century. The Chinese mercantile marine was located principally in the south, the former territories of the Sung, and here the native shippers and businessmen were free to develop their trading connections with the kingdoms of Indo-China.

In analysing the agrarian discontents which eventually proved fatal to the Mongols, we may perhaps discriminate between conditions in the North and those in the South.[25] The North had long been under barbarian sway; the power of the state had disintegrated; the Mongol nobles had seized much of the most valuable land, but the nearness of the capital familiarized the emperors and their advisers with the grievances of the cultivators in what may be termed the home provinces. In the far south, by contrast, the long survival of the Sung had ensured also the maintenance of that régime's State machine; the government of Peking, anxious to conciliate this conquered realm, left the Chinese landlords in possession of their estates and seldom ventured to interpose between them and the peasants. As the Mongol government grew weaker, the power of the landed class grew stronger, until oppression of the rural masses exploded in a series of popular risings of a kind which in the long history of China presage a violent change of dynasty.[26]

The first revolts broke out as early as 1325, and were led by leaders thrown up by the poorer classes, such as peasants, fishermen and artisans; they represented a rising of the poor against the rich, rather than a patriotic protest against foreign domination, and they spread through the towns and villages of central China. The government was unable to check the growing anarchy; there was no strong hand at the helm, the seasoned warriors of imperial days had died out and been replaced by young troops with no experience of war; a regular army was as usual at a disadvantage in a struggle with cunning guerrillas, and a thousand men were often incapable of flushing out from the hills and woods a band of fifty. As social disorder spread, the propertied classes were driven to look to their own defence; they raised volunteer forces to save their lands and mansions, and so deserved the gratitude of the imperial authorities, who in 1352 reopened the upper ranks of the bureaucracy to the native Confucian literati. At this juncture a characteristic Chinese disaster occurred; the Yellow River burst through its dykes, a vast labour force of 170,000 men was conscripted to repair them; harsh discipline and low pay provoked rebellion, and the rising of Kuo Tzu-hsing in Honan announced the impending fall of the régime. The rebels shifted their ground: their movement acquired a national rather than a social character as it gathered momentum; a change we may plausibly ascribe to the skill of the shrewder gentry in deflecting popular wrath away from themselves to their barbarian masters. In an incautious move, a tottering and foolish government chose to tighten the nationality laws and so outraged national sentiment and turned the rebellion into anti-Mongol channels. Kuo was doubtless a genuine social revolutionary, who hated the rich and drew support from the secret societies which have always proliferated in China and from monks who, possessing a superior education and in the eyes of the people dispensing semi-divine power, had carried into their monasteries the attitudes and sympathies of the villages, but he died in 1355 and his successor Chu Yuan-chang, the third peasant to found a Chinese dynasty,[27] broadened the class basis of the rebellion and welcomed such members of the gentry who were prepared to join in the fight against the foreigners.

Had the dynasty retained a modicum of political skill and military valour, it could have prolonged its existence for many years, for its enemies were many and quarrelsome; an adroit statesman could have detached the landowners from the peasants and the peasants from their masters, and a few timely concessions might have rallied to the throne the moderate elements who were disgusted by the growing disorder, which threatened the rights of property and the just harmony of the State and which was exploited, as usual, by self-seeking adventurers who combined the functions of patriot and bandit. But Toghan Temür, who by now had grown to middle age rather than manhood and who unworthily filled the throne of Kubilai, was foolish, lazy and indecisive; surrounded by eunuchs and lamas, he divided his time between women, boys and the chase, and remained the supine spectator of the steady shrinkage of the empire under his nominal control. The last days of Mongol rule may be compared with those of Manchu rule in 1911–12: a paralysed administration, a divided ruling clique, an explosion of national hatred of alien rule, and a popular revolution originating in the South, sweeping up through the Yang-tse valley, and finally engulfing the northern capital. Chu Yuan-chang was a bold soldier and an able political manipulator, who preferred persuasion to force; by a mixture of humanity and cajolery he disarmed the suspicious hostility of the gentry and enticed many of them within his party; he successively disposed of his rivals and absorbed their followers, and on seizing Nanking in 1356 he established a regular and alternative government as a rallying-centre for the Chinese nation, and at the same time cut the North off from its principal source of food. The reduction of the North threatened, however, to be a tougher task, for here the Mongols had been ensconced since the days of Chingis, a century and a half before, and the strength of their garrisons could be augmented by reinforcements from the

Mongolian homeland. But, with the fatality which seems to attend all falling régimes, the Mongol government of Peking was now imperilled by an attempt by the house of Ögedei to revenge itself upon that of Tolui; an Ögedeid prince marched on the Great Wall in 1360, and though he was soon killed in a mutiny, the commanders of Toghan Temür's armies quarrelled among themselves, the rivals Bolod Temür and Kökö Temür successively occupied Peking, and the civil war facilitated and made permanent the loss of the south to the Ming. When in the summer of 1368 the Ming forces moved northwards, their advance was almost unhindered; the defences of Peking were breached, the emperor Toghan Temür fled, first to the summer capital of Shang-tu beyond the wall, and then to K'ai-lu, where after uttering a pathetic lament for the vanished splendours of his cities, the beautiful plains and fresh greenery of his summer retreats, and exclaiming 'What wrong I have done thus to lose my empire!',[28] he died in 1370, 150 years after the armies of Chingis had chased the Chin from Peking. Kökö Temür maintained some resistance for a while in Shansi, and a few outlying Mongol garrisons held out in other provinces, but these remnants were driven into the hills of Kansu, and China, purified at last from barbarian rule, was reunited under the sceptre of the Ming.

The Chinese annalists, who pass lightly over this disagreeable episode in their country's history, ascribe the fall of the Mongols to corruption and decay; the seventeenth-century Mongol chronicler Ssanang Setzen, who has preserved or invented the lament of Toghan Temür, blames it on treason. A disinterested critic might easily reconcile these conflicting explanations and find a good deal of truth in each, and he would also perhaps ascribe to the Mongol era a merit which a patriot Chinese might condemn as a fault, namely, that during these years of alien domination, China was drawn into closer contact with the outside world than at any other stage of her history, that Turks and Persians filled her marts and sometimes governed her cities, and that Europeans, spanning the breadth of Asia, reached the shores of the Pacific and preached and traded among a people who had been but dimly known in the West as the mysterious 'Seres' of the ancients.[29] The single-minded devotion of John of Monte Corvino planted an outpost of Latin Christianity in the Far East,[30] in a few years he baptized 10,000 'Tartars' and converted George, prince of the Öngut, from the Nestorian heresy to Catholicism; he translated the psalter into the 'Tartar' tongue, which may have been either Mongol or Turkish,[31] and these noble labours were properly rewarded by Clement V with his elevation to the newly created archbishopric of Khan-Balik in 1307. The lonely pioneer was accorded seven other Franciscan friars as suffragan bishops, three of whom reached China; a second see was erected at Zaitun and filled for many years by Andrew of Perugia;[32] and of the intrepid missionaries who followed the long and dangerous route by land or sea to this new field of Christian endeavour, a special tribute is due to Odoric of Pordenone,[33] who left Venice in 1314 and after plunging via Trebizond and Tabriz into Il-khan Persia, sailed from Basra for India in 1322, passed down the coast of Malabar, was edified by the sight of the tomb of St Thomas, and after touching at Ceylon and Java, disembarked at Canton, a city, he says, as big as three Venices, perhaps ten years after his departure from Italy. Travelling through China, he was welcomed in city after city by his fellow Franciscans; at Khan-Balik, where he resided for three and a half years, he observed the ceremonial of the court, the vast hunting expeditions in the forests twenty days' journey from the capital, the speed and punctuality of the imperial posts, and the favour the Great Khan bestowed on the friars. Leaving Peking in 1328, he resolved to return overland; travelling through the Öngut country of Prester John, he followed the caravan route across the Tarim basin, approached sufficiently near Tibet to gather much information about its strange theocratic government of lamas,[34] and proceeding over steppe and sea, returned to Padua, in 1330, after an absence of sixteen years.

John of Monte Corvino died in 1328 or 1329, shortly after Odoric's departure from China; his successor Nicholas, appointed in 1333, met his death on the road somewhere in Central Asia, and the Alan community in Khan-Balik, who wrote in 1336 to Benedict XII at Avignon, complained that since John's death, they had had no ecclesiastical chief.[35] In response, the Pope despatched another Italian Franciscan, John of Marignolli,[36] in 1339, who travelled safely through the territories of Kipchak and Chagatai,[37] reaching Peking in 1342. Received in audience by Toghan Temür, he presented the Khan with some large European horses, whose bulk surprised Chinese and Mongols alike, accustomed as they were to the small, wiry animals of the steppes.[38] After a stay of five years, Marignolli sailed in 1347, returned slowly via the coasts of India, and presented his report to Innocent VI at Avignon in 1353. As late as 1370 Urban V nominated a theologian of Paris, William of Prato, to the see of Khan-Balik, but it does not appear that he ever took up the appointment; the fall of the Mongol dynasty two years before closed a chapter in East–West relations; the growing disorders in Central Asia blocked land communication between Europe and China, and the Latin missions in the Far East slowly atrophied and died. There is little evidence of anti-Christian persecution on the part of the new Ming rulers, but the Christian faith, whether in its Catholic or Nestorian form, made small impact on the Chinese; the converts were mostly foreigners (Mongols, Turks, Alans), who were swept away along with their cults in the nationalist reaction after the successful Ming revolution.

Under the Mongols, China ceased to be land-bound, emerged from her seclusion, took to the sea and came out; at the same time, the Christians and the Muslims of the West came in. By land and by sea, the Middle Kingdom was linked to distant realms, was inspected, exploited and sometimes described by foreigners who revealed to an astonished public the existence of an ancient, literate and populous society at the other end of the world. Neither Christianity nor Islam captured the mind and soul of a secular if superstitious nation, but the 'Franks' of Western Europe were permanently impressed by the discovery of a vast pagan realm ripe, as they believed, for the harvest of the gospel, and when the routes across the steppes were closed by political upheavals and the conquests of Timur, they refused to accept exclusion and sought to find an alternative route by sea. The most striking consequence of the temporary Mongol domination of China was the launching of a persistent European 'quest for Cathay' which took the seekers round the Cape at the close of the fifteenth century and brought Ricci and the Jesuits to Peking two centuries after the extinction of the missions founded by Monte Corvino and the Franciscans in the Khan-Balik of the Great Khan.

9

Kipchak and Chagatai

In the settled kingdoms of Persia and China the Mongols were overwhelmed in less than a century at least in part by difficulties of governing of which their previous experience allowed them to form no conception. By contrast, in the khanates of Kipchak and Chagatai they ruled a simpler and less urbanized society, whose population was partly nomadic and whose governmental system was sufficiently primitive to be administered by men lacking the education and hereditary training of the mandarins of China and the bureaucrats of Iran. In consequence, Mongol rule put down deeper roots in these northern realms, and in Russia lasted for more than 250 years. The periods of Mongol dominance both in Russia and Central Asia present many instructive features: in the former country the khans may be said to have bequeathed a powerful political heritage to the tsars and shaped the serf-ridden society of Muscovy, in the latter they rebuffed the pressures of China and carried the Turkish peoples of the high steppe into the fold of Islam and within the ambit of Persian culture. The histories of Kipchak and Chagatai are ill-documented, but archaeological finds and the reports of foreigners fill many gaps and supply the deficiencies of native chroniclers.

When Batu returned from the great campaign in Central Europe in 1242, he laid the foundations, on the east bank of the Akhtuba, a tributary of the Volga, of the city or camp of Sarai, whose Persian name, meaning palace, was indicative of the *golden* residence of the khan.[1] From this point, strategically placed athwart the main route across the steppes, he might watch the changing political scene in Mongolia and keep the princes of Russia under observation and in dread of swift punishment if there were any interruption in their loyalty and tribute. Whatever hopes those princes might cherish of regaining their freedom as a result of conflict between Batu and Küyük were dashed by the latter's sudden death in 1248 and the subsequent division of the empire between Batu and Möngke. When Möngke despatched Hülegü on the great offensive against the Assassins and the Caliph, he required of Batu contingents of troops and financial levies from the subject peoples; a census was taken in the Russian lands, and even the city of Novgorod, which enjoyed a precarious independence, was required to furnish returns, a demand which produced riots and disturbances. No Mongol garrison was stationed in Novgorod, but the Russian governor, Alexander Nevsky, was ordered to suppress the tumults and exact the tribute. In his later years, Batu suffered a paralytic stroke; the regency was assumed by his son Sartak, a Nestorian Christian, whose accession to power encouraged the King of France to send William of Rubruck to strengthen him in the faith and open up the Kipchak steppes to the preaching of the friars. Batu died in 1255 or 1256; Sartak, then in Karakorum, was confirmed by Möngke as his successor, but he died on the way home in 1257 and his uncle Berke was enthroned at Sarai in his stead.[2] A devout Muslim, Berke was horrified by Hülegü's savageries at Baghdad in 1258 and feared the ambitions of a potential rival; the Kipchak troops fighting under Hülegü's command were ordered home, and the bad feeling between the cousins flared in 1261 to open war in the Caucasus, the uncertain boundary between their respective realms.

Had it not been for the dangerous threat from the Il-khans, Berke might well have resumed the offensive against Europe, broken off by Batu in 1242 on the death of Ögedei. An excuse, if excuse were ever needed for Mongol aggression, was provided by the reckless conduct of Daniel of Galicia, who about the time of Batu's death attacked the local *baskaks* or collectors of tribute and repelled a force sent against him by the Mongol governor. In 1258–9 a more formidable punitive expedition under Nogai, an able young commander and grand-nephew of Berke, invaded

156

Poland and followed the road from Cholm to Lublin and Sando-mir. Cracow, which next lay in their path, was plundered, but the citadel held out; Duke Boleslas fled, and the country as far west as Beuthen and Oppeln was devastated with Mongol thoroughness. Europe trembled; Pope Alexander IV preached a new crusade and summoned to the help of the Poles King Bela of Hungary, who might well fear a return of the dreaded 'Tartars' who had torn his kingdom to tatters eighteen years before. Yet, after failing to catch the elusive Daniel, the invaders withdrew.[3] The mounting power of Hülegü, whose troops were now on the march to the Mediterranean, was viewed with growing fear in Sarai, and Berke might well prefer to guard his southern borders to launching ambitious adventures in Central Europe. The death of Möngke in 1259, the repulse of Ked-Buka at Ain Jalut in 1260, the recapture of Constantinople by the Greeks under Michael Palaeologus in 1261, and the shrewd diplomacy of Baybars, the new master of Mamluk Egypt, transformed the military and diplomatic scene, and encouraged Berke to abandon further thought of expansion to the north and west and concentrate on checking the ambitions of the Il-khans on his Caucasian frontier. The quarrel between the two Mongol states was hailed with delight in Cairo and assured the survival of the Mamluk kingdom; Baybars welcomed in Egypt the Kipchak contingents from Hülegü's army who were unable to return directly to their own country,[4] and when the battle of the Terek (January 1263) had tipped the military balance against the Il-khans, Cairo and Sarai entered into a formal alliance on the basis of a common Muslim faith against barbarous pagans. By favour of the Byzantine Greeks, now again in possession of Constantinople, the two allies could communicate by sea through the Straits, or as a poetic conceit might have phrased it, the Volga flowed into the Nile.

During the decade of Berke's rule (1257–66) the most westerly of Mongol-dominated regions, which the Russians styled the khanate of the Golden Horde,[5] began to take shape. The heart of the realm was in the Lower Volga; Batu's foundation of Sarai was matched by a second city near by which came to be known as New or Berke's Sarai and which grew into a flourishing centre of international commerce with a mixed population of Mongols, Turks and Russians. The khans directly controlled the steppes of the Don and the Dnieper, the peninsula of the Crimea, and the northern slopes of the Caucasus; their influence if not their power extended south of the Danube into Bulgaria and Thrace, but their endeavours to snatch the Seljuk sultanate of Rum from their Il-khan rivals were unsuccessful and they early lost Khwarizm and Utrar to the house of Chagatai.[6] Though the threat to Europe evaporated after the brief incursion into Poland in 1259, they maintained their hold over the Russian principalities, which had not learnt unity from disaster and were as much apprehensive from the expansion of the Lithuanians and the Teutonic Knights in the north-west as from that of the Mongols. The policy of Sarai followed traditional Mongol lines: the native princes were left on their thrones provided they regularly paid the tribute, but the disloyal or the defaulting could be deposed and their territory administered by a Mongol governor, a practice imitated centuries later by the British in India. The clergy, if duly submissive and enjoining submission on their flocks, were protected and exempted from taxation; a new and stronger link was forged between the Russian people and the Orthodox Church, which stood forth as a national institution confronting the paganism or the Islam of the conquerors and the Latin-papal pressures emanating from the German lands and the Mediterranean.

The lands directly ruled by the khans were the least urbanized and least civilized of old Russia; the population long remained nomadic, agriculture was practised only intermittently, and here a new race of 'Tartars' emerged out of a fusion of Mongols and Turks, Slavs and Finns. The Mongol settlers proper were but a small minority; geographically far removed from their homeland, they were eventually swallowed up in a Turkish sea, and Turkish replaced Mongol on the coins of the Horde before the end of the thirteenth century.[7] Though Berke's immediate successors were mostly pagans, Muslim influences continued to press in, from Transoxiana, the Seljuk sultanate of Rum, and even from the Bulghars of the middle Volga. Since all these Muslim neighbours spoke varieties of Turkish, the ultimate victory of that tongue within the khanate was assured, and merchants and travellers in Kipchak speedily discovered that Turkish was more useful to them than Mongol in the ordinary transactions of commercial life.[8] For trade was the life-blood of the State, as every Mongol believed; the ruins of Sarai contain traces of caravanserais and workshops as well as of palaces, and a steady stream of glass, pottery and human merchandise flowed across the Black Sea and the eastern Mediterranean to Mamluk Egypt. This profitable traffic was facilitated by the adroit Genoese, who acquired a monopoly of trading rights in the Black Sea from the Emperor Michael Palaeologus who was only too willing to favour them against their rivals of Venice, the champions of the defunct Latin Empire. Genoese 'factories' arose at Kaffa and other Crimean ports; agents of the Republic appeared at Sarai as early as 1267, they sold Flemish tissues in its marts, and as well as shipping slaves to Egypt via Constantinople, they despatched the furs and grain of Kipchak to the cities of Western Europe.[9]

The personality and policy of Berke ensured him a lasting fame: his capital was long known as 'Berke's Sarai' and the meadows east of the Volga as 'Berke's steppe'. The Muslim historians bestow praise and attention on so distinguished a convert; the embassies exchanged between Sarai and Cairo introduced him to the notice of the Arabic-speaking world, and Baybars's envoys have left a vivid picture of the man. They found the Volga (they report)[10] as big as the Nile; the audience tent of the Khan, which held a hundred men, was covered with white felt and lined with rich hangings decorated with pearls; Berke they depict as having a large face, a yellow complexion and a sparse beard, and being dressed in a robe of Chinese silk and wearing a cap and red velvet boots; with a gold belt instead of a sword at his side. In his later years he confided the military affairs of the state to his brilliant and ambitious young nephew Nogai, who had already won renown in the Polish campaign of 1259; on the appeal of the Bulgarian tsar, who was threatened by the Byzantines, Nogai led a force of 20,000 men across the Danube in 1265, the imperial troops fled in terror, the Emperor Michael escaped back to Constantinople in a Genoese ship, the Mongols ravaged Thrace, and a dethroned Seljuk Sultan Kai-Kawus II, who was detained in a Greek fortress, was released, carried to Kipchak territory and granted as an appanage the city of Sudak in the Crimea. Profiting by this lesson, Palaeologus accepted and perhaps sought a Kipchak alliance, and the marriage of his daughter to Nogai was indicative of Constantinople's belief that the latter was the real ruler of Kipchak. On the Caucasian front, the battle of the Terek threw the Il-khans on the defensive; the death of Hülegü in 1265 may have encouraged Nogai and Berke to move into Azerbaijan, but they were repulsed by Abaka, on the river Kur; Nogai lost an eye, and Berke his life, at Tiflis in Georgia in 1266. Though Nogai lived for another thirty-three years, he never aspired to the throne of Kipchak, a strange diffidence which is perhaps explained by a custom or superstition which excluded from the supreme power one who suffered from a physical defect or infirmity.

Berke was succeeded by his nephew Möngke-Temür, a son of Batu's, whose adroit diplomacy, backed by suitable military action, elevated the khanate of the Golden Horde to the rank of an independent Power. He maintained the alliance with Mamluk Egypt but made peace with the Il-khans, perhaps under pressure from Kubilai; his friendship with Michael Palaeologus was gratifying to that emperor, who feared the enmity of Charles of Anjou; by interfering in the struggles of the Mongol princes in Central Asia and supporting Kaidu against the Chagatai Khan Barak, he was enabled to shake off the remaining fetters of political servitude to the Great Khan, whose name and titles no longer appeared on the Kipchak coins. From the warring and divided princes of Russia he had nothing to fear and much to expect: the death of Daniel of Galicia in 1266 removed the only native ruler of skill and spirit; the martial Lithuanians, sweeping from the Baltic to the Dnieper, drove the alarmed Russians to plead for help from their pagan overlords, and the commercial republics of Novgorod and Pskov, though free from the presence of Mongol garrisons, were hard pressed to fend off the combined hostility of the Danes and the Teutonic Knights. In such unfavourable circumstances, the Russian lands could not hope to recover their freedom, and their princes were nominated and deposed, rewarded and punished, and required to furnish tribute and troops as the khan demanded. When Möngke-Temür died in 1280, the khanate was strong, independent and prosperous, and surrounded by loyal allies or docile friends, and its regular contacts with Egypt had carried to the northern steppes the religious and cultural influences of the world of the eastern Mediterranean. Mosques and palaces were constructed in the Crimea by Egyptian architects; the mosaics and wall-paintings uncovered in Sarai have earned for that capital from the Russians the perhaps pretentious title of 'the Pompeii of the Volga', and the nomadic element in the population of Kipchak was steadily reduced by the growth not only of agriculturists but of a new urban class of traders, craftsmen and artisans. These changes were accompanied by the appearance of a type of feudalism; the khan issued *yarliks* or grants to the lesser nobility or *tarkhans*, small landowners whose estates were exempt from taxation in return for military service by themselves and their tenants, but the freedom of the cultivator was replaced by peasant serfdom, an institution later borrowed and almost universalized by the Russians of Muscovy.

The death of Möngke-Temür, which was caused by the unskilful removal of a boil from his neck, cleared the path for the ambition of Nogai, who perhaps debarred from taking the khanate for himself, aspired to reign as a kind of mayor of the palace.[11] Möngke's younger brother Töde-Möngke, who succeeded him, a pious incompetent who became a Muslim and a Sufi in 1283, devoted himself to religious exercises and willingly relinquished the management of the state to the masterful general. The kingdom of Nogai assumed the character of an independent principality: it extended westwards from the Don across the flat cornlands of the Ukraine as far as the mouth of the Danube and the foothills of the Carpathians, and it cast its shadow over the plains of Hungary and the Balkan kingdoms of Serbia and Bulgaria, an area almost identical with that of the Gothic kingdom of the fourth century which was swept away by the irruption of the Huns. Its ambitious prince might easily aspire to renew the Mongol aggression against Europe, and in Hungary conditions were favourable to his designs. Laszlo or Ladislas IV, who ascended the throne of St Stephen in 1272 at the age of ten, was the son of a pagan Cuman princess; the boy displayed a strong predilection for his mother's kinsfolk, surrounded himself with Cuman concubines, welcomed the proffered support of Nogai, defied the clergy and magnates, arrested the papal legate, and virtually renounced the Christian faith for Asian shamanism. Pope Nicholas IV denounced his apostasy and preached a crusade against him in 1288, after Nogai had led a Mongol army into Transylvania and Töle-Buka, a nephew of the reigning khan, invaded Poland and advanced on Sandomir, perhaps to forestall Polish succour being brought to the Christian party in Hungary. But there was no Batu or Sübedei present to repeat the dazzling triumphs of 1241. Nogai and Töle-Buka failed to co-ordinate their efforts; the invaders were halted and then repelled;[12] the Christian or feudal armies hunted their apostate sovereign through his kingdom, until in 1290 Ladislas

161

was killed by a disaffected Cuman at the age of twenty-eight. After anarchy of twenty years, the ancient line of Arpad was annihilated in 1310, and under the new Angevin dynasty Hungary was steered back to Christianity and to civilization. Neither Hungary nor Poland was ever again seriously menaced by Mongol occupation, and these events may be said to have completed the cycle begun by Batu's drive across the Volga and Dnieper into Russia in 1240. After lying for fifty years under the shadow of the 'Tartar fury', Latin Christendom escaped into an atmosphere of freedom and security in which the arts of peace could flourish and produce in a few generations a renaissance of learning and science.

When Nogai and Töle-Buka returned from their campaign in the West they found Töde-Möngke sunk in religious torpor and surrounded by shaikhs and fakirs. In 1287 he abdicated the throne in favour of Töle-Buka, who perhaps in the hope of erasing the memory of his recent unsuccessful operations, reopened war with the Il-khans and attempted to seize the disputed province of Azerbaijan. He failed here also, and this finally discredited him and played into the hands of his rival. A party gathered round the young prince Toktu, a son of Möngke-Temür, and, when the khan, awakening to his danger, ordered his arrest, the youth fled to Nogai, whose intervention decided the issue. Töle-Buka was lured into an ambush and killed (1290); Toktu assumed the throne, and Nogai was richly rewarded with the revenues of the Crimean cities.

Toktu was young and inexperienced, and Nogai doubtless expected to find him a docile pupil. Within and without Kipchak, the great viceroy was treated as the real khan. The Russian chroniclers give him the title of Tsar;[13] the Franciscan missionaries in the Crimea speak of him as a co-emperor; the Venetians appealed to him to help break the Genoese trade monopoly in the Black Sea; he imposed his own candidate on the throne of Bulgaria, and forced the king of Serbia into the position of vassal. But the new khan was a strong and able youth, unwilling to fill second place; he reacted sharply, not to say savagely, to an attempt by the princes of north Russia to play him off against Nogai, and when Genoa appealed to him to defend her rights in the Crimea, he demanded an explanation from Nogai, who answered with a declaration of war: 'Our horses are thirsty and desire to drink from the Don.'[14] Toktu advanced against the veteran kingmaker, but on the banks of the Pruth he encountered defeat and fled eastwards; Nogai in pursuit paused to punish the Genoese by looting Kaffa and Sudak, but the khan eluded his grasp, re-formed his army, and in 1299 brought his opponent to battle again, this time probably at the Kagamlik, a small stream which falls into the Dnieper near the modern town of Kremen-chug.[15] Nogai, either over-confident or sluggish from advancing years (he was in his sixties), was defeated and killed, but a Russian soldier who brought his head to Toktu was himself put to death with the comment, 'A commoner is not entitled to kill a king!' In Russian and Turkish folklore this remarkable soldier, who made kings but never himself assumed a royal title, was long remembered as the 'Kalin-Tsar', or fat lord; the tribes who were grouped under his leadership continued to bear his name, and his descendants, the Nogai Horde, who eventually settled east of the Ural river, ascended the throne of Kipchak in the person of the *amir* Edigü.

Toktu had liquidated a rival and restored order and unity in his kingdom, but the curious co-kingship of Nogai had weakened the state and the self-confidence of the ruling class. Though he maintained friendly relations with the Byzantine Empire and married a daughter of the Emperor Andronicus, Toktu damaged his commercial prospects by renewed clashes with the Genoese, and the plunder of Kaffa by his troops in 1308 dealt a blow to the trade of the Black Sea region. Only a piercing insight into the future could have discerned that the final destruction of the Seljuk sultanate of Rum in 1300 would leave the way clear for the rise of Ottoman power in Asia Minor and that that power would block off the Kipchak khanate from Egypt and the Mediterranean to its permanent detriment. No unusual penetration was needed, however, to detect a novel restlessness among the Russians, en-couraged by the spectacle of Mongol fighting Mongol; the *baskaks* or tax-collectors could no longer travel with safety in pursuit of their duties, and the khan was obliged to charge the native princes with the task of levying and transmitting to Sarai the tribute extorted from the subject peoples. In his last years, Toktu gave much attention to the Russian problem; he contemplated, it is conjectured,[16] abolishing the seniority of the Grand Duchy of Vladimir and placing all the Russian princes on the same level of co- and equal vassalage, and in 1312, in order to study the situa-tion on the spot and perhaps preside over a meeting of the princes,

163

he resolved on a personal visit to northern Russia, a thing no successor of Batu had ever undertaken. Proceeding by boat up the Volga, he fell ill and died; Russia never received this formidable guest, and no future khan was tempted to leave the security of Sarai and the steppes for the perilous forests and marshes of the north.

The long reign of Toktu's successor, his nephew Özbeg (1313–41), is lauded as a golden age by the Muslim chroniclers who rejoice that under him Islam was finally and permanently enthroned as the state religion. The conversions of Berke and Töde-Möngke were personal and did not commit the régime, but after Özbeg there was no further vacillation; the issue was decided, Christianity and Buddhism in their various forms retired discomfited, and the stolid adherents of paganism among the Mongol notables could only delay what they could no longer prevent. Within a year the court of Cairo was gratified to hear that no unbelievers were left in Kipchak.[17] Özbeg graciously betrothed a princess of his house to the Mamluk Sultan Nasir, and when he himself married a daughter of the Emperor Andronicus III, he insisted that his bride profess herself a Muslim.[18] Yet he was prepared, for political or commercial reasons, to maintain friendly relations with Christian powers. The Genoese were allowed to rebuild the walls of Kaffa, which in 1318 was raised by the Pope to an episcopal see; the Venetians were permitted to erect a colony at Tana at the mouth of the Don; Pope John XXII expressed his thanks to the Khan for his protection of the Catholic missions, and the Franciscan envoy John of Marignolli, pausing at Sarai in 1339 on his way to China, presented to Özbeg a magnificent war-horse, a papal gift from Avignon. But neither Özbeg's foreign policy nor his relations with the Russians issued in success. His intervention to maintain the Mongol protectorate over Bulgaria and Serbia was indecisive; the peace concluded in 1323 between the Mamluks and the Il-khans weakened the ties between Cairo and Sarai, and Abu Sa'id repulsed Özbeg's attempts to occupy Azerbaijan; while the citizens of Tver rebelled against the Mongol tax-commissioners in 1327, after two grand-dukes had been executed, and were suppressed by Prince Ivan Kalita, who was rewarded with the grand ducal throne and chose to reside not at Vladimir but at Moscow, the future seat of Tsardom and patriarchate, centrally situated both for war and commerce by the head waters of the Volga and the Oka.[19]

Whatever might be the outward success and prosperity of his reign, the wisdom of hindsight enables us to discern that during these years the Golden Horde had passed its peak. The feverish unrest of the Russians could never be allayed, and the favour conferred on Ivan Kalita was the first step in the march to national supremacy of the Grand Duchy of Muscovy. The fall of the Il-khans of Persia could not be turned to advantage by Özbeg, who was no more successful than his predecessors in winning territory south of the Caucasus; the long-disputed province of Azerbaijan was destined never to be annexed to Kipchak. On the southern shores of the Black Sea the occupation of Brusa by the Ottoman Turks under their aged and gallant eponymous founder Othman in 1326 announced the establishment of a new Muslim military power; the capture of Nicomedia and Nicaea in 1330 by his son and successor Orkhan assured to his people control over Bithynia and the Asiatic shores of the Bosphorus and pointed the way to the passage of the Turks into Europe, which was achieved in 1357 with the crossing of the Hellespont and the seizure of Gallipoli. Özbeg, as a pious Muslim, had perhaps neither the wish nor the will to check the spread of this new *ghazi* state, nor could he have foreseen that it would so soon engulf extensive regions of Anatolia and the Balkan peninsula, yet its success condemned the Golden Horde to perpetual restriction to the Eurasian steppes and exclusion from the civilized lands of the south.

Özbeg died in 1341; his name is perpetuated in the mixed Mongol-Turkish tribal confederacy of the Uzbeks, whose land Uzbekistan is now a republic of the Soviet Union;[20] his elder son Tinibeg, who reigned for a year or two, was dethroned and killed by the younger Janibeg, whose rule of fifteen years (1342–57) was rendered tragically memorable by the ravages of the Black Death, which spread like a fuse along the trade routes from inner Asia and cost the lives of millions. When the plague had passed and the nation struggled into new life, Janibeg, profiting by the anarchy in Persia, struck southwards through the Caucasus and captured Tabriz,[21] but he died on his way back from the campaign, and his conquests were lost by the ill fortune or incompetence of his successor Berdibeg. The Horde itself threatened to go the way of the Il-khans, and the house of Jochi foundered in civil wars, assassinations and palace revolutions. The line of Batu became extinct in 1359; a new kingmaker, a second Nogai, arose in the person of Mamak or Mamai, and competitors from the White Horde[22] of Siberia, the descendants of Orda, strove to seize the throne of Sarai. The expulsion of the Mongols from China in 1368 deprived the empire of even a nominal head who might adjudicate in these disputes; Mamak, who was not himself of royal blood, kept alive a semblance of the Kipchak State and put up and pulled down 'do-nothing khans', until his ascendancy was challenged by Toktamish,[23] who restored the Horde to a semblance of its ancient glory. A nephew of Khan Urus, a protégé of Mamak's, who put his father to death, Toktamish as a youth led the life of a fugitive and sought help from the great Timur, who had reigned at Samarkand since 1369. Timur granted him the lordships of Otrar, Sabran and Sighnak on the Jaxartes; at Sighnak[24] he caused him to be proclaimed Khan in 1377 and furnished him with men and supplies sufficient to conquer Kipchak. Mamak was caught at a disadvantage; encouraged by the disintegration of the khanate, the Russian princes refused in 1371 to make the customary journey to Sarai to pay tribute and do homage, and when Mamak attempted to punish this insolence, he was crushed by the forces of Dmitri Donskoi, the Grand Duke of Moscow, at Kulikovo Pole, 'the field of curlews', in the Don valley in 1380, the first major victory the Russians had gained over their Mongol tyrants.[25] Reeling from this blow, he was attacked by Toktamish near the shores of the Azov Sea; defeated, he fled to Kaffa, where he was killed by the Genoese, and the victor ascended the throne of Kipchak.

The vision of freedom, which had flashed before the Russians on the morrow of Kulikovo, was instantly blotted out by the prompt action of Toktamish. He demanded in 1381 the total submission of the princes, and when this was boldly refused, he poured his armies into Russia and repeated the horrors of Batu's invasion 140 years before. Moscow resisted, was tricked into surrender, its inhabitants slaughtered and its treasures looted. A similar fate befell Riazan, and it would be tedious to enumerate all the towns which were left smoking ruins. The Russian people might well lament this fresh calamity, which struck them at a time when the ravages of the past had been repaired, but though their recovery was impeded, this ordeal was the last of its kind, as Toktamish was foolish enough to forget his obligations to Timur and to seek territorial aggrandisement at the expense of the great conqueror. Timur swore vengeance on his ungrateful pupil, and a war began which was fought round Khwarizm, Transoxiana, the Caucasus and the Kipchak plains.[26] After formidable preparations, Timur set out in 1391 from Samarkand, crossed the empty lands to the north of the Caspian Sea, attained the land of the Bulghars, where there being no night in summer the Muslims were dispensed from the obligation of midnight prayer, and learning that Toktamish was on the western side of the Yaik or Ural, he attacked with his accustomed success. Toktamish fled, leaving his camp and harem in possession of the enemy; a shattering blow was struck at the Horde: Sarai was sacked, and Timur feasted on the banks of the Volga, 'which had once been [says his annalist] the seat of empire of Jochi, son of the great Chingis Khan, whose throne he had the satisfaction of mounting'.[27] Yet he made no effort to annex the lands of the Horde and contented himself with installing a docile puppet as khan in the place of Toktamish. The latter regrouped his forces, concluded an alliance with Sultan Barkuk of Egypt, invaded Shirvan, and provoked a second assault from Timur, who inflicted another defeat on him on the banks of the Terek in 1395. Marching northwards, the conqueror reached Yeletz, a Russian city on the upper Don, though Moscow was beyond his grasp;[28] he savagely massacred the non-Muslim population of Tana, ravaged the lands of the Circassians and Alans, destroyed Astrakhan and burnt Sarai, whose people, says the chronicler, were driven like sheep before his army.[29] After this crushing disaster, Toktamish was reduced to the life of a wandering fugitive; years later he sought a reconciliation with Timur, who retained some faint affection for his former protégé and actually engaged to restore him to the throne, but he died in 1405 before he could fulfil his promise, and Toktamish perished obscurely the next year in the wilds of Siberia.

With him died the greatness, unity and prosperity of the Horde. The wounds Timur inflicted on Kipchak were never healed; Sarai never rose again to its former glory; the colonies of Venice and Genoa on the Crimean coasts, if not totally ruined like Tana, were left facing a desolate hinterland, and the trade which had once flowed through Constantinople across the Black Sea and the Russian steppes towards Transoxiana and the Far East was reduced to a feeble trickle and could no longer be reinforced by commercial intercourse with Egypt and Syria. The khanate itself shivered into fragments; a last attempt under Edigü (1399–1419) to repair its unity came to grief at the hands of the Lithuanians. New centres of limited power arose at Kazan, Astrakhan and the Crimea, which last survived under the protection of the Ottoman Sultans down to the time of Catherine the Great; these divisions and mutual animosities favoured the Russian bid for independence, and when in 1480 Ivan III, the Grand Duke of Muscovy, refused to kiss the stirrup of the khan in accordance with ancient custom, a Mongol army for the last time approached Moscow. Fearing attack from his rival in the Crimea, the khan Ahmad withdrew, and this event is commonly taken as marking the final attainment of Russian independence. In 1502 the khan of the Crimea captured Sarai, and the Golden Horde disappeared from history 265 years after the mighty armies of Batu had crossed the Volga.

During this long period of time Mongol power lay like a dead weight across the prostrate body of Russia. So harsh and humiliating an experience must inevitably have left marks upon that body, but the modern Russians are patriotically unwilling to allow more than a *negative* impact upon their nation's development, and they would doubtless endorse the comment of Pushkin: 'The Tartars had nothing in common with the Moors. If they conquered Russia, they gave us neither algebra nor Aristotle!'[30] They reduced the land to slavery; they extorted vast sums in tribute; they forced its soldiers to fight in their armies; they impoverished it by carrying off its craftsmen and artisans to enrich and embellish their own barbarous camp-courts. The Russian princes trembled at the khan's frown and prudently made their wills before setting forth on the perilous journey to Sarai to render personal homage to their savage overlord. The principal effect of the Mongol conquest was to wrench Russia round from Christendom and compel her to face east; since the incursion of the Cumans she had been cut off from her Byzantine mentor to the south, the rise of the pagan power of Lithuania blocked her outlet to the Baltic, as a vassal of the Horde she looked across the barren steppe towards Mongolia, and was for centuries deprived of cultural nourishment from the advancing nations of central and western Europe. Politically, Mongol example riveted on Russia the yoke of centralized absolutism; the title 'tsar', with its implication of unlimited and irresponsible autocracy, was first employed by the

Russians to describe their foreign tyrant the khan, and only later was it transferred to the first of their native princes, the grand duke of Muscovy, who rose to the primacy by his success in restoring the independence of his country. Russia regained her sovereignty, but lost the freedoms she had enjoyed in the early Kievan period of her history; the Russian, like the Mongol, tsar was not restrained by a powerful aristocracy, an independent Church, the liberties of chartered towns, the bold self-confidence of a free peasantry, or the legal limitations defined and enforced by an ancient and revered system of jurisprudence. The *boyars* or nobles were dependent on the grand duke for bounty in the form of landed estates from the territory retrieved from the Mongols; the Orthodox clergy preached the virtues of submission to the prince who fought for the faith against the accursed infidels, the spoilers of the land and the enemies of the cross of Christ; the necessity of providing the state with a regular flow of taxes and soldiers impelled the grand duke to employ his *boyars* as tax-gatherers and recruiting-sergeants in a vast country where distances were great and trained officials few, and the harsh institution of serfdom was gradually pressed upon the peasant masses. I cannot indeed detect in the culture of modern Russia any arts or sciences borrowed from the Turks and Mongols; to Asia the Russians acknowledge no obligations, but for her long and doleful subjection she exacted in time a full revenge; when the invention of firearms and artillery had placed the peoples of the steppe at last at a military disadvantage,[31] she expanded far beyond the Volga and the Urals across the Eurasian continent and in the nineteenth century finally broke the power of nomadism in its ancient homeland.

Yet the historian may still inquire why, when the Mongol leadership of the Horde came to make the decision which faced all the heirs of Chingis in the end, it opted for Islam and not for Christianity.[32] Of all the Mongol realms, that of Kipchak alone abutted on Christian lands, and one might have expected it to be exposed to the attraction of Byzantine-Slav culture. Christian influence was indeed not negligible there. The Nestorian clergy, who followed their Turkish disciples wherever they went, scored a striking success by converting Sartak, and if Batu's family had been thoroughly christianized, the western Mongols might have become acceptable to Europe and entered Latin society as the once pagan Germans had done before them. The Orthodox Church was not unmindful of its duty to protect its flock and evangelize the heathen; an episcopal see was erected at Sarai in 1261 to minister to the spiritual needs of the Russian colony in that city, and the khans on occasion employed its bishops as ambassadors to Byzantine Constantinople.[33] But it was the Latins, here as elsewhere, who were the most vigorous and pertinacious in missionary activity;[34] the Franciscans appeared in Kipchak as early as 1258, to preach and build churches; the Catholic element was strengthened by the multiplication of Genoese trading stations on the Crimean coasts;[35] Latin bishoprics were created at Kaffa,[36] Tana and elsewhere, and the Avignon Popes, in their letters to the khans,[37] supported the work of the friars and sought safe passage for those proceeding to more distant mission fields in Persia or Central Asia or China. Despite Berke's decision for Islam, his successors long hesitated before finally renouncing the shamanism of their fathers. The defeat of Christianity[38] in an area where its prospects seemed favourable, is perhaps attributable to the mutual enmities of the Nestorians, the Orthodox and the Catholics, the inferiority of the Russians to the Persians and Chinese in the scale of civilization, which rendered their religion unattractive to the conquerors, the presence of Islam among many of the Turkish peoples within the territory of the Horde, the influence of Muslim Egypt, whose agents were frequent and numerous at the court of Sarai,[39] and the example of Ghazan in Persia, which may have assisted Özbeg a few years later to embrace the faith of Islam. Whatever might be the motives of the khans, their conversion to Islam was of decisive effect. It imposed a permanent and insurmountable barrier between them and their Russian subjects; it raised the struggle for Muscovite independence into a crusade for Orthodox Christianity, and it prevented the Turco-Mongol peoples of Kipchak from being integrated into Christian Europe as the Hungarians and Bulghars had been and the Lithuanians were about to be.

The Golden Horde never became an urbanized or civilized state, for it was set in a region of pasture and desert which knew only markets and caravan stations but no true cities, settlements of ancient tradition governed by a bureaucratic class. All that lay behind it was a faint memory of the Khazars and the Scythians and of incessant nomad invasions. Yet its contacts with civilization were slightly more numerous than those of the khanate of Chagatai, which of all the Mongol principalities is the least known to history.[40] Its very boundaries are uncertain: the *ulus* of Chagatai originally comprised the basin of the Ili and extended from Kashgaria in the east to Transoxiana in the west, and its northern territories overlapped with the southern borders of the White Horde of Siberia. Unlike the other Mongol states, it had no access to the sea, and its population, mainly Turkish-speaking, was and remained largely nomadic. No great cities acted as centres of culture, education and government, but the famed Silk Road passed through the region, and its khans drew substantial revenue from the market-oases and commercial towns like Besh-balik and Almaligh. The Mongol ruling class here preserved a way of life closely resembling that of their old homeland, for Chagatai, like Kipchak, was no old traditional sedentary society governed, as in China and Persia, by a class of hereditary professional civil servants. The political life of Chagatai tended to swing between two points: the khans who resided on the steppe in the valley of the Ili were commonly conservative adherents of Mongol tradition, and often sympathetic to Christianity or Buddhism, those who migrated to Transoxiana fell under the influence of the cities, Persian in speech and Muslim in faith, and forswore the *Yasa* for Islam.

The Chagatai khanate was distracted, not only by this cultural and religious conflict, but by the attempts of the house of Ögedei to regain power in it, and the occasional intervention of the Golden Horde and Yüan China, and these incessant wars, depopulated the land, stifled commercial life, weakened the peasantry, endangered the security of the roads, and encouraged the murderous depredations of the Jatah or Jetes, nomadic brigands who in the fourteenth century were the scourge of Central Asia.[41] Ögedei's grandson Kaidu, an able prince, established after the death of Möngke a veritable suzerainty over the whole vast area between Kipchak and Mongolia; he protected the cultivators against the nomads, rebuilt the town of Andijan in Farghana on the Jaxartes, endeavoured to set the current of trade flowing again through his dominions, and confirmed Mahmud Yalavach and his three sons in the government of Bukhara and Samarkand. Kaidu died in 1301, fighting against his kinsman in China; his son Chapar proposed (a bold suggestion!) to Khan-Balik that the Mongol Empire be

171

transformed into a federation of free-trade states,[42] but was speedily dispossessed by Duwa, his Chagatai rival, and after the latter's death by his son Kebek, who completed the disintegration of the ancient *ulus* of Ögedei. Kebek, who reigned from 1318 to 1326, was a prince of ability; he preferred, without adopting Islam, to live in the civilized and urbanized district of Transoxiana; he built a palace (Mongol *Karshi*) near Nakhshab, from which the modern town Karshi takes its name;[43] he took over the monetary system of Persia and struck coins which were long known as *kebeki* after him.[44] His brother and successor, who bore the Buddhist name of Tarmashirin (1326–34), became a Muslim convert under the new name of Ala ad-Din; neglecting the steppe, he resided for four continuous years, in winter and summer, in Transoxiana; despising the poorer easterly regions of his kingdom and barred by the Chinese, the Il-khans and Kipchaks from expansion in any but a southerly direction, he followed earlier examples and led his armies over the high mountains into Afghanistan and the Punjab. Chingis and his immediate successors had been deterred from invading India by the heat of the plains, but the house of Chagatai was bolder; the Indus was repeatedly passed, Multan and Lahore were more than once plundered, Ghazna was attacked in 1326, and in 1329 Tarmashirin threatened, if he did not actually enter, the city of Delhi, which was defended by Sultan Muhammad b. Tughluk.[45]

The conversion of Tarmashirin displeased the nomads of the Ili valley; a revolt hurled him from the throne and replaced him by his nephew Changshi, a loyal adherent of the *Yasa*, and an anti-Muslim reaction permitted the Catholic missionaries for the last time to strive for the evangelization of Central Asia. The gospel was freely preached, churches were built, a son of the khan was baptized, and in 1338 the Avignon pope Benedict XII appointed the Franciscan Richard of Burgundy to the see of Almaligh. Muslim revenge was swift: the new bishop, five of his companions, and an Italian merchant named Gilotto, were killed by a mob in 1339 or 1340, and although John of Marignolli, who passed through the district in 1342 on his way to Peking, was protected by his status as legate or papal envoy from a like fate, the Muslim tide was rising and the 'seven martyrs of Almaligh' were never avenged. These religious dissensions split the khanate; the eastern half, where the conservative Mongol element was strongest, seceded, and in Transoxiana, where the Turkish amirs were now enthusiastic Muslims, the descendants of Chagatai became the puppets of a turbulent aristocracy. The khan Kazan was over-thrown in 1347 by the amir Kazghan, a kingmaker who impartially bestowed the nominal monarchy of Transoxiana on members of the houses of Chagatai and Ögedei; Kazghan, profiting by the fall of the Il-khans after the death of Abu Sa'id in 1335, forced the Kart prince of Herat into vassalage and restored Turkish supremacy over the Iranian element that was rising to the surface as Mongol pressure was removed, but his murder in 1357 enabled Tughluk Temür, a real or supposed member of the line of Chagatai, who about 1345 had seized power in Moghulistan, by professing Islam to snatch in 1360 at the throne of Transoxiana and so to reunite the ancient *ulus* of the son of Chingis. In 1361 Tughluk Temür, organizing his conquests, bestowed the governor-ship of Samarkand on his son Ilyas and appointed as the latter's vizier an able young soldier from a family which also claimed descent from Chingis. The young man was lame and was known as Timur Lang, which the Europeans have transformed into Tamerlane. In a few years he had embarked on his spectacular career as world conqueror; after proclaiming himself in 1370 the successor of Chagatai. Two years earlier the Mongol dynasty in China had fallen; the Il-khans were no more; Timur aspired to reign over Kipchak as well as Chagatai, and before he died in 1405 he brought nearly all the Mongol realms under his monarchy.

The rise of Timur may properly be considered the end of the Mongol age of conquest, for although his career rivals that of Chingis, his racial background is more Turk than Mongol and whereas Chingis was a pagan, Timur was a devout Muslim. Moreover, Timur was scarcely a nomad, a creator of a steppe empire, but rather the product of an islamized and iranized society and some of his most savage blows were struck at the Mongol principalities of Eurasia. The frightful barbarities he committed, his towers or pyramids of heads, his revolting butchery of prisoners and civilians, which might perhaps be excusable in Chingis, an untutored pupil of a harsh school, can hardly be forgiven in a man whose background was the educated and sophisticated society of Transoxiana. He posed at times as a champion of Islam against the unbelievers, and Jews and Christians indeed suffered terribly at his hands, yet he was no whit less ferocious towards his fellow-Muslims from Ankara to Delhi. His career was a singularly barren one. The great Chingis at least created an empire that imposed order and peace and a rudimentary civilization on Asia for over a century: Timur's kingdom vanished with his life, and his imperialism was imbued with no purpose other than the agglomeration of sheer power built on the corpses of millions. Till the advent of Hitler, Timur stood forth in history as the supreme example of soulless and unproductive militarism.

IO

The Mongol age in retrospect

The Mongol conquests, which shook the globe, were of a scope and range never equalled. The Mongols were invading Japan and Java thirty years after their armies stood on the frontiers of Germany and the shores of the Adriatic. After we have allowed for the military genius of Chingis, the world's greatest 'organizer of victory', the geographical advantage of campaigns launched from the steppe, and the weakness and confusion of the states that were attacked and demolished, the result is still marvellous and in a sense not fully explicable. The political landscape of Asia and half Europe was altered by this tempest of nomadic barbarism, the last and most violent civilization was called on to endure; the strength and distribution of the principal religions of the world were permanently changed; whole peoples were uprooted and dispersed and the ethnic character of many regions transformed for ever; Asia was opened up to European penetration by land and sea, and these contacts, once made, were later renewed on the initiative of the West, which in its search for a new way to the Far East discovered both America and the sea route to India round the Cape of Good Hope.

Ethnically, the most striking result of the Mongol conquests was the wide dispersal of the Turkish race over Western Asia. The Turkish entry into Islam had begun long before the Mongol age, and the occupation of Baghdad by the Seljuk chief Toghril Beg in 1055 signalized the coming of a third Muslim people, after the

Arabs and Persians, who were to dominate the greater part of Dar al-Islam down to the first World War. But the Mongol invasions speeded up this process, in consequence of the deliberate policy of Chingis himself. The Mongols were not a highly prolific people; their barren country has never supported a large population, and Chingis from the outset did not hesitate to augment his military power by admitting to his armies such Turkish tribes on whose fidelity he could depend and many of whom passed swiftly from foes to allies. The Keraits and the Naiman, the Oirats and the Uighurs, were not ashamed to serve so mighty a master, and their example was followed, as Mongol power spread westwards, by the Karluks and the Kanglis, the Bulghars and the Kipchaks, until the Turkish element in the Great Khan's war machine far outnumbered the original and native Mongol. By the time of Möngke virtually all the Turkish peoples of Asia were incorporated in the Mongol Empire, a circumstance from which flowed important consequences. (1) The Turkish nations, being in general at a higher level of civilization than the illiterate Mongols, acted as pace-setters in this matter; they provided Chingis not only with soldiers but with clerks, administrators and teachers, and the decrees of the Khans were published in a script derived from Turkish, or more precisely, Uighur. (2) The Turkish language advanced across Asia with the Mongol armies, most of whose troops were Turkish-speaking; the speech of the Seljuks and Cumans,[1] already common in parts of Persia, Azerbaijan, Anatolia and the Russian steppes, was powerfully reinforced by the newcomers; the Mongol speakers were always a minority and were eventually swallowed up in the Turkish sea, and the language of the conquerors, unlike the Arabic of the early age of Islam, shrank back into its Mongolian homeland and left Turkish dominant over the Eurasian steppe and beyond.[2] Even the name Tatar, once so terrible from its association with the Mongols, has been strangely carried across Asia and conferred on certain ethnic groups living now in the Soviet Union who, whatever racial strains may be contained within them, speak dialects that are unmistakably Turkish.

Since the ninth century, when Turkish slaves were first employed in the armies of the Abbasid caliphs, the Arabs and Persians had gradually been displaced from the political leadership of Western Asia. The Persian dynasties of the Samanids and

Buyids were succeeded by the Ghaznavids and Seljuks, and the Mongol period appears in retrospect as but a short break in the series of Turkish régimes. Whatever his real or fancied claims to Mongol descent, the great Timur was a Turk in race and spirit; the Mamluks of Egypt were commonly the offspring of Turkish Kipchak slaves; the Golden Horde of Russia grew progressively turcicized, as did the khanate of Chagatai, and in the sixteenth century the three mightiest thrones of Islam (the Ottoman Empire, the Safavid of Persia, and the Great Mogul of India) were filled by families of Turkish speech and origin. Almost all branches of the Turkish race were by then Muslim, and the more civilized of them had become strongly impregnated by Persian culture. Although a Persian National State did not arise till after the fall of the Safavid dynasty, Persian art and literature captivated the Ottomans and the Moguls, and the Arabs, whose political independence survived only in the deserts of Arabia, were depressed to the level of a poor third in the scale of Islamic nations. The Turks had already risen to prominence before the conquests of Chingis and his successors, but without those conquests their political triumphs in the Perso-Arab lands would have been slower and more protracted: in particular, it was the Mongol intrusion into Asia Minor which by breaking to pieces the old Seljuk sultanate of Rum, opened the path of supremacy to the greatest of Turkish monarchies, the Ottoman, whose six centuries of existence make it the longest-lived of Islamic empires.

As exponents of genocide, the Mongols were the most notorious since the ancient Assyrians, who exterminated or deported whole nations, and their loathsome record in killing was unsurpassed till the Nazi massacres of our own day. Christian and Muslim chroniclers agree in this bloody tale of savagery; their tones are hushed and saddened as they narrate horrors outside all their previous experience, and few today can read unmoved Juvaini's sombre comment that so many human beings had been slaughtered that the deficiencies could scarcely be made good by the Day of Judgment. Our emotions are so deeply stirred by the recital of these butcheries that their effect can be exaggerated, nor should we forget that they were restricted in time and locality. The worst horrors were perhaps perpetrated during Chingis's campaign in the West, and the massacres were largely confined to the province of Khurasan, where some famous cities never rose again from their ashes; on a slightly smaller scale the destruction was repeated during Hülegü's invasion forty years later, but on this occasion it is questionable if the ruin of such cities as Baghdad and Aleppo was more damaging than the smashing beyond repair of the intricate irrigation system of Irak, which for centuries had distributed the waters of the Tigris and the Euphrates over a naturally barren land. Southern Persia escaped devastation by timely submission, and its local dynasties were permitted to reign as vassals of the Khan; Asia Minor and the Caucasian kingdoms suffered spasmodically, and Syria was only briefly in Mongol occupation. In China, though our information is less precise, the early fighting was accompanied by the usual atrocities, but by the time of Möngke a humaner policy prevailed, and under Kubilai the final offensive against the Sung was conducted with no greater violence against civilians than was common in the warfare of that age. Such is the resilience of the human spirit that in thirty or forty years the poignant memory of the bloody invasions was dulled by the passage of time and the growth of a new generation, and notwithstanding the fears of Juvaini, the ranks of the dead were filled by a natural increase of population and the current of life resumed its accustomed flow.

In the course of their almost miraculous march to world empire the Mongols collided with three religious societies or cultures; their attitude towards them was hesitating and ambivalent, for they were torn between loyalty to their ancestral shamanism, which was consecrated by the *Yasa* of Chingis, and the powerful attraction of a superior and literate creed, possession of which seemed the hall-mark of a higher culture. Of these three religions (Buddhism, Islam and Christianity), which divided among them the spiritual allegiance of Asia, Islam emerged from the Mongol tempest the most strengthened and Christianity the most weakened. I shall discuss in turn the impact of Mongol imperialism on each.

(1) Buddhism, the oldest of the three creeds, has oscillated between the loftiest theosophy and the most debasing superstition. A religion without belief in a personal God, a future life and an immortal soul is beyond the comprehension of most Westerners; the Jew, the Christian and the Muslim are alike disgusted by the seeming paradox of an *atheistic* faith, but Asian devotion, always alert to escape from the manifold evils of a social order uncom-

178

monly rich in misery, has been willing to follow the four Paths to the extinction of sorrow and desire in the serene delivery of Nirvana. The philosophy and example of the Buddha was reinforced and perpetuated by the monkish order, whose mendicants in their yellow robes, shaven heads and begging-bowls carried the message of the Founder from Ceylon to Japan and from the Himalayas to the island of Formosa. Expelled after a long struggle from the land of its birth by a revivified Brahmanism, Buddhism divided, in the manner of religions, into rival sects, the most prominent of which received the names of Mahayana and Hinayana, the greater and lesser Vehicle. The former entered China at the beginning of the Christian era and was forced to compete with the ethical state system of Confucianism and the strange rituals and practices which lurk in Taoism.[3] The Chinese as a people have never been powerfully affected by religion; no one state religion has ever been officially adopted by them, but Buddhism came closest to national acceptance. Yet as a creed of foreign origin and antagonistic to the Confucian ideology, Buddhism was exposed to some degree of popular or official hostility, and in 845 a decree of the T'ang emperor suppressed it throughout the Middle Kingdom. The blow was severe but not mortal: the cult went underground and surfaced later after the fall of the T'ang, but its adherents sought a new field of expansion among the Turkish peoples of Central Asia and with them it moved westwards towards Transoxiana and eastern Persia. Under the barbarian dynasties which succeeded the T'ang, Buddhism re-entered China, and the Mongols found the three cults (Buddhism, Taoism and Confucianism) sharing the moral or spiritual education of the Chinese people.

The Mongols were naturally most strongly affected at the outset by the religious beliefs and practices of China, the only civilized nation they knew for many years. The example of Chingis, who sought wisdom from the sage Ch'ang Ch'un, directed their attention and patronage to the Taoists;[4] the Confucian literati, who embodied the national tradition, steadfastly declined to truckle to barbarians of any race, but the Buddhists, whose claims and loyalties were universal, early obtained the favour of the new masters of China. Mukali, the able general whom Chingis had left in command in China when he campaigned in the West, was impressed by Chinese culture; he extracted from the khan in 1219 a decree exempting the Buddhist monks from taxation,[5] a steady stream of Chinese defectors to the Mongol cause strengthened the Buddhist element in Karakorum,[6] and the Mongol invasion of Tibet after 1240 introduced the successors of Chingis to the peculiar Tantric or Lamaistic form of Buddhism which had already turned that remote and isolated highland into an unprogressive theocracy.[7] The Mongol leadership swung from Taoism to Buddhism: the Regent Töregene, who governed the empire from 1241 to 1246, gave the Buddhist monks precedence over their rivals, Kubilai's second son, born in 1243, was given a Buddhist name, the Great Khan Küyük conferred the title of Master of the State on Na-mo, a Tibetan lama, a series of conferences at Karakorum or Peking between representatives of the two cults was held to have resulted in the defeat of the Taoists, the influence of the lamas grew, and under Kubilai and his Tibetan adviser Phags-pa, Lamaistic Buddhism rose to an official and privileged position in the Empire.[8]

Secure in this powerful patronage, Buddhism seemed destined to win striking victories all over Asia and perhaps even to return to its Indian birthplace, whence it had been expelled. If Möngke was indifferent to the claims of the competing faiths, his brothers Hülegü and Kubilai were zealous Buddhists; the former's conquests carried his religion into Persia; under his grandson Arghun (1284–91) the land was covered with temples and stupas, priests and monks were imported from India, and Muslims, Christians and Jews doubtless viewed with horror the rapid spread of 'idolatry'.[9] In the same undocumented obscurity, Buddhism was received in the dominions of the Golden Horde; the evidence of its presence consists of little more than the statement that Özbeg marked his conversion to Islam in 1313 by putting to death some *bakshis*,[10] but this suffices to affirm that under the Mongols Buddhism first penetrated Europe. Clearly, Buddhism made little appeal west of the Altai,[11] where Islam was already rooted in the minds and hearts of the people, and when official support was withdrawn, its temples were deserted, its priests and monks dispersed, and its converts promptly reverted to their former faith. But in eastern Asia Mongol example and precept firmly and permanently enthroned Buddhism in China; by Kubilai's death the number of yellow-robed monks in his dominions was estimated at 200,000, his successors of the Yüan line nearly all bore Buddhist names or titles, and the Confucian historians of the dynasty, who are of course prejudiced witnesses, deplore this foreign corruption, the excessive influence of the lamas, and the insupportable burden placed on the State by clerical tax exemptions. Of Kubilai's successors, some had sufficient statesmanship to recognize the wisdom of conciliating the Confucians: Buyantu restored the examination system in 1313, and Tok-Temür (1328-9), who spoke and wrote Chinese, repaired the broken chain of tradition and sanctioned the revival of the customary veneration of Master Kung, which has been maintained through a hundred generations. As the only nomads who governed the whole of China, the Mongols bequeathed to it a double heritage: they cemented so powerfully the structure of the Chinese state that it never subsequently disintegrated, even under pressure from barbarians by land and Europeans by sea,[12] and they inserted Buddhism so tightly into interstices of Chinese society that if it has never been fully synthesized with Confucianism and Taoism,[13] it has persisted as the religion commanding the deepest loyalty of the most populous nation on earth.

(2) If Buddhism, despite its failure in the West, emerged from the Mongol experience stronger than it entered it, far different was the fate of Asian Christianity, whose bright prospects were unexpectedly clouded. The Nestorians, though like the Buddhists expelled from China under the T'ang, successfully preached their gospel to many Turkish clans; the Mongols first learnt of the faith of Christ through their Christian Turkish neighbours, notably the Uighurs, and the marriages of the Khans to Turkish princesses introduced that faith into the bosom of the ruling family. Töregene, the mother of Küyük, may or may not have been a Christian, but Sorkaktani, a Kerait princess and the mother of Möngke, Kubilai and Hülegü, certainly was, and Hülegü's celebrated wife Dokuz Khatun displayed a zeal for her Nestorian faith which is gratefully acknowledged by all contemporary Christian chroniclers of the East. The tolerant Khans listened to the exhortations of missionaries and allowed mass to be celebrated at their courts and often in their presence, but with the exception of Sartak, the son of Batu, none certainly received baptism, though reports of the conversion of one khan after another circulated through Christian Europe and Asia. When, at the earnest insistence of the popes, Franciscan and Dominican friars arrived at Mongol courts to

reinforce the efforts of the Nestorians and the Greeks,[14] hopes rose high; Latin hierarchies were created in China, Persia, Central Asia and the Crimea, and never had Christian propaganda been so vigorous throughout the Asian continent. The Crusades had already reminded the Catholic West of the existence of the Armenians, Maronites, Jacobites, Copts, Ethiopians and other Oriental Christian communities who had been largely isolated from the Greek and Latin Churches by the spread of Islam, and the persistent legend of Prester John,[15] reflecting the Turkish conversions of pre-Mongol times, kept alive the sanguine expectation of evangelizing half the known world. Yet this expectation was never realized: despite the heroic efforts of such devoted missionaries as John of Monte Corvino and Andrew of Perugia, Christianity not only failed to make permanent conquests in eastern Asia, it lost ground heavily in the Muslim world, where once-flourishing churches sank to the level of small tolerated minorities.

This humiliating defeat, from which the Christian religion never recovered, may be attributed to a variety of factors. The missionaries of Christ operated with very slender resources; they were never numerous, volunteers for such arduous and dangerous enterprises were not easy to recruit, and they rarely if ever had behind them the power and drive of an organized territorial State. They were in competition with two formidable rivals in Buddhism and Islam; and the politic Mongol rulers were sharply conscious of the unwisdom of embracing a creed anathema to the majority of their subjects, and Kubilai doubtless spoke for them all in his candid avowal to the Polos of the reasons for his unwillingness to receive baptism. The Christian preachers did not speak with one voice: the Latins and Greeks regarded each other as schismatics, and both repudiated the Nestorians as heretics; in China they were more concerned and more successful in stealing from each other than in converting pagans, and the story of the Önguts, or White Tatars, whose Prince George was persuaded by John of Monte Corvino to renounce the errors of Nestorius for the Catholic truth of Rome, reveals the sectarian weakness of Christianity in Mongol China.[16] More surprise may be felt at the failure of Christianity to gain a foothold in the Khanate of the Golden Horde, so close to Europe and the Byzantine-Russian Orthodox domain, but the cultural level of the subject Slav lands was not sufficiently high to excite Mongol respect and emulation and the pressure of Islam from east of the Volga was considerable.[17] By the end of the fourteenth century Christianity in every form had faded out of Asia; its disappearance was hastened though certainly not caused, by some brief, spasmodic and scattered persecution,[18] and its last feeble sparks were extinguished in the tempest of Timur's conquests.

(3) The collapse of Asian Christianity was inextricably connected with the Muslim *revanche* which swept over the west and centre of the continent as the Mongol hurricane subsided. Islam at first had seemed unfavourably situated. Its conquests before the days of Chingis had stopped short of Mongolia; the victory of the Kara-Khitay had thrust it back beyond the Oxus; the Mongol ruling family had few Muslim connections; the dietary laws of Islam conflicted with the ordinances of the *Yasa*, and the Mongols, jealous of potentates whose authority seemed to clash with or encroach upon that of the Great Khan, marked out the caliphate for destruction. Though the Muslims benefited from the general toleration, Chagatai was strongly hostile to them, and Hülegü marched against Baghdad, slew the caliph, and bereft Sunnite Islam of its titular head. The Latin Christians were more fortunate, in that the Pope was beyond the reach of these redoubtable pagans, and could with safety ignore the command of Küyük that he should present himself in person as a humble suppliant at the court of Karakorum, nor was Rome in danger of suffering the fate of Baghdad. Yet Islam slowly established an ascendancy over the men of the steppe and its success was confirmed by the accidents of history. Its pre-Mongol Turkish conversions had given it a broad and solid base of operations at the western end of the Eurasian pastures; part of the Uighur confederacy and all the Bulghars and the Seljuks had accepted the religion of the Arab prophet, and the Turkish auxiliaries who rode westwards with the khans were mostly zealous Muslims whose example could scarcely fail in time to sway their masters. Moreover, Islam penetrated more subtly and more permanently even in Yüan China. The Chinese were already familiar with the *Hui-hui*,[19] a name perhaps concealing that of the Uighurs, who were the first Muslims to settle in China; in the Seljuk age refugees from Transoxiana, among them an ancestor of Sayyid Ajall, carried the Law and the Koran to the Middle Kingdom, and the

large, mountainous province of Yunnan was islamized before it was sinized.[20]

The Islam that conquered the Mongols in the West, as exemplified by the decisive conversions of Ghazan in 1296 and Özbeg in 1312, was a persianized Islam, for the ascendancy of the Arabs in the Muslim world, long threatened, finally perished in the sack of Baghdad in 1258, which destroyed the Arab dynasty of the Abbasids and the metropolis of Arabic culture. The Arabic language indeed remained the vernacular speech in the lands west of the Tigris; it retained a religious prestige as the tongue of the Prophet and the vehicle of divine revelation, and Koranic commentaries and works of theology continued to be composed in it throughout the domain of Islam. But secular Arabic learning retreated from Baghdad to Cairo, where it flourished anew under the patronage of the Mamluk sultans and darted its rays into the shadowed negro lands of Africa. In eastern Islam Persian arose to unchallenged predominance; the poet Firdawsi had already done for it what Dante did later for Italian and Luther for German, and the Turks and Mongols, moving west across the Oxus, encountered a literature and a civilization vastly superior to anything in their previous experience.[21] The clerks, secretaries and officials the barbarians perforce employed to govern the land and collect its revenues insensibly conveyed to their more intelligent or curious or receptive masters an appreciation of Persian culture, which was diffused by its own power and attraction far beyond the borders of Iran. In Asia Minor it travelled in the wake of the Mongols into this now turcicized land and it thus imposed itself upon the Ottomans, whose literature was ever afterwards influenced by Persian models, while refugees from the invasions of Chingis and Hülegü carried it beyond the Indus into the Muslim principalities of the Gangetic plain, whose art and letters it moulded down to the last age of the Moguls. Persian became almost the official language of the Mongol court; Küyük's reply to Innocent IV and Möngke's letter to Louis IX were composed in it, Muslim merchants in China employed it in their commercial transactions, and under the Great Khans it enjoyed the status, in the words of a modern critic,[22] of the *lingua franca* of Asia.

Not only did Persian Islam take captive its conquerors: the faith of Muhammad won, during the ascendancy of the Mongols, a triple victory over the pagan nomads, the Christian Crusaders and their oriental brethren, and the Isma'ilian heretics. Islam's conquest of the Eurasian steppelands was indeed incomplete; it failed to advance north-east of the Altai and never penetrated Mongolia itself, but it gathered up nearly all the Turkish peoples, who had once seemed likely to follow Christ or Buddha, and its achievement in converting so many descendants of the great Chingis was a signal triumph. The Franks in Outremer would doubtless have succumbed to a Muslim *revanche* had the Mongols never intervened; their numbers were few, their leaders were disunited, their territories were strung out thinly along the Syrian coast, and the diminution of reinforcements from Western Europe must have condemned them to ultimate extinction. But the Mongol defeat at Ain Jalut in 1260 revived at a critical juncture the drooping hopes of Islam; the quarrel of Berke and Hülegü paralysed the Mongol offensive and supplied the Mamluks of Egypt with a welcome ally in the north, and the Muslims, gathering strength and courage, held Syria against the Il-khans and turned to crush the remnant of the Crusaders, equally with the pagans the enemies of the true faith. The Christian communities of the East, the Armenians and Maronites, the Copts and Nestorians, were involved to a greater or lesser extent in the fall of the Latin colonies in the Levant. They had supported, or at least sympathized with, their co-religionists, the intruders from the West, and some of them, notably the Armenians, had dreamed of a Mongol-Christian alliance that would not only return Jerusalem to Christian possession but deal a perhaps fatal blow to Islam and restore the religion of Christ to the primacy it had enjoyed in the Near East before the coming of Muhammad.[23] The triumph of the Mamluks in Egypt, the halting of the Mongol advance to the Mediterranean and the expulsion of the Latin Crusaders from the Asian mainland dispersed this mirage; a victorious Islam pressed heavily on the defeated and dispirited Christians, and mass conversions reduced the eastern churches to the tiny remnants they are today.[24] The catastrophe of Oriental Christianity is vividly illustrated by the disappearance of the Syriac language, the descendant of ancient Aramaic which became the ecclesiastical or liturgical tongue of the non-Hellenic churches of Asia. The last noteworthy author to write in Syriac was Bar Hebraeus, or Abul-Faraj, a Jacobite churchman and learned polymath who died at Maragha in 1286 and whose universal chronicle[25] is a valuable memorial of the Mongol age. By the fourteenth century Arabic was the universal speech of those regions for all communities, and a language whose history goes back to Assyrian times and which had been carried as far as China is spoken today only in a few villages of the Anti-Lebanon.[26]

The third victory was won over the divisive forces of Alid sectarianism or Shi'ism, which in the century before the Crusades had brought into existence the rival Caliphate of the Fatimids and torn Egypt, Syria and the Maghrib away from Sunni orthodoxy. This bitter schism had admitted the Frankish Crusaders into the Muslim East and facilitated the advance of the Mongols into Persia, since the Isma'ilis in these lands had given birth to the new sect of the Assassins, whose ferocious fanaticism, directed from impregnable castles in the Elburz mountains and the hills of North Syria, terrified the Islamic world. To the Mongols the grand master of the Assassins was as much a rival to the Great Khan as the Caliph of Baghdad, and Hülegü's overpowering might crushed the Persian branch of the order and exterminated its devotees. The Syrian branch survived longer, but was eventually rooted out by the Mamluks of Sultan Baybars, who by repulsing the Mongols and restoring the Abbasid line of caliphs, asserted his championship of an uncompromising orthodoxy. Some traces of the once mighty Isma'ilian movement may be discerned here and there in modern Islam, but as a serious threat to the unity of the Faith it died during the Mongol period.

Such victories have their price, and the Islam that emerged from the fires of this ordeal was narrowed, restricted and closed. During the four centuries from 800 to 1200 Islam had enjoyed a cultural predominance; the science and philosophy of the Greeks, commonly filtered through a Syriac channel, had fertilized the mind of the Muslim world and stimulated it to an impressive creative activity, and Arabic acted as the *lingua franca* of scholarship and letters over a wide segment of the globe from Spain to Transoxiana. In medicine and mathematics, in history and geography, in logic and philology, in music and astronomy, in physics and chemistry, the men of many races who wrote in Arabic enriched mankind by extending the horizons of knowledge and improving the techniques of inquiry, as for instance, by the use of the so-called Arabic numerals. The brilliant culture of Islam shone the more brightly by contrast with the stagnant

Byzantines and the barbarous Latins. Through Muslim Spain and Sicily the writings of Aristotle and the great Arabic thinkers, scientists and commentators were introduced into the West to inspire the intellectual awakening which culminated in the Renaissance. But with the death of Ibn Rushd (Averroes), the last great philosopher of Islam, in 1198, the primacy of Arabic-Muslim culture may be said to have come to an end. The invasions, first of the Turks and then of the Mongols, and the long and bitter struggle against Isma'ilianism, had forced the Muslim orthodox to close their ranks, systematize their theology, cease to tolerate freedom of speculation, and discourage intellectual effort not directly related to the furthering of religious piety. In the new schools or *madrasas*, a product of the Seljuk age, little was taught save the Koran and theology; the professors were exponents of an unbending scholasticism, and al-Ghazzali, the Aquinas of Islam, conducted a lifelong campaign against a 'philosophy' which he considered no better than atheism. In the post-Mongol age theology won a resounding victory; free scientific inquiry was virtually suppressed, and Islam shut itself up in its past.[27]

In consequence, the intellectual and scientific primacy of the Old World was slowly transferred to Western Europe, but this cultural shift was due to a number of circumstances in addition to the relative decline of Islam. In the first place, the Latin West escaped Mongol conquest, a piece of good fortune which has perhaps never been given its due weight. The tide of Mongol invasion rolled up to the borders of Germany and Italy and then receded. Had Rome and Florence suffered the fate of Kiev and Baghdad, it is hard to see that the Renaissance could ever have occurred. By an equally lucky chance, the Mongols never attacked and captured Constantinople, and that city, the repository of what was left of Greek culture, which had indeed suffered dreadfully from the Latin Crusaders in 1204, survived in Byzantine possession till 1453, long before when many of its scholars and artists had carried with them into Italy and beyond the seeds from which would spring a new birth of classical learning and philosophical thought. The eastern half of Christendom sank beneath the Tatar blows, and when Orthodox Russia and Catholic Hungary and Poland slowly came forth lamed and disabled, the Christian Balkans were overrun by a new Asian enemy, the Ottoman Turks, and Constantinople became the capital of a Muslim

Empire. Thus Western Europe, free from the scourge of barbarian attack since the Viking raids, was able to develop the arts and sciences and steal a march on the Christian nations of the East, who languished under Tatar or Turkish servitude. The unequal evolution of the two halves of Europe originated in the Mongol age has never been rectified since. The West pressed ahead to a more dynamic future, through Renaissance and Reformation, scientific and industrial revolutions, while the East stagnated under alien tyranny, in despotism, serfdom and ignorance.

The Mongol conquests had the further consequence of impelling the West, from mixed motives of trade and religion, to seek direct access to the Far East, first by land and then by sea. So long as the Mongol Empire dominated Asia, the highways across that landmass were safe and well-policed: less than sixty years after John of Plano Carpini and his companions set out from Lyons in 1245 on one of the boldest ventures ever undertaken by Europeans, a Franciscan friar was Archbishop of Peking and the Polos were employed in the civil service of Mongol China. When the political unity of the Empire crumbled and the wars between Berke and Hülegü in the 1260s foreshadowed the ruin of the *Pax Mongolica*, travel overland across Asia became once more slow, dangerous and obstructed, and the more enterprising Europeans, chiefly Italians, cast about for an alternative route to the East. In the vague geography of that age, Africa might be considered as no more than a large island washed by the waters of the Indian Ocean and its circumnavigation might bring the voyager within easy distance of India and China. Before the thirteenth century closed and while Kubilai still reigned in Khan-Balik, the pioneer attempt was made by the Vivaldi brothers of Genoa: they sailed in 1291 through the Straits of Gibraltar down the west coast of Morocco past Cape Nun, after which all trace of their expedition was lost.[28] They blazed the trail: after a long interval, others followed. The Mongol dynasty fell, the Asian trade routes were blocked, the Mamluks and the Ottomans successively controlled the eastern Mediterranean, but Ming China was finally reached by sea in 1514 by the adventurous Portuguese in the wake of Diaz and Da Gama.

While unbroken Mongol supremacy lasted, it facilitated a mingling of cultures on a novel scale. The Christians of the West, already carried by the Crusades to the eastern shores of the

Mediterranean, discovered a vast pagan empire at the other end of Asia; the wealth and urban populousness of China made a deep and permanent impression; the remote land of silk, hitherto a vague legend, acquired precise reality; merchants sought a share of its markets; missionaries wished to shine the gospel light into its heathen darkness, and even the islands of Japan and Java appeared for the first time on the maps and charts of Europeans. The appearance in thirteenth- and fourteenth-century Europe of guns[29] and the compass[30] *may* be a consequence of Chinese contacts, but no firm evidence of the transmission of these fateful inventions from east to west has yet been produced, and independent discovery in Europe or Islam is not excluded. Communication between China and Persia was maintained by land and sea until long after the fall of the Mongol dynasty. Chinese ships sailed as far as Ormuz in the Persian Gulf until the mid-fifteenth century; Persian merchants frequented the cities of coastal and inland China, carrying with them the Persian language and the Muslim faith, but this intercourse was productive of little permanent effect, and the introduction of Chinese paper money was confined to a brief period and a small locality. Some advantage, easy to assert but difficult to trace, might accrue from the mixture of languages which the conquests brought about. The decrees of the Great Khan were published in more than one tongue; the Il-khan Ghazan is said to have been familiar with Arabic, Persian, Chinese and 'Frankish'; an inscription in the village of Keuyang Kwan, forty miles north of Peking and dated 1345, is engraved in six languages including Uighur and Sanskrit,[31] and the great historian of Mongol Persia, Rashid ad-Din, owed to his linguistic versatility his ability to expand a history of the Mongols into a history of the world.

The historian who is struck by the comparison between the Arab conquests of the seventh century and the Mongol conquests of the thirteenth, may be surprised at the failure of the latter to issue in the creation of a new civilization. If the Arabs, like the Mongols, were illiterate barbarians when they embarked on the building of an empire that eventually stretched from Spain to India, they speedily educated themselves in the schools of the Greeks and Syrians, and later the Persians and Indians, and the philosophical and scientific treatises that were composed in the Arabic language in Baghdad and Samarkand, Cairo and Cordova, carried the human mind to new heights, while the graceful domes and minarets of mosques and colleges transformed the skyline of eastern cities. The Mongols totally failed to match this achievement. Their original barbarism was indeed softened by example of their better-educated neighbours and subjects; their leaders acquired a tincture of letters; the culture of China and Persia in particular left its impress upon them, but the Mongol language never became the vehicle of a sophisticated literature, nor was it widely propagated beyond its first homeland and it was easily defeated in competition with Persian and Uighur Turkish. The failure of Mongol to rise to the level of Arabic may be attributed to the fact that the Mongol Empire was created by a soldier and legislator whereas the Arab Empire was created by a prophet. Muhammad was in the eyes of his followers the mouthpiece of God; the divine revelations which he delivered to mankind in his mother tongue consecrated the Arabic language as the speech of Allah and his angels, and the Koran could not with propriety be recited or quoted in any language other than the one in which Gabriel had made known the commands of God to his Apostle. Whenever Islam was established, Arabic inevitably followed and grew into a universal tongue, understood if not spoken by Turks and Berbers, Persians and Indians. If Arabic represented the Law and the Prophet, Mongol represented the Law only, and though the *Yasa* was venerated as the bequest of Chingis to his people, no Bible or Koran was composed in his language, which thus could claim no special status as the speech of heaven. So long as the Mongol realm held together as a unity, the language of the khans enjoyed an imperial fame, but from 1260 or so onwards that realm was split down the middle, the western half turned Muslim and the eastern Buddhist, and as these religions, unlike Mongol, possessed sacred scriptures, the linguistic as well as the political unity of the Empire was finally shattered.

Finally, in the history of war and of the relations between sedentary and nomadic societies the Mongol conquests were the end of an epoch. Since the dawn of civilization the cultivators of the soil and the dwellers in cities had been threatened by periodic assault from the mounted horsemen of the steppe; the 'barbarians', whose invasions are a constant recurring theme of the histories of China and India, Greece and Persia, Rome and Byzantium, enjoyed for centuries a parity of weapon power and superiority in mobility over their enemies. The military techniques of the Mongols were comparable to those of the ancient Huns or Scythians, but as they were employed with greater skill and more proficient leadership, the results were commensurably more startling. But the Mongol victories were at once the most spectacular and the last that were won by barbarism over civilization. While the Mongol Empire still stood, the new inventions of gunpowder and firearms were applied to the art of war; the battle would in future no longer be decided by the skilful aim of the archer and the swiftness of his horse, and as metalwork was not a craft that could be practised on the steppe, the nomad lost at last the military advantage he had so long exploited. The gun was a monopoly of civilization; and a single burst of artillery could disperse or destroy a small army of archers. In the course of the seventeenth century, Russia and China, two nations which had suffered most from nomad aggression, moved in from either end of Asia to corral these recalcitrant shepherds of the steppes; the treaty of Nerchinsk in 1687, which fixed the Amur river as the boundary of their respective empires, deprived the Mongol- and Turkish-speaking peoples of the opportunity of playing one off against the other, and Russian colonists and Chinese peasants gradually came to outnumber the native owners of flocks and herds. Nomadism was silently controlled; its military power was broken, and its horsemen rode out to conquest no more. Yet in the strange whirligig of fate, the present quarrel between Russia and China may permit the Mongols to recover, not indeed their capacity for aggression, but their political freedom from both the giant Powers which have divided and dominated them for so many decades.

Appendix 1
The Secret History

The *Secret History of the Mongols* is our main, indeed our only, native source of information respecting Chingis Khan and his extraordinary career. So far as we know, it was the first Mongol *book*, as the Koran was the first Arabic book. It was compiled from oral tradition, by someone who was well acquainted with the Conqueror's early life. Passages of it are in alliterative prose, indicating that they were recited or sung in tribal assemblies before being committed to writing. The title 'secret' probably means 'private', that is, the book was not to be circulated in any form among non-Mongols. It was treated with veneration, not only as embodying a good deal of tribal lore, but also as containing many of Chingis's instructions and pronouncements.

Neither the author nor the date of composition is known. Several guesses have been made at the former, but the total lack of evidence makes the pursuit of this inquiry at present fruitless. More important to the historian is the date of the book, and in recent years much attention has been given to this problem, which would appear to be nearer solution than that of the authorship.

The only clue in the *History* itself is the statement that it was finished in the Year of the Rat. But which Rat year? It could be 1228, 1240, 1252 or 1264. The first was the year after Chingis's death and before the election of Ögedei. The *History* contains a short account of Ögedei, but does not mention his death, which occurred in December 1241: hence some have assumed that the book was completed in 1240. For 1252 there is little to be said, though Grousset argued (*L'Empire mongol*, 1941, 230, 303) that Chapter 255 contains a hint of the succession of the

House of Tolui to the grand khanate, an event signalized by the election of Möngke in 1251. In 1951 Hung ('The Transmission of the Secret History', *HJAS*) decided for 1264, mainly on the ground that Chapter 247 refers to the Chinese city of Hsüan-te chou as Hsüan-te fu, a name it did not officially acquire till 1263. Waley in 1960 ('Notes on the Yuan-ch'ao pi-shih', *BSOAS*) detected in Chapter 274 references to fighting in Korea in 1248, and Ledyard in 1964 ('The Mongol Campaigns in Korea', *CAJ*), building on this, argued persuasively that the *History* could not have been written before this date: the Rat Year must therefore be 1264. This still left unexplained why the compiler never mentioned Ögedei's death and ignored the reigns of Küyük and Möngke. Moreover, the *History* alleges that this particular Rat Year was also the year of a great *kuriltai* or Diet, but the annals of Kubilai, which are full and accurate, make no mention of a *kuriltai* held in 1264 at Köde'e-aral, the place given in the *History*,[1] nor is there any record of a *kuriltai* in 1240 or 1252. De Rachewiltz suggested in 1965 ('The Dating of the Secret History', *Monumenta Serica*) that the *kuriltai* was the one summoned in 1228 which elected Ögedei as Great Khan in 1229. The *Secret History* was compiled, he argued, in order to commemorate the great deeds of Chingis; it would be put in hand soon after the Conqueror's death in August 1227, and nothing would be more fitting, natural and convenient than that the pious work should be done while all the Mongol princes were gathered to mourn his passing and choose his successor, since never again, in all probability, would so many people who knew the details of his career be assembled together and available for questioning. According to this theory, the *History* was originally no more than a biography of Chingis and ended with the statement that 'he ascended to Tengri (heaven)', the mention of his death being taboo. Years afterwards, certainly not before 1241, a short life of Ögedei was tacked on to it; this life is pro-Tolui in tone and tendency, and represents Ögedei as a weak man dominated by Chagatai, so it could hardly have been published in his lifetime.

No Mongol chronicles were drawn up under Küyük and Möngke. Under Kubilai, however, the collection of historical records was undertaken in earnest, no doubt under the influence of Chinese practice. Scholars and scribes were probably employed to compile them in both Mongol and Chinese. As Kubilai could not read Chinese, he would check the Mongol text before authorizing the Chinese translation, which became the basis of the *Yüan shih*, the dynastic history drawn up after the Ming revolution of 1368. At least one copy of the *Secret History* must have been left behind in China after the expulsion of the Mongols, and from it the Ming scholars made a transcription in Chinese characters and a translation into vernacular Chinese, as well as dividing the book into sections or chapters. From whatever cause, the Mongol original subsequently perished; yet it is not strictly correct to say that the *Secret History* survives only in its Chinese form. The *Altan Tobchi*, a Mongol chronicle of the late seventeenth century, incorporates the greater part of the text of the *Secret History*: it is noteworthy, as confirming the theory that the life of Ögedei was a later addition, that it reproduces none of the passages relating to him.

Appendix 2
Did the Mongols use guns?

War is notoriously a great stimulus to technological invention, and in modern times every great European conflict has resulted in the appearance of new or improved weapons, culminating in the atom bomb which emerged at the end of the second World War. In view of the scope and magnitude of the Mongol wars, it is natural to ask if any new type of armament came out of them, more precisely, if they hastened the coming of firearms, that is, weapons in which gunpowder or a similar explosive is used to propel a bullet or projectile of stone or metal from a gun or cannon.[1] Before the Mongol conquests, there is scarcely a trace of them; there is no evidence that either side used them during the Crusades, but by the fourteenth century firearms are found being employed in the armies of Europe and China. Were the Mongols directly or indirectly responsible for this innovation, which was to transform the art of war and much else besides, or did it spring up independently and simultaneously in East and West?

It must be said at the outset that the evidence is tantalizingly inconclusive. Documents cited by early inquirers sometimes turn out to be forgeries[2] or of a later date than was originally thought. The precise meaning of the terminology employed frequently eludes us; new inventions are commonly named after older, more familiar things (thus the word 'cannon' is from the medieval Latin *canna*, a tube or reed), and it is often impossible to decide whether, for example, the word 'gun' in a particular passage refers to the new firearm or the old-style catapult or ballista. The path of the inquirer is sometimes blocked by a thick undergrowth of legend, as in the case of the monk or magician Berthold

Schwarz, 'Black Berthold', who was reputed to have discovered gun-powder in mid-fourteenth-century Germany but who is as mythical as Pope Joan.[3] In evaluating evidence from China,[4] peculiar difficulties arise from the nature of the Chinese language and the fewness of Western scholars who possess an expert knowledge of it.

The explosive nature of gunpowder, by which we understand a mixture of saltpetre, sulphur and charcoal, was no doubt discovered accidentally, perhaps in China, whose soil is in places like the alluvial plains near Peking heavily impregnated with saltpetre and a wood fire lit on such ground might well bring about an explosion.[5] This powerful force was most likely employed harmlessly in the manufacture of fire-crackers and fire-works before it was adapted to military purposes, probably not until the Sung period, but the 'fire-arrows' (*huo shih*) so frequently named in the wars of that time, were in all likelihood no more than flamethrowers and incendiaries of the 'Greek fire' type compounded of naphtha and quicklime. The Chinese character *p'ao*, now meaning 'cannon', was written for centuries with the radical for 'stone', indicating that it meant a stone-throwing catapult or ballista, long before it was written with the radical for 'fire', when it may be presumed to mean a true gun.

However, gunpowder is one thing, firearms quite another, nor is it certain that the Chinese were pioneers in both. The Sung period appears to have been one of remarkable military innovation, chiefly in the form of new explosives and incendiaries, fire-arrows and smoke bombs used by the Sung troops in their wars against the Ch'i-tan and Ju-chen, barbarians who controlled most of North China before the coming of the Mongols. These conflicts around 1200 possibly speeded up the transformation of the catapult into a gun. According to the *T'ung Chien Kang Mu*, a collection of Chinese historical records originally compiled in the 11th century and revised in later times,[6] the Ch'i-tan, defending the city of Lo-yang against the Mongols in 1232, used a 'thunder-bomb' (*chen t'ien lei*), an iron vessel filled with gunpowder and discharged from a catapult by the igniting of the powder. It exploded with a noise that could be heard 100 *li* (thirty-three miles) away; it blew the besiegers to pieces, and its splinters pierced metal armour. Making allowance for exaggeration (modern shells are not heard exploding thirty miles away), 'it is possible to grant [says Partington] that some sort of explosive bomb was concerned'.

On the basis of this fact, if fact it be, a rickety structure of speculation and guesswork has been built, intended to show that a few years later the Mongol armies brought firearms into Europe. Among the Mongol generals commanding in North China was the great Sübedei Bahadur, their most brilliant strategist, who five years later (in 1237) led the massive invasion of Russia and Eastern Europe under the nominal command of Chingis's grandson Batu. It is assumed that the Mongols, always quick to learn from their enemies, were soon employing 'thunder-bombs' themselves and that Sübedei would have a supply with him when he marched westwards. Some recent writers have boldly asserted that gunpowder, or even cannon, were used at the battle of the Sajo (11 April 1241), when the Mongols annihilated the Hungarian army under King Bela.[7] Of this there is not the slightest evidence. The Europeans who faced this fearful and unexpected attack were quite capable of noting Mongol tricks, stratagems and novel military devices: how, for instance, the mobility of the Mongol troops was enormously increased by their practice of bringing with them plenty of remounts, so that pursuit of the enemy was never hindered by exhausted horses, and how at the battle of Liegnitz in Silesia, fought two days before that of the Sajo, they choked and disabled the Polish troops by releasing a toxic gas in the form of black, stinking smoke. Had some kind of artillery been employed, it is hardly likely to have escaped contemporary record, but the Polish and Hungarian chroniclers are silent.[8]

It is certain that the Mongol high command was impressed by technological devices of a military kind, and they conscripted engineers all over Asia and attached them to their armies. Chinese, Muslims and Europeans were all employed in armament works and as military advisers. In 1259 Chinese technicians produced a 'fire-lance' (huo ch'iang): gunpowder was exploded in a bamboo tube to discharge a cluster of pellets at a distance of 250 yards.[9] We are getting close to a barrel-gun. A great deal of attention has been given to the siege of Hsiang-yang in 1273, which was fully described by the Chinese and Persian historians as well as by Marco Polo. Impatient at the resistance of this strongly fortified Sung city, Kubilai Khan sent to his cousin, the Mongol Khan of Persia, asking for engineers and powerful machines to assist him in reducing it. What was sent was not, however, cannon but enormous trebuchets, mangonels or slings which threw stones of 150 pounds weight capable of smashing through walls seven or eight feet thick. The towers were demolished and the city surrendered.[10] P'ao were also employed in naval warfare between the Sung and the Mongols, but the term still applies to missiles discharged from wooden siege-engines rather than from guns. Yet in the two Mongol invasions of Japan in 1274 and 1281 'fire-barrels', possibly guns with iron barrels fired by gunpowder, were employed along with the traditional catapults and incendiaries, and an illustration in a Japanese work, said to date from 1292, shows what appears to be a kind of bomb bursting in front of a Japanese archer.[11]

Gunpowder slid unobtrusively into Chinese history; it probably came into widespread use in the reign of Kubilai (1260–94), and by 1280 was already being stored in arsenals, as is shown by the story told of an accidental explosion in that year which wrecked the building and killed four tiger-cubs belonging to the Chief Minister next door![12] It was already known in Europe, and even if we reject the story that Roger Bacon discovered it, the strange cipher-recipe contained in his *Epistola de secretis operibus naturae* (dating probably from 1265–6) would indicate that he knew of its composition, even if he was ignorant of its use as a propellant.[13] If the invention passed from China to the West, the Muslim peoples may well have been intermediaries: saltpetre was known to the Persians and Arabs as 'Chinese snow' (*thalj al-Sin*), and by the mid-thirteenth century a new word *barud* has been coined to describe the explosive mixture of which saltpetre was the most important ingredient.[14] But the chain of transmission is hidden, and independent discovery in East and West cannot be excluded.

There can be little doubt that firearms also appeared in China during the Mongol period (1260–1368). 'Between 1280 and 1320 [says Dr Needham] is the key period for the appearance of the metal-barrel cannon', though he confesses that 'it might have appeared first among the Arabs or the Latins'.[15] From the 1320s onwards real guns were cast in Western Europe,[16] but the earliest dated Chinese examples are several years later, one of 1356 and an iron bombard of 1377.[17] Far from having been manufactured for the Mongols, these early Chinese guns appear to have been produced by the Ming revolutionaries who brought the great national revolt to a successful conclusion in 1368. Earlier, there is more evidence of the use of gunpowder by the Sung than by the Mongols. In view of their force and novelty, the new guns should have been of more advantage to the Mongols than they apparently were. Possibly the Mongols were inhibited psychologically from making fuller use of artillery: like the Mamluks later, they may have felt that such mechanical devices detracted from the human element of personal bravery which should always predominate in war. Is there an echo of this in Mao Tse-tung's well-known assertion that even in a nuclear age, it is in the last resort men who matter?

To the question 'Did the Mongols use guns?' the answer must be a qualified negative. To the further question, 'Did they introduce gunpowder and firearms into Europe?' the reply can only be that there is no firm evidence at all and that it is wholly improbable. That gunpowder appears to have been first used both in China and the West in the late thirteenth century and firearms about a century later might indicate that one learnt of it from the other, but no documents exist to prove it. The wars in North China involving the Ch'i-tan, the Ju-chen, the Mongols and the Sung seem to have been the testing-ground for a number of new technological devices,[18] but these were used *against* the Mongols rather than by them. Like clocks and movable printing, the time and place of their origin must be recorded as unknown in the present state of our knowledge.

Abbreviations

AHR	*American Historical Review*
CAJ	*Central Asiatic Journal*
EI	*Encyclopedia of Islam*; 1st ed., 4 vols, 1913–36; 2nd ed. in progress
HJAS	*Harvard Journal of Asiatic Studies*
JA	*Journal Asiatique*
JAH	*Journal of Asian History*
JESHO	*Journal of the Economic and Social History of the Orient*
JRAS	*Journal of the Royal Asiatic Society*
JWH	*Journal of World History*
REI	*Revue des Études Islamiques*
SI	*Studia Islamica*
TP	*T'oung Pao*

Notes

Preface

1 Perhaps I ought to exempt from censure under this category the late Harold Lamb's *Genghis Khan, Emperor of All Men*. Originally published in 1927, it went through several editions and foreign translations. Lamb specialized in biographies of colourful historical characters (Hannibal, Charlemagne, Justinian, Tamerlane, Babur); his racy, journalistic style is not to everyone's taste, but he had travelled extensively in the Middle East, he was a man of wide reading and immense industry, and his work is not disfigured by serious errors.

2 I am afraid I cannot amend this sentence even after the appearance of Walter Chapman's *Kublai Khan, Lord of Xanadu*, New York, 1966.

3 Actually, the first biography of Chingis to appear in Europe was the *Histoire du grand Genghiscan*, Paris, 1710, compiled mainly out of Persian sources (Juvaini and Rashid) by Pétis de la Croix, Oriental interpreter at the court of Louis XIV.

4 In two memoirs read to the Institut in 1822–4 under the title 'Les relations politiques des princes chrétiens avec les empereurs mongols'.

5 On the dispute over the date, see I. de Rachewiltz, 'Some Remarks on the Dating of the *Secret History of the Mongols*', *Monumenta Serica*, 24, 1965. Dr de Rachewiltz highly praises the recent (1962) edition of the *Secret History* by the Hungarian Mongolist Ligeti.

6 I may note here that the work of Soviet scholars is slowly becoming known in the West. A series of booklets in English, under the general title of *Fifty Years of Soviet Oriental Studies* (Moscow, 1968), provides succinct summaries of Soviet achievements in these fields: the one on 'Mongolic Studies' is a particularly useful conspectus.

Chapter 1: Eurasian nomadism

1 Lattimore, *Studies in Frontier History*, Oxford, 1962, 459.

2 For a vivid description of this Sahara of Asia, see Cable and French, *The Gobi Desert*, London, 1942, the report of two intrepid women missionaries. In Mongol, *gobi* is not a proper name, but a generic term for a strip of hard clay with a scattering of gravel, distinct from steppe and sand-desert.

3 Kizil-kum and Kara-kum are the Red and the Black Desert respectively, in the Turkish language.

4 The Himalayas were often known as the Indian Caucasus, 'That vast sky-neighbouring mountain of milk-snow', *Sohrab & Rustem*.

5 The gap of Dzungaria or Jungaria, a name said to be derived from the Dsongars, who formed the left wing (*dson*—left; *gar*—hand) of the Mongol army when it invaded this region, covers roughly the basin of the Ili river: the name is no older than the sixteenth century.

6 But not of pigs, because the oak, from whose acorns these animals are chiefly fed, is not found even in the forests which line the steppes, and pigs cannot be driven for long distances when on migration.

7 In the Altai, the temperature is often below freezing-point on more than 200 days of the year.

8 The horse-drawn war-chariot, in which spokes replaced the solid wheels invented by the Sumerians, made its appearance among the Indo-European nomads around 1000 BC. The Chinese acquired it soon after, as the horse remains in the Shang and Chou tombs testify. E. G. Pulleyblank, 'Chinese and Indo-European', *JRAS*, 1966.

9 This change probably occurred between 400 and 200 BC. Lattimore dates 'the relatively sudden appearance of horse nomads [by which he means horse *riders* as distinct from drivers of chariots] hostile to the agricultural Chinese between the fifth and third centuries BC', *Inner Asian Frontiers of China*, 168. Cf. H. G. Creel, 'The Role of the Horse in Chinese History', *AHR*, 70, April 1965, and E. Erkes, 'Das Pferd in alten China', *T'oung Pao*, 36, 1942.

10 The stirrup may not have been invented much before the beginning of the Christian era. A *metal* stirrup would not have been invented by nomads: the word originally meant to 'step up' by putting one's foot in a loop of rope or leather thong. Its coming led to a shortening of the saddle between pommel and cantle, so that the rider could twist and turn and fire to the side and rear without falling off his mount. Lattimore, *op. cit.*, 465–6, note, citing W. W. Arendt, 'Sur l'apparition de l'étrier chez les Scythes', *Eurasia Antiqua*, Helsinki, Vol. 9, 1934. Cf. Grousset, *L'Empire des Steppes*, 37, note, & Lynn White, *Medieval Technology & Social Change*, Oxford, 1962, 15–17, who notes that the earliest mention of the stirrup in Chinese literature is AD 477, quoting Pelliot, *T'oung Pao*, 24, 1926.

11 In the nomenclature of the steppes, six to ten tents or households (Turkish *yurta*) form a camp, literally 'home', several camps a clan, several clans a tribe (*uruk*), several tribes a people (Turk. *il*, Mong. *ulus*).

12 The most recent descriptions of ancient nomad life, based on archaeological finds, will be found in A. L. Mongait, *Archaeology in the USSR*, 1955; Eng. tr. 1961, G. Vernadsky, *The Origins of Russia*, Oxford, 1959, Ch. 1, and E. D. Phillips, *The Royal Hordes*, London, 1965. The picture is highly generalized: the details given are not to be applied to *every* nomad tribe in *every* age.

13 See the learned article by J.-P. Roux, 'Tängri. Essai sur le ciel-dieu des peuples altaïques', *Revue de l'histoire des religions*, 149–50, 1956.

14 Shamanism arose among the forest people of the north and spread southwards to the steppes, where it still survives the repression of the Soviet authorities, the enemies of all religions and superstitions. See M. Eliade, *Shamanism*, 1951; Eng. tr. 1964.

15 J. A. Boyle, 'A Form of Horse-Sacrifice among the Mongols', *CAJ* X, 1965.

16 A. Waley, 'The Heavenly Horses of Ferghana', *History Today*, 1955.

17 See E. H. Minns, 'The Art of the Northern Nomads', *Proc. Brit. Acad.* 1942, M. I. Rostovtzev, *The Animal Style in South Russia and China*, Princeton, 1929, Tamara T. Rice, *Ancient Arts of Central Asia*, London, 1965, and Karl Jettmar, *Art of the Steppes*, Eng. tr. 1967.

18 Among the objects found in the seventh-century Anglo-Saxon burial ship at Sutton Hoo in Suffolk in 1939 was a purse decorated with a bird of prey in a style strongly reminiscent of nomad art.

19 On the complicated problems of Central Asian philology, see Sir Gerard Clauson, *Turkish and Mongolian Studies*, London, 1962. He vigorously repudiates the 'Altaic theory' which holds that Turkish and Mongolian are genetically related.

Chapter 2: The Turkish rehearsal

1 *Khan* is merely a shortened form of *kaghan*, and not, as was once thought, an inferior rank. (But see the entry in Doerfer, *Türkische und Mongolische Elemente im Neupersischen*, III, 141–80.) The Persians and Arabs transliterated *kaghan* as *khaqan*. Before the Juan-Juan, the highest title among nomads like the Hiung-nu was *shan-yü*.

2 Both these etymologies are rejected by Clauson, 'A Note on Qapqan', *JRAS*, 1956, who suggests that the search for meanings should be suspended until our knowledge of old Turkish has been greatly deepened.

3 *Yabghu, yavghu* or *jabghu* was a pre-Turkish title, possibly of Iranian origin, and is found on the coins of the Kushan kings of north India. Grousset, p. 127, note. It was a title of rank, as distinct from *tegin*, a title of birth conferred on princes of the reigning house.

4 S. Julien, 'Documents', *J.A.*, 1864, 331. Some details are added from E. H. Parker, *A Thousand Years of the Tartars*, London, 1924, 133–5, taken likewise from the Chinese sources.

5 The identity of the Avars with the Juan-Juan is not absolutely certain, and the question is complicated by Menander's distinction between the true Avars who stayed behind in Asia, and the pseudo-Avars who invaded Europe. See D. Obolensky's chapter, 'The Empire

and its Northern Neighbours', in the new (1966) edition of the Byzantine volume of the *Cambridge Medieval History*.

6   See the fragments of the Menander collected in C. W. Müller, *Frag. Hist. Grae.* iv, 200, and translated in Yule and Cordier, *Cathay and the Way Thither*, I, 205–12. The Byzantine authors disguise the name Istemi under such corrupt forms as Dizabul and Silzibul, the second and third syllables of which are almost certainly a slight distortion of the title *yabghu*.

7   Chavannes, 236. The yabghu's *ordu* was probably located in the valley of the Tekes, a tributary of the Ili river.

8   So reported, not by the contemporary Byzantine historians, but by Michael the Syrian, a twelfth-century writer, ed. and tr. J. B. Chabot, Paris, 1905, III. Cf. O. Turan, 'The Ideal of World Domination among the Medieval Turks', *Studia Islamica*, IV, 1955.

9   S. Julien, 'Documents', *JA*, 1864, 213–19. Cf. C. P. Fitzgerald, *Son of Heaven, a biography of Li Shih-min*, Cambridge, 1933.

10   V. Thomsen, *Inscriptions de l'Orkhon*, 99.

11   A tomb, two pillars and sixty-four lines of inscription, found near Urga (now Ulan Bator) in 1897, commemorate the Turkish statesman, who died about 730 at more than seventy years of age.

12   C. P. Fitzgerald, *The Empress Wu*, Melbourne, 1955.

13   *Mo-ch'o* is, of course, the Chinese transcription: his personal name was Kapghan or Kapkan, on which see the articles by Sinor and Clauson in the *JRAS* for 1954 and 1956.

14   Bilge's original name in Chinese transcription was Mo-ki-lien. He figures on the monuments as Bilge-kaghan, 'the wise kaghan'.

15   H. A. R. Gibb, *The Arab Conquests in Central Asia*, London, 1923.

16   Talas (in Arabic Taraz) lay near the present town of Jambal in the Kazakh republic of the Soviet Union. It was an important commercial centre in medieval times.

17   The first Nestorian missionaries reached China in 636 and were received by T'ai-Tsung, the second emperor of the T'ang dynasty. Moule, *Christians in China*, London, 1930.

18   The Sogdians were Iranian-speaking Zoroastrians living mainly in Transoxiana. They established commercial colonies or trading stations in the Chu valley and (according to Pelliot) as far east as Lop-Nor. Professor E. G. Pulleyblank adduces evidence ('A Sugdian Colony in Inner Mongolia', *T'oung Pao*, 1952) of their presence in Mongolia in the days of Turkish domination there.

19   The *kaghans* carefully define the limits of their conquests—'it is only by little that I failed to reach Tibet'—they warn their people against the Chinese, who 'have words as smooth as milk' and urge them to avoid the snares and lures of civilized urban life—'O Turkish people, it will be death if you say, Let us settle to the right [=the south], not in the forest but the plain.' See the texts in Thomsen, and cf. L. Bazin, 'Man and the Concept of History in Turkish Central Asia during the Eighth Century', *Diogenes*, 1963.

20 The Yenesei inscriptions, brief and dateless, were found in 1721, in the days of Peter the Great, in the present Soviet Autonomous Regions of Khakass and Tuva; the great Orkhon steles, unearthed in 1889, consist of three large dated memorials to Bilge-kaghan, his brother Kül-tegin, and his father-in-law, the minister Tonyukuk, and the Ongin stone, found in 1891 near a tributary of the river Ongin, was erected about 732-4 by an unnamed son to commemorate an unnamed father. On this last, see Sir Gerard Clauson, 'The Ongin Inscription', *JRAS*, 1957.

21 See the full and learned discussion by E. Chavannes, 'Le cycle turc des douze animaux', *T'oung Pao*, 1906, 51-122, supplemented by the later article by P. A. Boodberg, 'On the use of the Animal Cycle among "Turco-Mongols"', *HJAS*, 1938. Boodberg was inclined to regard it as a nomad, not a Chinese, invention; its origin has been ascribed to the Avars, the Indians and the Tibetans. The earliest instance of its use is in a letter written in 564 to the Regent of the Northern Chou by his mother, reminding him that he was born in the Year of the Snake and his brothers in the Years of the Rat and the Hare respectively.

22 As a specimen: 'In the Year of the Dog, the tenth moon, the 26th day, my father the *kaghan* left this life'.

23 In both cases, China was weak and divided, the Turks exploited the Byzantine-Persian feud, the Mongols the political anarchy in Russia and the conflict between the Khwarizmian Shah and the Caliph.

24 Istemi's statement to the Byzantine envoy Zemarchus that the Turks had received a divine mandate to invade the whole world is paralleled by the Great Khan Küyük's letter to Innocent IV (1246) that, as viceregent of God, he could rightfully claim the dominion of the globe. Centuries earlier, Attila had seen himself as universal king. O. Turan, 'The Ideal of World Domination among the Medieval Turks', *Studia Islamica*, IV, 1955.

25 The early Turks were not noticeably cruel, and their expansion was marked by none of the frightful massacres perpetrated by the Mongols. But their operations were commonly confined to the open steppe country and they rarely captured towns, whereas the Mongols seem to have deliberately adopted a policy of terror in order to frighten fortified cities into surrender.

Chapter 3: From Turk to Mongol

1 But see Clauson's objections to this and other etymologies, 'The Name Uyğur', *JRAS*, 1963.

2 The text of the inscription is given in Radloff, *Antiquités de l'Orkhon*, Helsingfors, 1892, 50-61. It is possibly referred to by Juvaini-Boyle, I, 54-5.

3 The most recent study, Geo. Widengren, *Mani and Manichaeism*, Eng. tr. London, 1965, has not superseded the authoritative work of Henri Puech, *Le Manichéisme*, Paris, 1949. The social impact on the

Uighurs of their new faith is discussed by A. von Gabain, 'Das uigurische Königsreich von Chotscho', in the *Proceedings of the German Academy of Sciences*, No. 5, Berlin, 1961.

4   The history of Chinese Manichaeism is summarized by Chavannes and Pelliot, 'Un traité manichéen retrouvé en Chine', *JA*, 1913, 99–199, 261–394. The community that Marco Polo found at Zaitun (II, 77), 'a people of whom no one knows what law they follow', was undoubtedly Manichaean.

5   The Uighurs seem to have abandoned a purely pastoral life, perhaps under the influence of Manichaean dietary laws, for Mani required the *elect* to live on fruits and juices, though the *hearers* (auditores) were permitted to eat meat. Chavannes and Pelliot, article cited, 268.

6   The explorer Albert von Le Coq found a rich collection of Manichaean manuscripts and frescoes at Khotcho (modern Kara-Khoja) in 1905. Some of the Turkish writings were in the old Orkhon runic script. See his *Buried Treasure of Chinese Turkestan*, London, 1928.

7   When the Chinese reoccupied Central Asia in the late seventh century, they organized the region in 702 in administrative areas and garrisons, one of which, Pei-t'ing, later received the Turkish name of Besh-balik. The town remained prominent down to the fourteenth century, when it fell into ruin. The Russians rediscovered it in 1908. *Enc. of Islam*, article 'Bishbalik'.

8   The Uighur princes seem to have styled themselves both *kaghan* and *iduk-kut*. Near Kara-Khoja is a place still known as Idikut-shahri, 'the Iduk-kut's Town'.

9   See the inventory of these finds in Sir Aurel Stein, *Innermost Asia*, Vol. 2, Oxford, 1928. The seventeenth chapter of this volume gives a concise history of Turfan.

10   A Chinese envoy, Weng Yen-te, who travelled through the Uighur kingdom in 982, has left a favourable and even flattering picture of its wealth and well-being. The people (he says) are honest and intelligent, and skilled in metal-working; the poor are fed at the public expense; the libraries are rich in Chinese books; there are fifty Buddhist convents and a temple of Mani, with 'Persian priests', and the inhabitants commonly live to a ripe old age. See his report, translated by Stanislas Julien, in the *Journal Asiatique*, Tom. 9, 1847.

11   Hsüan Tsang passed through Turfan in 630, on his way to India.

12   On the Sha-t'o, see W. Eberhard, *Conquerors and Rulers*, Leiden, 1965, Ch. 6. They were a small group of not more than three tribes; their armed forces numbered only 10,000 men. They copied the T'ang system of government, and were served mainly by Chinese officials. Though nominal Buddhists, they worshipped Tengri and followed many ancient Turkish practices, including the use of arrows as credentials and the game of football as recreation.

13   The confused interlude between the T'ang and the Sung is dealt with in O. Franke, *Gesch. des chin. Reiches*, II, 508 ff., and Wang Gungwu, *The Structure of Power in North China during the Five Dynasties*, Kuala Lumpur, 1963. Eberhard, *op. cit.*, 20, depicts it as a period of

great social change and mobility, marked by the emergence of a new class of small, 'middle class' gentry in the provinces and the spread of education to the merchant and artisan classes.

14 'Liao' from the river of that name; the word means 'iron' in Chinese. For an analysis of their rule, see Wittfogel and Feng, 'History of Chinese Society, Liao 907–1125', in *Transactions of the American Philosophical Society*, 36, Philadelphia, 1949, a long and learned disquisition which compares the Ch'i-tan with the Mongols in their relations with the Chinese.

15 Cordier, *Hist. gén. de la Chine*.

16 They developed a script of their own, but its character was hidden till two Ch'i-tan inscriptions, dating from about 1100, were discovered in Mongolia in 1922. Pelliot and Ker, 'Le tombeau de l'empereur Tao-tsung et les premières inscriptions en écriture k'i-tan', *T'oung Pao*, 1923.

17 Balasaghun, a Sogdian foundation, was the seat of the Kara-khanids in the tenth and eleventh centuries and of the Kara-Khitay in the twelfth. In the Mongol age it fell into ruin and was deserted; its precise location is unknown; it was probably not far from Kashgar. See Barthold's *EI* article 'Balāsāghūn'.

18 According to Pelliot, *T'oung Pao*, 1930, the correct spelling is 'Jürtchät': 'Ju-chen' is the Chinese form of the word.

19 E. Chavannes, 'Voyageurs chinois chez les Khitan et les Joutchen', *Journal Asiatique*, 1897, 378.

20 Said the Ju-chen chief, in reference to the Liao: 'Iron rusts, but gold always keeps its purity.'

21 Tokuz-Oghuz, a confederacy of nine (Turkish *tokuz* = nine) clans long settled between the Aral and Caspian Seas. The Persians and Arabs knew them as 'Ghuzz': their obscure history is traced in the *EI* article under that name, and see also James Hamilton, 'Toquz-Oguz et On-Uyhur', *JA*, 1962.

22 Jand, the original centre of Seljuk power, is described by the geographers of the eleventh and twelfth centuries as one of the great Muslim cities of Turkestan, and the Aral is often called in this age the Sea of Jand. It was ruined by the Mongols, and is now a decayed village.

23 See now the authoritative work of C. E. Bosworth, *The Ghaznavids*, Edinburgh, 1963.

24 On all these political changes in Central Asia, see the classic work of W. W. Barthold, *Turkestan down to the Mongol Invasion*, 1900; revised Eng. tr. 1958.

25 Barthold, 255. The conversion of the nameless Turks is mentioned by the chronicler Ibn al-Athir, 8: 396, ed. Tornberg, Leiden, 1867–76, who died in 1232.

26 See a summary of the medieval Muslim geographers' descriptions of Khwarizm (modern Khiva) in G. le Strange, *Lands of the Eastern Caliphate*, Cambridge, 1905, Ch. 32.

27 On this title, see Boyle's *Juvaini*, I, 62, note 4. *Gur* may be old Turkish *kür* or *kül*, meaning 'glorious' or 'heroic'.

28 The annals of the Kara-Khitay were related by the Persian historian

Juvaini in his life of Chingis Khan. *The History of the World Conqueror*, Eng. tr. J. A. Boyle, Manchester, 1958, Part 2, Chap. 10.

29 The Chinese include the Gur-Khans among their emperors, and call the dynasty the Western Liao, the only example in history of the retention of the imperial title by an alien line after it was driven out of China. Barthold, *Four Studies on the History of Central Asia*, Vol. 1, Eng. tr. 1956, 28.

30 Ibn al-Athir says he was a Manichaean. The Kara-Khitay did not persecute Islam, but presumably put all these world faiths on an equal footing as the Mongols did later. The oldest Nestorian tombs in this region are said to date from Kara-Khitay times. Barthold, *op. cit.*, 106.

31 Prester John was first heard of in Europe in 1145, when a Syrian bishop visiting Italy told the German chronicler Otto of Freising at Viterbo that a Nestorian priest-king named John defeated 'the Samiardi brothers, Kings of Persia' and advanced to the Tigris to help 'the church of Jerusalem', but was unable to cross the river and had to turn back. The reference is clearly to Sanjar's defeat in 1141, and no doubt there were Nestorians in the Gur-Khan's entourage. Otto seems not to have been impressed with the story, and concludes his summary with the words *Sed haec hactenus*, 'but enough of this'. In 1165 there was circulating in Europe a letter purporting to come from Prester John and addressed to the Byzantine Emperor Manuel Comnenus; the author is unknown, but his fiction spread the legend far and wide, and more than a hundred MSS. of the letter survive. In 1177 Pope Alexander III sent a letter from Venice to 'the king of the Indians', but the addressee, who is nowhere called a priest, was probably the Negus of Abyssinia. Little has been added in recent times to the exhaustive survey of the evidence by F. Zarncke, 'Der Priester Johannes', in the *Proceedings of the Saxon Academy of Sciences*, Leipzig, 1879, 1883, Vols 7 and 8. Cf. C. F. Beckingham, 'The Achievements of Prester John', inaugural lecture at the London School of Oriental and African Studies, 1966.

Chapter 4: Chingis Khan

1 Many descriptions of Mongolia are current today, but few surpass the careful, exact observations of two travellers of the last century, Huc and Prjevalsky. The former, a French Lazarist missionary, explored Tartary and Tibet in 1844–6, and his racy *Souvenirs d'un voyage dans la Tartarie, le Thibet et la Chine* (2 vols, Paris, 1850; Eng. tr. 1851) first exposed the recesses of Asia to the eyes of Europe. The latter, an officer of the Russian Army, undertook a scientific journey through the country in 1870–3: the English translation of his book *Mongolia* (2 vols, 1876) is enriched with valuable notes by Sir Henry Yule. Among his many discoveries was that of the oldest species of horse, since known as *Equus prjwalskii*.

2 The name Mongol is first met with under the T'ang, whose annalists refer to a tribe Mongwu or Mongwa. P. Pelliot, 'À propos des Cumans',

Journal Asiatique, 1920, 146. The Mongol language, like the Turkish, is older than the name, and it is probable that the Sien-pe, the Avars and the Ephthalites or White Huns, were of Mongol speech.

3 This fascinating chronicle, an artless picture of nomad life and manners, was probably compiled in the mid-thirteenth century: the Mongol text survives only in a Chinese transcription and partially in the text known as *Altan Tobchi*, ed. Cleaves, 1952. The only complete version in a Western language is Erich Haenisch's German translation, *Die geheime Geschichte der Mongolen*, 2nd ed. Leipzig, 1948. The first six chapters were put into French by Paul Pelliot and published posthumously at Paris in 1949. An abbreviated English version is in Arthur Waley, *The Secret History of the Mongols and Other Pieces*, London, 1963. Professor F. W. Cleaves of Harvard is preparing a full and annotated English translation. For the history of the *History*, see W. Hung, 'The transmission of the book known as "The Secret History of the Mongols"', *Harvard Journal of Asiatic Studies*, XIV, 1951. See also the valuable German commentary by Pavel Poucha, *Die geheime Geschichte der Mongolen*, Prague, 1956, and Appendix I above.

4 V. Thomsen, *Inscriptions de l'Orkhon*, Helsingfors, 1896, 140. Two groups, 'thirty Tatars' and 'nine Tatars' are mentioned. The name appears in the Chinese records in 842 under the form 'Ta-ta'. Possibly it was a general term used for tribes of Mongol speech till the conquests of Chingis led to its being supplanted by the name of the conquerors. Yet the Mongols were universally known as Tatars when they broke into Europe, the identification being helped by a confusion with Tartarus, the classical Hell, whence these dreadful hordes were believed to have originated, and in this way the form 'Tartar', with two r's, became common. The name was later loosely and incorrectly applied to certain *Turkish* peoples in the Russian Empire, e.g. Volga Tatars, Crimean Tatars, and in the USSR an autonomous Tatar Republic exists with its capital at Kazan.

5 The Merkits, a Turco-Mongol people, had their pastures in the valleys of the Selenga Basin, east of Lake Baikal. They were at least partially christianized.

6 The Keraits were located on the upper Onon, were converts to Nestorianism since the year 1000 (for which fact, if it be a fact, the only authority is Bar Hebraeus, Eng. tr., 184) and were almost certainly Turks. Their titles are Turkish, and Toghril ('Crested goshawk'?) is not a Mongol name.

7 The date of Chingis's birth is not quite certain. One tradition makes it the Year of the Pig, which in this twelve-year cycle, might be either 1155 or 1167. The Persian historian Rashid ad-Din, a high authority since he had access to the Mongol records of the Il-khans, gives the date as 1162, and the eighth centenary was celebrated in Mongolia in 1962. I follow Pelliot, who after his usual meticulous examination of the evidence, decides in favour of the Pig year, and in this case 1155 is certainly far too early. See his *Notes on Marco Polo*, Vol. 1, Paris, 1959, article 'Cinghis', 284 ff.

8 The life of Temujin has been traced in several European languages since the early eighteenth century, when Louis XIV's orientalist Pétis de la Croix compiled his *Histoire du grand Genghiscan*, Paris, 1710, Eng. tr. 1722, out of the Persian and Arabic sources. Père Gaubil, a French Jesuit missionary in China, translated the relevant portion of the Chinese dynastic history of the Mongols in his *Histoire de Gentchiscan*, Paris, 1739. Thereafter there was a lull of more than a century until the German Erdmann produced his detailed and ponderous *Temudschin der Unerschütterliche*, Leipzig, 1862, and R. K. Douglas compiled a *Life of Chingis Khan*, London, 1877, out of three Chinese biographical sources. Krause, *Cingis Khan*, Berlin, 1922, is a useful modern translation of the relevant portion of the *Yüan Shih*. In our own age, the social and economic background of the great conqueror's career has been carefully examined, as in B. J. Vladimirtsov's *Life of Chingis Khan*, 1922, Eng. tr. London, 1930; Fr. tr. Paris, 1948, which may be considered the standard biography, Ralph Fox's *Genghiz Khan*, London, 1935, which utilizes modern Russian studies, René Grousset, *Le Conquérant du monde*, Paris, 1944, Eng. tr. New York, 1966, and H. de Fernandy, *Tschingis Khan*, Hamburg, 1958.

9 Barthold and Vladimirtsov. The former put forward in 1896 the theory that the clash between Chingis and Jamuka was a class conflict between the nomad aristocracy and the ordinary tribesmen; the latter, while not fully accepting this, argued that at the beginning of the twelfth century the old clan community was being broken up and replaced by what he called 'feudal nomadism'. This interpretation has been sharply attacked by L. Krader, 'Feudalism and the Tartar policy of the Middle Ages', *Comparative Studies in Society and History*, I, 1958, who points out the total absence of a lord-serf relationship among the Mongols, and has now been abandoned by Soviet scholars, according to A. M. Belentisky, 'Les Mongols et l'Asie centrale', *Journal of World History*, 5, 1960. Cf. Owen Lattimore, 'The Social History of Mongol Nomadism', in *Historians of China and Japan*, London, 1961.

10 *Noyan* is a title applied both to civil and military chiefs, governors, commanders in the field, etc. See Pelliot and Hambis, *Histoire des campagnes de Genghis Khan*, Leiden, 1951, 178.

11 Many are the explanations which have been given of this celebrated title, first conferred, it seems, at a tribal assembly in 1194 and merely confirmed at the grand national *kuriltai* in 1206. Pelliot held it was derived from the Turkish *tengiz*, meaning 'ocean' and thus implied a sovereignty as wide as the sea which was supposed to surround the earth. It could therefore be translated as 'oceanic' or 'universal khan'. See his article 'Cinghis' referred to above. The correct Mongol form of the word is Chinggis; the more familiar European corruption Genghis or Jenghiz has come through the Arabic, which has no letter 'ch' in its alphabet. See also Erich Haenisch, 'Genghis Khan', *Collectanea Mongolica*, Wiesbaden, 1966.

12 *Nökör* (plural *nököd* or *nököt*) has the meaning of client, free warrior, warrior-knight, antrustion. Originally it meant a companion (cf. the

Latin *comes*), a fighter who moved about freely from lord to lord offering his services and who was neither a subject nor a mercenary.

13 The Wang-Khan was certainly the best-known Christian prince of Asia, and his royal title *Wang* or *Ong* might easily be confused with 'John' in its various Asian forms.

14 See an exhaustive article by F. W. Cleaves, 'The historicity of the Baljuna Covenant', *HJAS*, 1955. Among those who visited Chingis at Baljuna was a Muslim merchant named Hasan, who was trading in sable furs and squirrel hides: this was the first and peaceable contact of the great conqueror with Islam, which had not yet penetrated his country.

15 For the Chinese campaigns of Chingis, see H. Desmond Martin, *The Rise of Chingis Khan and his Conquest of North China*, Baltimore, 1950.

16 Peking ('northern capital') was not then the considerable metropolis it afterwards became, but a relatively small frontier town. The massacres are discreetly concealed in the *Dynastic History*, compiled in the reign of Kubilai, who atoned for his grandfather's crimes by his wholehearted adoption of Chinese manners and culture.

17 Küchlüg died in Sarikul or Sirikol ('yellow lake'), a mountain region named after the lake (*kol*) in which the Pamir river rises, according to Rashid ad-Din; in Badakhshan, according to Juvaini, tr. Boyle, I, 67 and note.

18 The Mongols knew all Muslims as 'Sarts', a Turkish word meaning merchants which the nomads applied to all of Perso-Muslim culture who came among them, usually on business. As these traders commonly came from Islamic countries, *sart* or *sarta 'ul* became synonymous with 'Muslim' and is used in the *Secret History* for the Khwarizmians, the first Muslim people the Mongols fought. See Barthold's article 'Sart' in the *EI*.

19 Our information about this bloody struggle is drawn principally from Ibn al-Athir, Juvaini, Nasawi and Rashid ad-Din, whose narratives have been subjected to minute criticism by Barthold in his *Turkestan down to the Mongol Invasion*.

20 Barthold rejected the Bukhara 'sermon' as 'quite beyond belief' (*Turkestan*, 410), on the ground that Ibn al-Athir, our earliest contemporary authority, does not mention it. The argument from silence is always risky: the story is not altogether implausible.

21 For the colourful and romantic career of this valiant young prince, in whom the statesman was submerged by the soldier, we have the biography compiled by his secretary Nasawi (French trans. Houdas, *Vie de Djelel-ed-Din Mankobirti*, Paris, 1895), who entered his service after his return from India in 1223. Nasawi is fullest on the affairs of his native Khurasan, and his narrative vibrates with the horrors of the invasion.

22 If the fifteenth-century Persian historian Mirkhwand is to be believed, the Mongols might also be encouraged by learning of the deep divisions within Islam: he alleges they were begged by Sunnite Muslims

to root out the heretic Shi'ites from the town of Kumm, which lay in their path.

23 The first news of the Mongols reached Western Europe through a letter of the Queen-Regent of Georgia to Pope Honorius III in 1224, printed in Baronius-Raynaldus, *Ann. Eccles.* ed. Theiner, Vol. 20, 1870, under that year. Shortly before, the Georgians had congratulated the Latins on the capture of Damietta from the Muslims in the Fifth Crusade 1219. See W. E. D. Allen, *History of the Georgian People*, London, 1932.

24 Maragha, the old capital of Azerbaijan, lies on fertile, well-watered slopes some miles from Tabriz. *EI* article 'Maragha'. The Mongols here were guilty of their usual tricks: prisoners were forced to lead the assault on the walls, and when, after massacring the population, they evacuated the town, they returned shortly afterwards and killed all those who had crept out of hiding.

25 Derbend was known as Bab al-Abwab ('gate of gates') by the medieval Arabs and Persians, the 'gates' being the passes through the Caucasian mountains at the western end of the Caspian Sea. Derbend was at once a town, a fortress, a harbour and a pass.

26 The Alans or Ās were an ancient Iranian race inhabiting the Northern Caucasus and are first mentioned (by Ammianus Marcellinus) as having been defeated by the Huns in 371. Converted to the Christian faith in the tenth century by Byzantine missionaries, they were members of the Orthodox Church at the time of the Mongol invasion. See the article 'Aleni' in Pauly-Wissowa, Ibn al-Athir *sub anno* 617/1220, and Bretschneider, *Medieval Researches*, II, 84–90.

27 The Cherkes or Circassians were a group of Ibero-Caucasian peoples, organized today in several autonomous regions of the Soviet Union, and living chiefly in the Kuban valley. At first Christians, they went over to Islam in the sixteenth century, and are today Sunni Muslims.

28 The Kipchaks, the Cumans of the Byzantines and the Polovtsians of the Russians, were a tribal confederacy who long possessed the steppes north of the Black Sea. They remained nomadic, uncivilized and illiterate, and our only clue to their language (a Turkish dialect) is contained in the Codex Cumanicus, a thirteenth-century word list preserved in St Mark's, Venice. See Pelliot's learned pamphlet, 'À propos des Cumans', reprinted from the *Journal Asiatique*, Paris, 1920.

29 See G. Vernadsky, *Kievan Russia*, New Haven, 1948, 235–9. Three Russian princes were captured, laid on the ground and covered with boards, on which the Mongol leaders feasted while their victims suffocated.

30 On Sudak, Sugdak, or Soldaia, see Bretschneider, II, 84.

31 On Gurganj, see Le Strange, *Lands of the Eastern Caliphate*, 447–9. The geographer Yakut said in 1219 he had never seen a mightier or more beautiful city: a year later it was totally ruined, not perhaps by deliberate Mongol action as by floods caused by the breaking of the dams, itself due to the lack of competent men to carry out the annual repairs. Barthold, *Turkestan*, 437. The episode became celebrated, and Plano Carpini's reference to the flooding of 'Orna' (a place otherwise unknown) probably refers to Gurganj.

32   On the changing course of the Oxus, consult Le Strange, 455-8, and the *EI* article 'Āmū Daryā'. Since the sixteenth century the river has emptied itself into the Aral Sea.

33   Browne, *Lit. Hist. of Persia*, II, 438; *Cambridge Hist. of Iran*, V, 312.

34   Ibn al-Athir, *sub anno* 618/1221.

35   Langer and Blake, 'The Rise of the Ottoman Turks', *Amer. Hist. Rev.* 37, 1932.

36   On Nishapur, an ancient city named after King Shapur, see Le Strange, 383-7. Yakut thought it the first city of Khurasan; it was later rebuilt, but never regained its former importance.

37   See the article 'Bāmiyān' in the *EI*, and Le Strange, 418-19. It was once a flourishing Buddhist centre; its monasteries are said to have housed 1,000 monks, and two colossal figures of the Buddha, carved out of the cliffs on which the town stood, exited the wonder of travellers. Chingis forbade anyone to live in Bamiyan again; the site was renamed Mo-balik, 'the accursed city', and was uninhabited in Juvaini's day, forty years later.

38   Barthold, *Turkestan*, 439-40. The Ghurid kingdom having been destroyed by Muhammad Shah in 1215, the Ghurids, who were mainly Persians and Afghans and strongly anti-Turkish, were unwilling to assist his son, and the Mongols, as always, exploited these differences to their advantage.

39   Parwan was the name of a town and a pass through the Hindu Kush. Yule-Cordier, *Cathay and the Way Thither*, IV, 209, 257.

40   See Nasawi's colourful account of this dramatic incident, 138-41 of Houdas's translation.

41   Herat was a great centre of trade in medieval days and rose to fresh life later under Timur and his successors. See the *EI* article 'Harāt', and Le Strange, 408-9. It was reconquered after the rebellion by the general Aljigidei or Eljigidei, who as Mongol governor of Persia some time later wrote to Louis IX of France in 1248 proposing a Mongol Christian alliance against Islam. See above, p. 97. A *History of Herat*, composed about 1320 by one Saifi, was discovered in 1944: *Camb. Hist. of Iran*, V, 315.

42   On the dreadful depopulation of eastern Persia let Juvaini speak: 'Even though there be generation and increase until the Resurrection, the population will not attain to a tenth part of what it was before.' Boyle's translation, I, 97.

43   For this famous meeting between the conqueror and the philosopher, see Arthur Waley, *The Travels of an Alchemist*, London, 1931. The narrative of the journey and discussion was compiled by Ch'ang Ch'un's disciple Li Chih-Chang. The sage was specifically summoned from his home or hermitage in Shantung, in 1219: it took him three years to reach the camp of Chingis at the foot of the Hindu Kush; his route is carefully checked by Bretschneider, I, 35-108. Born in 1148, Ch'ang Ch'un died in the same year and month as Chingis himself, i.e. August 1227.

44   A shrewd comment by an illiterate pagan, whose god (*Tengri*) was the blue sky itself.

45 Grousset, 309, citing the *Secret History*.
46 E. Haenisch, 'Die letzen Feldzüge Cinggis Hans', *Asia Major*, IX, 1933.
47 *EI* article 'Djuči'. Cf. Pelliot, *Notes sur l'histoire de la Horde d'Or*, Paris, 1950.
48 The precise date of Chingis's death is taken from the Chinese dynastic history. The cause is unknown, but a few months earlier he suffered injury in a fall from his horse while hunting and this may have contributed to his end.
49 The classical reader will recall the sacrifices of the Scythians at the burial of their kings as recounted by Herodotus, IV, 71–2. Cf. J. A. Boyle, 'A Form of Horse-Sacrifice . . .' *CAJ*, 1965.
50 Juzjani, *Tabakat-i Nasiri*, Eng. tr. H. G. Raverty, London, 1881, 1077–9. Juzjani, who died about 1260, came of a Persian family of officials and after serving the Ghurids, retired to India in 1226 and rose to high office under the Slave Kings of Delhi. On the alleged portraits of Chingis, see Father Mostaert's article, 'À propos de quelques portraits mongols', *Asia Major*, IV, 1927.
51 On the organization, equipment, strategy and tactics of Chingis's impressive military machine, see H. D. Martin, 'The Mongol Army', *JRAS*, 1943, and the learned notes of Pelliot to his translation of the *Cheng-wu*, a military history compiled (in Chinese ?) under Kubilai about 1285, *Hist. des campagnes de Genghis Khan*, Leiden, 1951: it is apparently abridged from the Mongol chronicle *Altan Debter*. The acute Franciscan Plano Carpini laboured to gather every scrap of information on the Mongol fighting forces which would enable the Christian nations to understand the enemy and put up a better defence: see the translation of his report in C. Dawson, *The Mongol Mission*, London, 1955.
52 For the *yams*, see the details in the travels of Friar Odoric, Yule-Cordier, II, 232–4, and P. Olbricht, 'Das Postwesen in China unter der Mongolenherrschaft', *GAF*, Wiesbaden, 1954, II, 232–4. Cf. Bretschneider, I, 187, note.
53 On the sacks of ears, there are examples in Russia (Bar Hebraeus, 398, who speaks of 270,000 right ears!), at Magas in the Caucasus (V. Minorsky, 'Caucasica III', *BSOAS*, 1952), and at Liegnitz in Silesia in 1241, when nine sacks of ears were collected (G. Vernadsky, *The Mongols and Russia*, New Haven, 1954, 55).
54 For the utter paralysis of mind and will that terror of the Mongols induced, see the oft-quoted story in Ibn al-Athir, *sub anno* 628/1231, translated in Browne, *Literary History of Persia*, II, 430. A Mongol soldier took a man prisoner but had not a weapon to kill him. 'Lay your head on the ground and do not move', he commanded him, and went away to fetch a sword. When he returned, he found the man still there and killed him.
55 Notably by Sir Basil Liddell Hart, the most distinguished of recent British historians of war. See his chapter on Chingis in *Great Captains*, London, 1927, and his article 'Mongolian Campaigns' in the 1946 edition of the *Enc. Brit.*

NOTES TO PAGES 67–70

56   See his life, drawn from Chinese sources, in Abel-Rémusat, *Nouveaux mélanges asiatiques*, Vol. 2, Paris, 1829. His original Turkish name is unknown: we have only the Chinese form.

57   The lesson was learnt some years before Chingis's death: the oldest monument with a Mongol inscription is a stone engraved with five lines in Mongol in the Uighur script, which dates from about 1220, and is now in the Hermitage Museum, Leningrad.

58   See a collection and translation in E. Chavannes, 'Inscriptions et pièces de chancellerie chinoise de l'époque mongole', *T'oung Pao*, 1904, 1905, 1908.

59   See his life in Abel-Rémusat, *op. cit.*, a brief notice in Bretschneider, I, 9–11, and Igor de Rachewiltz, 'Yeh-lü Ch'u-ts'ai', in *Confucian Personalities*, Stanford, 1962. He died in 1244 at the age of 55, having served throughout the reign of Ögedei as well as Chingis.

60   *Ortak* or *ortag* ('partner') was a member of an association of *Muslim* merchants: few non-Muslims engaged in Asian trade. See the introduction to H. F. Schurmann's *Economic Structure of the Yüan Dynasty*, Cambridge, Mass., 1956.

61   Consider the career of Mahmud Yalavach, a Muslim merchant from Khwarizm, who was a member of the embassy sent by Chingis to Sultan Muhammad in 1217 to organize commercial relations between the Mongol and Khwarizmian empires. After the Mongol conquest he was appointed governor of Transoxiana, in which capacity he laboured to repair some of the damage wrought during the invasion. His son Ma'sud later succeeded him in this office. Barthold, *Turkestan*, 396, note, and his article 'Čaghatay Khan' in the *EI*.

62   *Yasa*, *yassa*, *yassak*, means law, order, regulation, prohibition. The fragmentary evidence concerning it is assembled by V. A. Riasanovsky, *Fundamental Principles of Mongol Law*, The Hague, 1965, and G. Vernadsky, 'The Scope and content of Chingis Khan's Yasa', *HJAS*, 1938.

63   Chiefly the Persians Juvaini and Rashid, and the Egyptian Makrizi (died 1441). The last two assert that the *Yasa* was promulgated after the overthrow of Wang-Khan in 1206. Riasanovsky, *op. cit.*, 26–7.

64   A. N. Poliak, 'The Influence of Chingis Khan's Yasa upon the general organization of the Mamluk State', *BSOAS*, 1941. Makrizi is our principal authority for the 'reception' of the Yasa in Egypt.

65   Thus when the Öngut chief Alakush-tegin was killed for supporting the Mongols against the Naiman, Chingis took the family under his protection and gave the son his own daughter in marriage. Grousset, *L'Empire des Steppes*, 314.

66   Hence the regard he seems always to have had for the Uighurs and the Ch'i-tan, the most civilized representatives of the Turco-Mongol nations. He undoubtedly deplored the backwardness of his own people.

Chapter 5: The Mongol drive into Europe

1 For the name Jochi (Mongol for 'guest'), see Pelliot, *Notes sur l'histoire de la Horde d'Or*, Paris, 1950, *sub nomine*. The *EI* article 'Djuči' summarizes his career.

2 The story is found only in Juzjani (tr. Raverty), 1101. Rashid says Jochi was ordered to conquer the lands raided by Jebe and Sübedei, but failed to move; Chingis, incensed, sent Chagatai and Ögedei against him, but at this moment arrived the news of Jochi's death.

3 See the *EI* article 'Čaghatay Khan', and Barthold, *Four Studies in the History of Central Asia*, tr. Minorsky, I, Leiden, 1956, 45-7. His eldest son was killed at Bamiyan in 1221, and the place was totally destroyed as a punishment.

4 Mahmud was at once an official and a merchant: Barthold, *Turkestan*, 396, note, identifies him as a member of Chingis's embassy to Khwarizm in 1217-18. He was presumably a Muslim Turk, since Yalavach is Turkish for 'envoy'.

5 For the history of the khanate, whose centre was at Almaligh in the Ili valley, see Yule-Cordier, IV, 160-6, and Barthold, *Four Studies*, I. Thirty descendants of Chagatai ruled in a space of 130 years; 'revolutions, depositions, murders and usurpations seem to have succeeded each other with a frequency unusual even in Asiatic governments' (Yule-Cordier, 161). Chagatai princes reigned at Kashgar till as late as 1678, when the Kalmuks put an end to the dynasty.

6 His name became *tabu* after his death (Carpini could never discover it), and he was referred to simply as Yeke-noyan, 'great chief'. *The Vinland Map and the Tartar Relation*, New Haven, 1965, 76.

7 Ögedei, Ogday, Oktai, Ogotay, Uguday are the common variants of the name, the vowels of which are constantly transposed in the European forms and the etymology of which is obscure.

8 Karakorum (Turkish, 'black rock') no doubt derived its name from the Karakorum mountains, as Juvaini and Rashid assert. Juzjani describes it as a cold place where no trees would grow. The Chinese knew it as Ho-lin, their transcription of *Korum*. Abandoned in 1289 and forgotten for six centuries, its ruins were excavated by the Russians in 1889. See the article 'Caracorum' in Pelliot's *Notes on Marco Polo*, I, 1959. The place is said to have been selected by Chingis in 1220, but Ögedei was the first to reside there regularly.

9 The wars in China are related in the *Yüan Shih*, the Mongol dynastic history, and this source is summarized in the ninth volume of Père de Mailla's *Histoire de la Chine*, a valuable example of eighteenth-century French Jesuit sinology. De Mailla's work was published as far back as 1779, yet I know of no more recent summary of the Chinese sources. For the general Chinese background see Otto Franke, *Gesch. des chinesischen Reiches*, Berlin, 1930, Vol. 5. Rashid ad-Din adds some details, which are given in D'Ohsson, *Hist. des Mongols*, Vol. 2.

10 De Mailla, IX, 132.

11 The labours of Ch'u-ts'ai were supplemented by Chin Kai or Chen-hai, a Nestorian Kerait whom Plano Carpini called the 'chancellor' of the empire under Ögedei. The *Yüan Shih* indicates that no edict was issued in North China without Chin Kai adding a version in the official Uighur script. The narrative of Ch'ang Ch'un's travels reveals his high rank and influence. Bretschneider, I, 60 and note.

12 Our scanty information relating to the Mongol wars in Korea has been collected and criticized in W. E. Henthorn, *Korea, the Mongol Invasions*, Leiden, 1963, which is based on the *Koryo-sa*, a collection of Korean annals published at Seoul in three volumes in 1956. See also G. Ledyard, 'The Mongol Campaigns in Korea', *CAJ*, 9, 1964. Korea, known to the Chinese as Kao-li, is the Solangka of the Mongols and is found under that name in the Latin (Carpini and Rubruck) and the Persian (Juvaini and Rashid) writers of the age. The meaning of 'Solangka' is uncertain, but *solonga* is the Mongol for 'weasel' and the Koreans were celebrated as fur-trappers.

13 *Darughas* (from Mongol *daru*—to press, stamp or seal) were properly commissioners of police charged with the maintenance of public order and sometimes with the collection of taxes, the holding of a census, and the recruitment of local troops. The title long survived in Safawid Persia and Mogul India. See the *EI* article 'Dārūgha'.

14 The distinction between Irak Arabi and Irak Ajami is a commonplace of medieval geography. The former is Irak proper, with its centre at Baghdad; the latter is the province formerly known as Jibal. *Ajami*, the common Arabic term for 'non-Arab', was specifically applied to the Persians: hence the phrase 'Persian Irak'.

15 Diyar Bakr, 'the abode of Bakr', a celebrated tribe who once encamped there, was the region watered by the Tigris from its source to its great bend south; its capital was Amid.

16 Jalal is said to have checked the Mongol advance at Ispahan, but three years later the enemy returned and made a night attack on his camp, while he lay in a drunken sleep. The place of his death is not known: it was a village near Mayyafarikin. Many refused to credit he was dead, and several pretenders arose claiming to be the last of the Khwarizm-Shahs.

17 See the new (1966) Byzantine volume of the *Cambridge Medieval History*, Chap. 14, and W. E. D. Allen, *History of the Georgian People*, London, 1932, summaries which are beholden to Brosset's collection of Georgian sources, *Hist. gén. de la Géorgie*, 4 vols, St Petersburg, 1849–58.

18 See the eloquent eulogy on Simeon in the Armenian chronicler Kirakos of Ganjak, who narrates the events of the century 1165–1265 (Fr. tr. Brosset, 1870–1). He was a great builder of churches, and armed with the *tamgha* or seal of the Great Khan, he and his people moved about freely and were treated with great respect by the Mongol officials. His success perhaps encouraged King Hayton to initiate his policy of a Christian-Mongol alliance. Cf. J. A. Boyle, 'Kirakos of Ganjak on the Mongols', *CAJ*, 8, 1963.

19 On Baiju, see Pelliot, 'Les Mongols et la Papauté', *Rev. de l'Orient chrét.*, 1924, 303 ff.

20 Erzurum, Arz al-Rum, 'the Roman place', enjoyed great prosperity under the Seljuks and was the capital of a Turkish *malik* or subordinate prince. *EI* article 'Erzurum', Le Strange, 117.

21 Chagatai was hated by his Muslim subjects because, as guardian of the *Yasa*, he punished brutally infractions of the law, particularly those enactments relating to ablutions and the ritual slaughter of animals, which ran counter to the *shari'a*. Yet he employed Muslim ministers and officials. Barthold, *Four Studies*, I, 1956.

22 The Volga-Bulghars were kinsmen of the Danube-Bulghars, who migrated to the land which still bears their name in the mid-seventh century. 'Volga' and 'Bulghar' are doubtless the same word, but which was derived from which is uncertain. The Bulghars of the Volga were long vassals of the Khazar State, and won their independence when the latter was destroyed by the Russians in 965. *EI* article 'Bulghār'.

23 The date of their conversion to Islam is unknown, but was certainly before 921, when Ibn Fadlan reported to the Caliph Muktadir on the results of his mission to this most northerly of Muslim peoples. M. Canard, *La Relation du Voyage d'Ibn Fadlan*, Algiers, 1958. Their location in such high latitudes, where the winter days were short and the nights long, posed difficult questions of canonical law in connection with the five daily prayers and the fast of Ramadan.

24 Russian archaeological work on the site of Old Bulghar (see the references in the *EI* article) reveal it to have been a flourishing city with a population of perhaps 50,000.

25 Sübedei had a personal motive for revenge: he had been ambushed by the Bulghars on his expedition round the Caspian in 1223 and suffered heavy losses. Ibn al-Athir, *sub anno* 620 (AD 1223–4), 12, 254; for Chinese confirmation, Bretschneider, I, 295–6.

26 I shall not pretend to have solved the vexed question of the relations between the Bashkirs and the Hungarians. The Bashkirs have always lived on the lower slopes of the Urals, north of the Kirghiz Steppe; the Autonomous Bashkir Republic is found there today on the maps of the Soviet Union, and its people are Turkish-speaking Muslims, Islam having reached them in pre-Mongol times from the Bulghars to the west. An ancient tradition asserts that the Magyars, who migrated to Hungary in the ninth century, were a branch of the Bashkir race; Muslim writers invariably call the Hungarians 'Bashkurts'; European travellers like William of Rubruck speak of Great Hungary or Old Hungary, 'the country of the Pascatir', and Matthew Paris specifically names 'Hungaria Magna' as one of the first kingdoms subdued by the Mongols when they burst out of Asia. Yet Magyar is a Finno-Ugrian language, albeit with a strong admixture of Turkish, and this philological discrepancy has not been explained. See C. A. Macartney, *The Magyars in the Ninth Century*, Cambridge, 1930, reprinted 1968, the medieval references collected in Bretschneider, I, 326–8, and the article 'Bashdjirt' in *EI*.

27 I refer again to Pelliot's magisterial article, 'À propos des Cumans', *JA*, 1920; the most thorough and exhaustive treatment of the subject.

28 The anecdote comes from the *Yüan Shih*. Bretschneider, I, 312.

29 The great Mongol campaign in Europe in 1237–42 is known to us from many contemporary sources, which I shall presently notice. But to my knowledge only one modern scholarly monograph has been devoted to it, G. Strakosch-Grassmann, *Der Einfall der Mongolen in Mitteleuropa*, Innsbrück, 1893, a meritorious work which the passage of nearly eighty years has rendered in part antiquated and which is principally concerned with the invasions of Poland, Moravia and Hungary. The Mongol conquest of Russia has been excellently treated in G. Vernadsky, *The Mongols and Russia*, New Haven, 1953, for which the numerous Russian chroniclers of the thirteenth century have been laid under contribution. See also Bertold Spuler, *Die goldene Horde*, 2nd ed. Wiesbaden, 1965, chapter entitled 'Batu'.
30 Often quoted, this melancholy comment has not been traced to its source. Howorth, *Hist. of the Mongols*, I, 139, attributes it to the 'chronicler of Kostroma', but Vernadsky, in a letter to me (7 March 1965) suggests that by this description is meant the Hypatian Codex, but states that the words are not found in it.
31 See the *Chronicle of Novgorod*, Eng. tr. Camden Soc., 1914, for Russian reaction to the approach of 'the accursed godless ones' to the Venice of the North.
32 Matthew Paris, *Chronica Majora*, ed. Luard, Rolls series, III, 488–9. The monk of St Albans, perhaps our greatest medieval historian, is remarkably well informed about the Mongols and collected a large number of letters and reports relating to them. See my article, 'Matthew Paris and the Mongols', in *Essays in Medieval History presented to Bertie Wilkinson*, Toronto, 1969.
33 Except for some minor fighting against the Circassians and other tribes of south Russia.
34 See the narrative of the Russian chronicler quoted from Karamzin's collection by Bretschneider, I, 318.
35 'I have heard [wrote Batu to King Bela] that you have taken the Cumans, our dependants, under your protection. I charge you to cease harbouring them, and to avoid in favouring them making an enemy of me. It will be much easier for them, who have no houses and live in tents, to escape, than for you who live in houses and are settled in towns. How can you fly from me ?' This menacing missive was delivered to the king by the hand of a renegade Englishman in the Mongol service.
36 Boleslav IV, the titular king of Poland, governed the provinces of Cracow and Sandomir, Conrad of Mazovia, Henry the Pious of Silesia, and Miecislav of Oppeln, divided the rest of the country between them. The anxiety of the last three to safeguard their own domains prevented them from co-operating with Boleslav, and the Mongols, as was so often the case, were able to deal with their opponents one by one.
37 On the disorganized state of Hungary under Bela IV, see D. Sinor, *History of Hungary*, London, 1959, Ch. 8.
38 The principal native authority for the Mongol invasion of Poland is Matthias of Miechow, or Mekhosky, whose *Tractatus de duobus Sarmatiis* was first printed in 1517. He supplies the facts on which D'Ohsson has

based his spirited narrative. *Hist. des Mongols*, II, 120–58. See also the more recent examination of the evidence by the Japanese Mongolist Iwamura Shinobu, 'The Mongol Invasion of Poland', *Toyo Bunko*, X, 1938, where the relevant Latin texts are translated.

39   Several writers (Wolff, Howorth, Grousset) give Ögedei's grandson Kaidu as Baidar's partner, but Pelliot has shown this to be an error, since Kaidu was born in 1230 and would have been a child of little more than ten at this time. *Notes on Marco Polo*, I, 125.

40   The Mongols swept through Moravia in less than a month, long enough, however, for a legend to grow that they were repulsed by Yaroslav of Steinberg from the citadel of Olmutz, where 'Peta' (Baidar) was killed. The story is probably based on the events of a quite different campaign in 1253, and Baidar in any case lived to be present at Küyük's inauguration in 1246. Juvaini, I, 244. The Czech historian Vadar Novotny has set the record straight in a study published at Prague in 1928, but as I am ignorant of Czech, I can only refer to Vernadsky's note in *The Mongols and Russia*, 56.

41   The Mongol conquest of Hungary is documented from many sources of varying reliability. (1) *Hungarian*. Roger of Varadin, *Carmen Miserabile*, the doleful cry of an Italian-born churchman who endured many miseries as a fugitive from the Mongol killers. Often reprinted, the best edition is in the *Scriptores Rerum Hungaricarum*, Budapest, 1938, II, 551–88. Thomas of Spalato, *Hist. Salonitanorum Pontificum*: the author lived 1200–68, and was archdeacon of Spalato, ancient Salona, modern Split. His ecclesiastical history of the place has a chapter 'De peste Tartarorum', describing the Mongol incursion from Hungary into Dalmatia. I consulted this work in the older *Script. Rer. Hung.*, Vienna, 1748, Vol. 3. (2) *Latin Western*. The correspondence of Frederick II in the fifth volume of Huillard Brébolles, *Hist. Dipl. Frid. Sec.* Paris, 1859, 1139–54. The Chronicle of Alberic of the Three Fountains, *MGH*, Script. 23, 1874. Matthew Paris, *Chron. Maj.*, Rolls series, Vols 4–6. (3) *Persian*. Juvaini, tr. Boyle, and Rashid follow their Mongols into the lands of the Franks: not unnaturally events are transposed and errors abound, as Minorsky points out, 'Caucasica III', *BSOAS*, 1952. (4) *Chinese*. The *Yüan Shih* briefly describes the campaigns in the West, the first occasion, I apprehend, on which the Chinese have taken extended notice of events in Europe. It is not always easy to identify European names under their Chinese transcriptions: see Bretschneider's elucidations, I, 323–32.

42   Though as he had won the battle of Liegnitz in Silesia on 9 April, he could scarcely have arrived in time to take part in the battle of Mohi two days later.

43   See the brief but vivid description of the battle in the new source, probably Friar Benedict the Pole, published in *The Vinland Map and the Tartar Relation*, New Haven, 1965, 82–3. The Chinese life of Sübedei depicts him as rallying a dispirited Batu, who had suffered heavy losses at the bridge and proposed to retreat: 'Prince, you may retreat if you wish, but for my part I am resolved not to return till I have reached the

Danube.' Bretschneider, 331. Juvaini, I, 270, has Batu ascending a hill and praying to Tengri for victory, like Chingis.

44   See the text of the letter, with its flattering references to the different nations, in Matthew Paris, *sub anno* 1241. The chronicler Alberic asserts (p. 943 in the edition in the *Monumenta*) that earlier 'the King of the Tartars' (Batu ?) wrote to Frederick urging that he come to take a position at his court, on which the Emperor commented that he knew enough about birds and how to be a good falconer. No text of such a letter has come down to us.

45   After seeking help from the Duke of Austria, who exacted too high a price, Bela fled to Croatia and from Zagreb wrote (May 1241) to the Pope, the Emperor and Louis IX of France begging for a crusade against the savage invaders of his kingdom. In reply, Frederick blamed the Pope for his inability to help.

46   When the first reports of Mongol atrocities in Hungary reached France, Queen Blanche asked her son what was to be done, to which Louis IX replied: 'If these people, whom we call Tartars, should come upon us, either we will thrust them back into Tartarus, whence they came, or else they will send us all to heaven.' Matthew Paris, *sub anno* 1241. Yet the same accurate chronicler had discovered that the true form of the name was Tatar, not Tartar.

47   Among the wild rumours that flew over Europe was one alleging that the Mongols were descendants of the Lost Tribes of Israel and so were being assisted by the Jews, who were said to be smuggling arms to them concealed in wine-casks across the German border. Matt. Paris, IV, 131-3. Alternatively, they were represented as the tribes of Gog and Magog who had been shut up by Alexander the Great behind the 'Caspian' (i.e. Caucasian) Mountains and had now broken out. For this legend, see G. Cary, *The Medieval Alexander*, Cambridge, 1956, 130-1. The Dominican missionary Ricoldo di Monte Croce gravely assures us that the name 'Mongol' is derived from Magogoli and that the Tartars cannot bear the mention of the name of Alexander! *Peregrinatores quattuor*, ed. J. C. M. Larent, Leipzig, 1864, 118-20.

48   Two ingenious tricks are noted in Hungary: the Mongols set dolls or puppets dressed as soldiers on riderless horses to give the impression of greater numbers, and having captured at Mohi the great seal of the kingdom, they issued false proclamations in the king's name to confuse his subjects and prevent them mustering for further defence.

49   Gran (Latin Strigonium, Hungarian Esztergom) was the birthplace of St Stephen, the residence of the primate and often of the court, and the occasional meeting-place of the Diet. The Mongols burnt the town, but as often, failed to take the citadel, and the spring thaws obliged them to retire before the rising waters.

50   There is a curious parallel between the pursuit of Bela and that of Muhammad Shah twenty years before. In each case the fugitive found safety on an island, but whereas the Khwarizmian died soon afterwards, the King of Hungary lived to regain and restore his stricken kingdom.

51   There are signs that they intended to settle in Hungary, as the Huns

had done eight centuries before them: they minted there in 1241 the only coins found from that period. B. Spuler, *The Mongol Period*, Leiden, 1960, 13.

52 According to the *Secret History*, Sect. 275, the quarrel arose out of a dispute about precedence at a drinking-bout, when Küyük threatened to have Batu bastinadoed. It was probably but one expression of a long-standing feud between the houses of Jochi and Ögedei, which resulted in the palace revolution of 1251 and the disruption of the Mongol Empire.

53 Vernadsky, *op. cit.*, 54–5. Alexander acquired his famous sobriquet 'Nevsky' from the Neva battle. He repelled a second Swedish attack on the frozen Lake Peipus in April 1242.

54 The rumour is reported in Matthew Paris, *Hist. Anglorum*, ed. Madden, III, 38–9, in connection with the first Mongol mission to Innocent IV in 1248. It was probably unfounded, but indicates what contemporary opinion thought possible. The Pope had earlier accused Frederick of having 'by his own accord, plotted the invasion of the Tartars'.

55 Spuler, *Die goldene Horde*, 266–7.

Chapter 6: The Christian response

1 Plan, Plano, Pian Carpini is a village near Perugia, where he was born in 1182, the same year as St Francis.

2 Carpini wrote two reports of his journey on his return in 1247, and an abridgment of these was published shortly afterwards by Vincent of Beauvais in his *Speculum Historiale*, Book 32, under the title *Historia Mongolorum*. The complete text was published by M. d'Avezac only in 1839, in the fourth volume of the *Recueil des voyages*, as *Relation des Mongols ou Tartares*. W. W. Rockhill produced the first full English translation for the Hakluyt Society, London, 1900: another is contained in *The Mongol Mission*, ed. C. Dawson, London, 1955, reprinted as *Mission to Asia*, Harper Torchbook, 1966. A critical edition of the text is G. Pullé *Historia Mongolorum: Viaggio di F. Giovanni da Plan del Carpine*, Florence, 1913.

3 Benedict the Pole wrote a shorter account of the mission, included in Wyngaert's collection, *Sinica Franciscana*, Vol. I, Quaracchi, 1929, trans. Dawson, 79–84. For the theory that this was the basis of the new source recently discovered, see the introduction to *The Vinland Map and the Tartar Relation*, New Haven, 1965, hereafter cited as *TR*.

4 'Passing through the fire' was an old Turco-Mongol custom: the fire warded off any poison or other evil strangers might bring. The Byzantine envoy Zemarchus had to undergo this purification when he visited the Turkish khan in the Altai in 568. Yule-Cordier, *Cathay*, I, 208.

5 Töregene was either a Naiman or a Merkit: the sources disagree. She was probably a Nestorian Christian, and died soon after Küyük's election. See her life in Juvaini (tr. Boyle), Ch. 34.

6 Siremun (Solomon?) was the son of Ögedei's son Kochu, who died in China in 1236. He perished with other members of Ögedei's family in the palace revolution of 1251.

7 For their journey over the cheerless windswept steppes north of the Caspian and Aral Seas, they wore puttees round their legs to protect them from the sharp grass, like the modern cowboys and gauchos.

8 Sira-ordu ('yellow' or 'golden camp') was 'half a day's journey' from Karakorum, which the Carpini mission never saw. *TR*, 86–7. Juvaini (Boyle, I, 239) describes it as a place of 'cool waters and much grass'.

9 For the magical or symbolic significance of felt, see L. Olschki, *The Myth of Felt*, Berkeley, 1949.

10 I do not know why Vernadsky should say (*The Mongols and Russia*, 63, note 8) that Küyük 'could hardly have been over thirty at that time', when the *Yüan Shih*, which is most reliable on these details, states that he was born in 1206.

11 The text of Innocent IV's letters was first published by the Franciscan annalist Luke Wadding, *Annales Minorum*, Rome, 1636, *sub anno* 1245; Eng. tr. Dawson, *op. cit.*, 73–6. Both were dated March 1245.

12 Only the general tenor of this celebrated document was known until the original was discovered in the Vatican archives in 1920 and published by Pelliot in his 1922 article in the *Revue de l'Orient chrétien*. The first three lines are in Turkish, the rest in Persian, and the letter is dated by the Hegira year, AH 644 = AD 1246. Carpini had a Latin version prepared for the Pope. English trans. Dawson, 85–6.

13 See the section, 'The Mongol Imperial Idea', in Vernadsky, *op. cit.*, 92–9, and E. Voegelin, 'The Mongol Orders of Submission to the European Powers', *Byzantion*, 1941.

14 The preamble of Küyük's letter to the Pope ran: 'We by the power of the Eternal Heaven (*möngke tengri*), Universal Khan (*dalai khagan*) of the great [Mongol] nation (*ulus*), our order.' See Pelliot's careful analysis of these phrases in his article. Carpini translated *dalai khagan* as 'imperator omnium hominum', emperor of all men. The root meaning of *dalai* is supreme, limitless, without bounds; it later became the peculiar adjective of the ocean, and the chief magistrate of Tibet is, or rather was, styled the *dalai lama*. *Dalai Khagan* is the title given to Ögedei in the *Secret History*, Section 280.

15 See, for example, the experiences of Lord Macartney at Peking in 1793. J. L. Cranmer-Byng (ed.), *An Embassy to China*, London, 1962.

16 Much less is known of the Ascelin than of the Carpini mission. It probably left Europe in 1245 and returned in 1250, and its members included Simon of St Quentin, who wrote a report incorporated by Vincent of Beauvais in his *Speculum* (recently edited by J. Richard, *Histoire des Tartares*, in *Documents à l'histoire des Croisades*, Tom. 8, Paris, 1965), and Andrew of Longjumeau, who was later employed by Louis IX on a similar mission. Pelliot's article, 'Les Mongols et la Papauté', remains the fullest critical account.

17 For the location of Sitiens, see J. A. Boyle, 'The Journey of King Het'um', *CAJ*, 1964, 185, note 95.

18 D'Ohsson, II, 220–31.

19 Matthew Paris, *Chron.*, V, 37–8; *Hist. Angl.* III, 38–9. The Pope was rumoured to be trying to incite the 'Tartars' against the two anti-papal emperors, Frederick II and John Vatazes of Nicaea. Pelliot suggests that a change in Mongol policy followed the replacement of Baiju as governor of Persia in 1247 by Eljigidei, which took place at the time of the Ascelin mission. If, as is likely, Eljigidei was planning an attack on Baghdad, it would be useful to have the Crusaders create a diversion in Syria and prevent Muslim help being sent to the Caliph.

20 Salimbene, *Chronicle*, MGH, 32, 207. A fellow Italian Franciscan, Salimbene 'interviewed' Carpini at Lyons on his return; he tells us that 'the man who came back from the Tartars' dined out at many abbeys and friaries that winter on the strength of his travel stories.

21 Innocent rewarded Carpini with the bishopric of Antivari in Dalmatia, but a dispute with the Archbishop of Ragusa clouded his last years; he was obliged to return to Italy, where he died in 1252, at the age of about seventy.

22 The *TR*, 100–1, after analysing Mongol tactics and strategy, oddly recommends the nations of Europe to imitate the Maccabean kings, who sent out archers ahead of the main army and laid different kinds of ambush for the enemy; as the editor remarks, the Book of Maccabees is not a reliable manual of military art.

23 'There is great discord between them, and if this proceeds further the Christians may have respite from the Tartars for many years' (*TR*, 82–3). The writer goes on to observe that for a successful resistance against a future Mongol attack, 'peace between our rulers is absolutely necessary', an allusion to the struggle then raging in Italy between the imperialists and the papalists.

24 Carpini, in Rockhill, 29.

25 Joinville, *Vie de St Louis*, Eng. tr. Everyman, 168–9. The ceremony was allegedly performed by a Nestorian bishop named Malachy, but Matthew Paris (*Chron.*, V, 87) heard it was by Peter, an Indian Benedictine.

26 Bar Hebraeus, *Chron.*, tr. Budge, I, 411: 'And Ghoyuk (sic) Khan himself was a true Christian, and in his days the horn of many followers of Christ was exalted, and his camp was filled with holymen, and priests and monks.'

27 Boyle, *Juvaini*, I, 259. Rashid, a later authority, merely repeats the story.

28 See Matthew Paris's scornful remarks, V, 87. I fancy the doubts were rooted in a reluctance on the part of the Latins to allow heretics like the Nestorians the honour of converting the Great Khan.

29 Reinforced no doubt by over-enthusiastic reports like that of Sempad, the Constable of Armenia, who was received by Küyük in 1248 and was promised help against the Seljuks of Rum, of the rapid spread of the Christian faith among the 'Tartars'. See Sempad's letter to his brother-in-law Henry of Cyprus, taken from the chronicle of William of Nangis, in Yule-Cordier, *Cathay*, I, 262–3.

30 On Sorkaktani, see Pelliot's paper 'Seroctan', *T'oung Pao*, 1932. She lived to see her son Möngke elected Great Khan and died in 1252.

31 The place where Küyük died is not precisely located: Juvaini, I, 261, gives it as Kum Sengir (Turkish, 'sand promontory'), which must have been somewhere in the upper reaches of the Urungu. The date is from the *Yüan Shih*. See Pelliot's long note in 'Les Mongols et la Papauté', 3rd article, 196–7, and E. Blochet, 'La Mort du Khagan Kouyouk', *Rev. de l'Orient chrét.*, 23, 1922–3.

32 Andrew's missions are thoroughly investigated by Pelliot in his third (1932) article. The Regent's reply and Louis's reaction are given in Joinville, 258–9; incensed by Mongol arrogance, the King regretted having sent the mission.

33 D'Ohsson, II, 249 ff. The Turkish form of Möngke, which means 'eternal' and is the common attribute of Tengri, is Mangu.

34 'A woman viler than a bitch' is how he described her to Friar Rubruck. Dawson, 203. She was tried and executed not for treason but for sorcery.

35 In addition, Chagatai's son Yesu-Möngke was executed and replaced by the grandson Kara-Hülegü, who had been deposed by Küyük. When the latter died, his widow Orgina took over the government. Juvaini, I, 273–4.

36 Sinkur's campaign against these rebels carried the Mongols far north to a land where there was scarcely any night and the natives had fair hair and blue eyes. See the Chinese source, cited by Père Gaubil, *Hist. de Gentchiscan*, Paris, 1739, 104. Haakon II of Norway granted asylum to the Parossits, Permieks or Finns, at what date is uncertain. D'Ohsson, II, 186. The fanciful legend that these people lived on steam (Carpini, in Dawson, 30; *TR*, 74–5) derived from their practice of offering the steam of cooked meats to the souls of their dead. See G. Pullé's edition of Carpini, Florence, 1913, 181.

37 Vernadsky, *op. cit.*, 144–5, quoting the Hypatian Codex. Michael's martyrdom (he was canonized by the Russian Church) is described by Carpini, in Dawson, 10: he was kicked 'in the stomach against his heart' and afterwards beheaded. His loyalty was suspect because he had been a refugee in the West and his son had married a Hungarian princess.

38 Yaroslav, who was Grand Duke of Vladimir, attended Küyük's inauguration and died in Mongolia, of poison, according to Carpini in Dawson, 65. Alexander Nevsky went to do homage to Küyük in 1247 and was made by him Prince of Kiev.

39 Carpini, in Dawson, 70; Vernadsky, 146–7.

40 Rubruck's report, though in many ways superior to Carpini's, was less well known than his: it was not published by Vincent of Beauvais, though it was quoted by Roger Bacon in the *Opus majus*, and parts of it were included in Hakluyt. The full Latin text appeared along with Carpini's in 1839, and both travellers were put into English by Rockhill in 1900 and by Dawson in 1955.

41 At this point, Rubruck inserts seven chapters (2–8) on the manners,

dwellings, food, drink, clothing and laws of the 'Tartars', a valuable little sociological treatise.

42 Before they left Sartak's *ordu*, they were warned not to describe him as a Christian, 'for he is not a Christian but a Mongol'. Rubruck explains that Christianity 'appears to them to be the name of a race, and they are proud to such a degree that although perhaps they believe something of Christ, nevertheless they are unwilling to be called Christian, wanting their own name, that is, Mongol, to be exalted above every other name. Nor do they wish to be called Tartars, for the Tartars were another race.' Dawson, 121. A remarkable example of the accuracy of Friar William's observations.

43 This place, which Rubruck spells Cailac, was apparently north of the Ili river, near the later Russian station of Kopal. Yule-Cordier, *Cathay*, I, 288.

44 Dawson, 155. This confirms the theory that the empire at this time was a dyarchy. The interview was conducted with difficulty, since the interpreter was drunk and Möngke himself struck Rubruck as tipsy.

45 Dawson, 183-4. This is the first European description of Karakorum: the Carpini mission never got further than Sira-ordu.

46 The sources speak of *tuins*, which seems to be a Chinese word for Taoists ('men of the Tao, or Way'), but it was used for monks in general, and in this context, almost certainly Buddhist monks.

47 Unlike Küyük's letter to the Pope, of which we now have the original, Möngke's letter to Louis IX is known to us only in Rubruck's Latin version. Dawson, 202-4.

48 Dawson, 122. 'The Nestorians make a great rumour out of nothing. This accounts for their spreading the story that Sartak was a Christian, also Möngke and Küyük, just because they pay greater respect to Christians than to other people. And yet the truth is they are not Christians.' Cf. p. 123: 'As for Sartak, whether he believes in Christ or not, I do not know. But I do know he does not wish to be called a Christian, rather indeed does he seem to me to hold Christians in derision.' Yet we must be on *our* guard against Latin jealousy of the Nestorians, of whom Rubruck draws a most unflattering picture.

49 Dawson, 185. He was, as usual, well-informed: he states that campaigns were planned against the Assassins, the Caliph, the Seljuks of Rum, and Sung China.

50 Capital and residence of the kings of Little Armenia, built against the slope of an isolated mountain of the Taurus range. *EI* article 'Sis'.

51 Kirakos of Ganjak, who died in 1272. His narrative is summarized in Bretschneider, I, 165-72, and given more fully and with critical annotations in Boyle, *CAJ*, 1964, 175-89.

52 'Who was a Christian by religion.' But nothing else is said of him; his Christianity is not enlarged upon.

53 The wild horse is Prjevalsky's, which survives in the steppe country between Lakes Baikal and Balkash: the two-humped wild camel still roams the Gobi.

54 Under the name Sakmonia, i.e. Sakyamuni, 'the Sakya sage', one of

the several titles of the historic Buddha.

55　The dog-faced men are known to Carpini, in Dawson, 23, and the *TR*, 70-1. They spoke two words and barked every third! Marco Polo and Friar Odoric speak of dog-men in the lands round the Indian Ocean, and Ivo of Narbonne asserted that Batu had dog-faced warriors with him in Hungary. Matt. Paris, *Chron.*, IV, 27. Perhaps the explanation should be sought in the custom of totemism and the wolf-packs which hunt in the northern forests.

56　Hülegü is the Alau of Marco Polo and the Halaon of the medieval French writers, spellings which indicate that the 'g' is silent. His name does not occur among the commanders of the great European campaign of 1237-42, and the commission to subdue western Asia must have been his first major assignment, given him at the age of thirty-six or thereabouts. The Caliph Mustas'im, answering his summons to surrender, addressed him as 'Young man, scarcely entered upon your career'—Rashid, 235. See the *EI* article 'Hūlāgū', and Rashid ad-Din's biography of him, *Histoire des Mongols de la Perse*, tr. E. Quatremère, Paris, 1836, reprinted Amsterdam, 1968, pp. 85 ff.

57　Spuler, *Die Mongolen in Iran*, 48-67.

58　See the life of Korguz in Juvaini, II, Chs 28, 29. He appointed the historian's father *sahib-divan*, minister of finance, and such was the firm justice of his rule that 'the peasantry became so self-assured that if a great army of Mongols encamped in a field they might not even ask a peasant to hold a horse's head, let alone demand provisions and offering of food'.

59　Korguz named in 1244 a local prince Shams ad-Din Kart as ruler of Herat, an appointment confirmed by Möngke and Hülegü. Shams, an able and cultivated man, founded a dynasty which outlived the Mongols, patronized art and letters, and sponsored a revival of Persian culture in the old homeland of the Ghurids. See D'Ohsson, III, 129-31, and Spuler, *Die Mongolen in Iran*, 155-61.

60　Juvaini, II, 505. Yet his name Korguz is Turkish for 'George'.

61　His life in Juvaini, II, Chs 30, 31.

62　The Armenian author of *La Flor des Estoires*, composed around 1300, pretends that at Hayton's urging Möngke received baptism and sent Hülegü to attack the Caliph, 'our mortal enemy', to restore Jerusalem and the Holy Land to the Christians. *Recueil des historiens des Croisades*, Documents arméniennes, II, 1906, 164. Such self-deception was, I fear, only too common among eastern Christians at this time.

63　On Eljigidei, see Pelliot 'Les Mongols et la Papauté', 1932 article, where the text is given of his letter to Louis IX, delivered to the king in Cyprus in December 1248 by the hand of two Nestorian envoys. He did not replace Baiju, but was given by Küyük authority over him. He apologized to Louis for Baiju's rough treatment of Ascelin and his friars the previous year by saying that Baiju was a pagan surrounded by Muslim advisers, whereas he (Eljigidei) had been a Christian for some years. Eljigidei's loyalty to the house of Ögedei cost him his life: accused of complicity in the plot against Möngke, he was executed in 1251 or 1252, and Baiju recovered his full power of command, which he exercised till the arrival of Hülegü.

64   The contemporary Indo-Persian Muslim historian Juzjani alleges that Möngke became a convert to Islam in 1251. *Tabakat-i Nasiri*, tr. Raverty, London, 1881, 1181–2. Cf. Juvaini's account of Möngke's favours to the Muslims, II, 600.

65   On Dokuz Khatun, see Rashid, in Quatremère, 93–5. *Khatun* is the common Turkish word for queen, princess, lady; *Dokuz* means 'nine', but Cleaves suggests that it may represent the Mongol *tayus*, 'peacock'. She was a widow of Tolui, and therefore Hülegü's own step-mother, it being common Mongol practice for a man to take over his father's wives (except of course his own mother) after his death.

66   Möngke advised Hülegü always to abide by her advice. Rashid-Quatremère, 145.

67   According to Boyle (Juvaini, II, 596, note), the correct form of the name is Ked-Buka, which means 'fine bull'.

68   The elaborate preparations are detailed by Juvaini, II, 607–11, who joined the expedition in what is now Afghanistan and acted as adviser and *bitikchi* (secretary) to Hülegü.

69   *Khana* is the word used by Juwaini; it commonly means 'households', but Boyle suggests, II, 609, in this context 'teams'. Bretschneider, I, 113, translates simply 'a thousand engineers from China'. They were in charge, not only of the mangonels or siege-engines proper, but also of 'fire arrows', machines worked by a wheel, so that one bowstring pulled three bows.

70   The story of the destruction of the Assassins is the climax of Juvaini's book, II, 618–725; he does not go on to describe the fall of Baghdad. After the capture of Alamut he was allowed to examine the library; he carefully preserved copies of the Koran and astronomical treatises, but burnt all writings relating to the heresy and error of the Isma'ilians.

71   Juvaini, II, 725. He adds: 'And in truth that act was the balm of Muslim wounds and the cure to the disorders of the Faith.' The last sentence of his history runs: 'and may God do likewise to all tyrants!'

72   Born at Tus (hence his name) in 1201, he died at Baghdad in 1274; he was a Twelver Shi'ite who felt no distress at the fall of the Sunni Caliphate. Through his astronomical knowledge he ingratiated himself with Hülegü, who had great faith in the stars and built for him the famous observatory at Maragha in Azerbaijan. See the summary of his life and a list of his many works in G. Sarton, *Introduction to the History of Science*, II, Baltimore, 1931, 1001–13.

73   His name was Ibn al-Alkami. Juzjani says he betrayed the Caliph by weakening the defences of Baghdad and persuading Mustas'im not to escape down the river to Basra. Failing to get himself appointed governor of the city after its fall, he died of remorse three months later. But Ibn al-Tiktaka, who wrote around 1300, assures us that the vizier vainly strove to awaken the Caliph to the gravity of his situation, but his parsimonious master was unwilling to spend money in the defence of Baghdad. *Al-Fakhri*, Eng. tr. London, 1947, 321–2. Both historians were

partisans in the Sunni-Shi's quarrel, and it would be idle to determine now who is the more worthy of credence.

74 See the text of these exchanges in Rashid, Quatremère, 231–5.

75 The figures of the massacre vary wildly and increase the further away the writer is in time and place. Chang-te, a Chinese envoy sent by Möngke to Hülegü in 1259, says 'many tens of thousands were killed', Bretschneider, I, 138–9; Juzjani, living in India, puts it at 800,000; while Makrizi, the fourteenth century historian of Egypt, claims that 2,000,000 perished! The population of Baghdad, always considerable, had been swollen by refugees who poured into the city from the surrounding countryside in the vain hope of finding safety behind its walls.

76 The most famous story about the fall of Baghdad tells how the Caliph was shut up in a tower full of gold and silver and left to starve amidst his wealth. It appears in the Armenian historians Gregory of Akner and Hayton the Monk, and among Western writers in Joinville and Marco Polo, and has been versified by Longfellow in *Kambalu*, but cannot be traced back beyond 1300. Its source is doubtless Nasir ad-Din Tusi's account of the interview between Hülegü and Mustas'im. Hülegü set a gold tray before the Caliph and told him to eat it. On Mustas'im replying that gold was not edible, Hülegü asked, 'Then why didn't you use it to pay soldiers to defend you?' 'Alas,' said the Caliph, 'it was God's will.' 'What will happen to you,' retorted Hülegü, grimly, 'will also be God's will!' See J. A. Boyle, 'The Death of the Last Abbasid Caliph', *Journal of Semitic Studies*, 6, 1961.

77 The Muslim writers are curiously reticent about the mode of Mustas'im's death, but Juzjani's version (tr. Raverty, 1252–3) is plausible: Hülegü, he says, feared an earthquake if the Caliph's blood was spilt on the ground and therefore had him trampled to death. Kubilai put his rebel cousin Nayan to death in this manner, as we learn from Marco Polo. From the same superstitious motive, the Ottoman Sultans had their rivals and brothers strangled bloodlessly with a bowstring.

78 Rashid, 311.

79 'The Iberians (Georgians) effected a great slaughter', says Bar Hebraeus, 431. In a fourteenth-century Latin pamphlet, *De Modo Sarracero Extirpandi*, printed among the Armenian documents in the *Recueil*, a Georgian prince is alleged to have beheaded the Caliph, II, 535.

80 Kirakos of Ganjak, Fr. tr. *JA*, 1858, 492.

81 She rebuilt the churches and threw down the temples (*sic*) of the Saracens, says Hayton, *La Flor*, 169–70.

82 The island and the fort on it were called Shaha or Shahu. Hülegü and his son Abaka were both buried there. See Le Strange, *Lands*, 160–1. Some remains are still visible, according to E. F. Schmidt, *Flights over Ancient Cities of Iran*, Chicago, 1940.

83 Among them the rival Seljuk sultans Kai-Kawus II and Kilij-Arslan IV. The former, who had been beaten by Baiju at Köse-Dagh, presented to Hülegü a fine boot on which the Seljuk had had painted his own portrait, saying, 'Your slave dares to hope that his King will honour his head by placing on it his august foot.' Such abasement flattered the

conqueror, who forgave him his crime of resisting the Mongols. Rashid, 323.

84 On the role of these Christian auxiliaries, see the Armenian chronicler Vartan, Fr. tr. *JA*, 1860.

85 Makrizi, *Sultans*, I, 90, who is sometimes more picturesque than accurate, says that the streets were so encumbered with corpses that the Mongol troops marched over them.

86 On the Christian demonstrations in Damascus, see Hayton, *La Flor*, 171–2.

87 The Mongols bypassed Jerusalem, from the military point of view an unimportant town, but the Armenians, to whom the wish is made fact, allege not only that it was occupied but that Hülegü himself piously visited the Church of the Resurrection! Grigor of Akane, *History of the Nation of the Archers*, Eng. tr. Cambridge, Mass., 1954, 81.

88 The fullest text of this truculent missive is in Makrizi, I, 101–2, translated in Howorth, III, 165–6; a shorter version in Rashid, 343.

89 By deposing the Regent Orkina and recognizing Alghu, a grandson of Chagatai's, as Khan. Alghu acknowledges Arik-Böke as Great Khan, and expanded his power into Khwarizm and most of present-day Afghanistan, thereby making him a dangerous neighbour of Hülegü, who had espoused the cause of Kubilai.

90 According to Kirakos, Ked-Buka was left with 20,000 men; according to Hayton, *La Flor*, 172, 10,000.

91 On the perplexities of the Franks, who found it difficult to decide which were the greater evil, the Mamluks or the Mongols, see Runciman, III, 311–12. In April 1260, just after the fall of Damascus, the barons wrote to Charles of Anjou, Louis IX's brother, expressing great anxiety about the Mongol approach and asking for help. *Revue de l'Orient Latin*, II, 213–14. They may possibly have heard of the new Mongol invasion of Poland in 1259, which led Pope Alexander IV to preach a new crusade against the 'Tartars'.

92 Runciman, III, 308; *Les Gestes des Chiprois*, 751; *La Flor*, 173–4.

93 'Goliath's Spring', so named because of an old tradition that here David slew Goliath. *EI* article "Ayn Djālūt'.

94 The course of the battle and the fate of Ked-Buka are related differently by the Persians and the Egyptians. The former, writing under the Il-khans and therefore pro-Mongol, stress the enormous numerical superiority of the Mamluks, who outnumbered Ked-Buka's forces by ten to one, and represent the great *noyan* as being unhorsed, captured and brought before Kutuz who reproached him for shedding so much innocent blood; Ked-Buka proudly replied that if he died, he died by God's will, not the Sultan's, that Hülegü would avenge his death—'I am his slave, and not like you, my master's murderer!', in allusion to the means by which Kutuz had gained the throne. He was then beheaded. Rashid, 349–53. The latter, being naturally pro-Mamluk, assert that both sides were evenly matched, that superior Mamluk valour gained the day and that Ked-Buka was killed in battle. Makrizi, 104–5.

95 An uncle of the last Abbasid Caliph was recognized as Caliph under

the title of al-Mustansir and sent at the head of some troops to Irak in 1261, but was defeated and killed by the Mongols at Anbar. D. Ayalon, 'Studies in the Transfer of the Abbasid Caliphate from Baghdad to Cairo', *Arabica*, VII, 1960.

96 S. F. Sadeque, *Baybars I of Egypt*, Dacca, 1956.

97 See J. Richard, 'La conversion de Berke', *REI*, 35, 1967. According to one report, Berke was brought up a Muslim, his father Jochi having provided the child from birth with a Muslim nurse: according to another, he was converted as an adult by a shaikh or holy man of Bukhara. He was certainly a devout Muslim before he came to the throne of Kipchak: Rubruck says Batu was displeased at his brother's friendship with Muslim princes, and he notes that Berke would not allow pork to be eaten in his *ordu*. The bad relations between Berke and his nephew Sartak, who died soon after succeeding his father Batu, are said to have proceeded from religious differences.

98 He claimed the provinces of Arran and Azerbaijan, which having been overrun by the Mongols in Chingis's day were considered part of the heritage of Jochi, but had been occupied by Hülegü.

99 For the tortuous diplomacy of Michael Palaeologus, see A. A. Vasiliev, *Hist. of the Byzantine Empire*, Madison, 1952, 600–2. The Emperor was nervous of Hülegü, whose ambitions seemed to threaten the Greek Empire; he feared attack from the West by Charles of Anjou, who wished to restore the Latin Empire in Constantinople, and was therefore almost driven into alliance with the Mamluks and the Golden Horde, a military demonstration on his frontiers by Berke in 1265 hastening his decision.

100 The negotiations are summarized in Makrizi (tr. Quatremère), I, i, 181–211. Baybars reminded Berke that they were united by the common bond of Islam and should, if necessary, fight against their own kindred, as the Prophet himself had done.

101 See Rashid's account of the war in Quatremère, 391–401.

102 Grekov and Yakubovsky, *La Horde d'Or*, Fr. tr. Paris, 1939, 77. The battle of the Terek was fought in the winter of 1263–4.

103 See my article, 'The Decline of Christianity in Medieval Asia', *Journal of Religious History* (Sydney), 1968.

Chapter 7: Nomad imperialism

1 Arik-Boge or Arik-Böke, 'Arik the wrestler', was Tolui's youngest son by Sorkaktani and was forty-four in 1260. Boyle-Juvaini, II, 518, note.

2 Bretschneider, I, 158, where some unimportant discrepancies are noted in the contemporary accounts of Möngke's death.

3 Kaidu was the son of Ögedei's son Kashi. The longest-lived of the Mongol princes, save Kubilai himself, he died in 1301 at the age of nearly seventy, and his son Chabar submitted to Kubilai's successor Timur

in 1303. He drove the Chagatais out of Turkestan and made himself master of western Mongolia. Grousset, 404-10.

4   See the well-known description of the city in the second book of Marco Polo, who in the first book has also noticed Kubilai's summer residence at Shang-tu, the Xanadu of Coleridge's poem, ten days' journey from Khan-Balik beyond the wall. In selecting Peking, Kubilai was mindful that it had been the capital of earlier barbarian rulers of North China (the Ch'i-tan and the Chin) and that it was sufficiently near the edge of the steppe and desert to make movement to and from Mongolia relatively quick and easy.

5   The original meaning of *il* was friendly, peaceful, submissive; it also meant tribal group, realm or community, and in Hülegü's time was employed to signify a kingdom submissive or subordinate to the Great Khan. See Mostaert and Cleaves, 'Trois documents mongols des archives secrètes vaticanes', *HJAS*, 15, 1952, 454, and Quatremère-Rashid, 14-15.

6   Yule-Cordier, I, 166. The title but not the name of Kubilai appeared on the Il-khan coins until the reign of Ghazan. S. Lane-Poole, *Coins of the Mongols*, London, 1881.

7   He needed interpreters when conversing with Chinese scholars. H. Franke, 'Could the Mongol emperors read and write Chinese?', *Asia Major*, 3, 1953.

8   Sung China was known as Manzi or Manji, from *Man-tze*, barbarian, an appellation bestowed, of course, by the northerners, who were themselves styled in the south *Pe tai*, northern idiots.

9   This siege made history and gave rise to many legends. Two Muslim engineers from Aleppo constructed powerful siege-engines which finally reduced the place, but Marco Polo alleges (II, 62) that these machines were the work of his father and uncle. On Bayan, see F. W. Cleaves, 'The Biography of Bayan . . .', *HJAS*, 19, 1956.

10   See the introduction to H. F. Schurmann, *Economic Structure of the Yüan Dynasty*, Cambridge, Mass., 1956, one of the few European treatises on the internal conditions of Mongol China: it is essentially a translation of, and commentary on, two chapters (93 and 94) of the *Yüan Shih*, which deal with taxes, transport and currency.

11   Murdoch and Yamagata, *History of Japan*, I, 491-592; Sir George Sansom, *A History of Japan*, London, 1958, I, c. xx, and N. Yamada Ghenko, *The Mongol Invasion of Japan*, New York, 1916. Marco Polo (III, 2) has fused these two expeditions into one: see K. Enoki, 'Marco Polo and Japan', *Oriente Poliana*, Rome, 1957. The second was a more formidable affair than the first, since it was manned by troops released from mainland China by the end of the Sung war in 1279. Some extracts from the Japanese sources are given in Yule-Cordier, *Marco Polo*, II, 260; see also A. Pfitzmaier, 'Die Geschichte der Mongolen Angriffe auf Japan', in the *Proceedings of the Vienna Academy of Sciences*, LXXVI, 1874.

12   The conquests and invasions of the lands of south-east Asia are summarized in H. Cordier, *Hist. gén. de la Chine*, Paris, 1920, II, Ch. 18. Marco Polo describes the conquest of Burma or Mien (II, 42) and Champa (III, 6), which he claims to have visited, but excuses the Great

Khan's failure to subdue Java on the ground of the distance and the perils of navigation, III, 7, on which see further the old but still useful article by W. P. Groeneveldt, 'The Expedition of the Mongols against Java', *China Review*, IV, 1875-6. For the speed with which Kubilai built up a navy out of the remnants of the Sung fleet, see Lo Jung-pang, 'The Emergence of China as a Sea Power in the late Sung and early Yüan periods', *Far Eastern Quarterly*, XIV, 1954-5.

13   See W. Eberhard, *Conquerors and Rulers: Social Forces in Medieval China*, 2nd ed., Leiden, 1965, Ch. 5.

14   The traditional examinations in the Confucian classics were suspended after the Mongol conquest and not resumed till 1313. H. Franke, article cited, *Asia Major*, 1953.

15   On the employment of foreigners in China, see Ch'en Yuan, *Western and Central Asians in China under the Mongols*, tr. L. C. Goodrich, Los Angeles, 1966. The author, who was born a subject of the Manchu empire in 1880 and ended as an academic administrator under the Chinese People's Republic, measures all people by the yardstick of Confucian élite, and foreigners are praised or blamed, noticed or ignored, in so far as they were or were not assimilated.

16   Marco Polo, II, 60. But Pelliot may well be right in suggesting that Polo was no more than an official in the Salt Administration at Yangchow. *Notes*, II, 834, 876.

17   Fanakat in Persian, Banakat in Arabic, was a town near the Jaxartes, ruined by Chingis and rebuilt in 1392 by Shah Rukh, whence its new name Shah Rukhia. It was not far from Shash, the modern Tashkent. Cordier, *Hist. de la Chine*, II, 314, and *EI* article 'Banākat'.

18   Marco Polo's scathing account of this cruel, rapacious and lecherous tyrant (II, 8) is confirmed from the Chinese sources, where he figures in the *Yüan Shih* under the rubric 'villainous ministers'. Bretschneider, I, 272. He was assassinated in 1282, and posthumously degraded by Kubilai, who regretted the trust he had placed in him. See H. Franke, 'Ahmed', *Oriens*, II, 1949.

19   Shams ad-Din was born in Bukhara in 1211, was carried off as a boy by Chingis, employed under Ögedei and Möngke, and died governor of Yunnan in 1279. He was also known as Sayyid Ajall, a title indicating his descent from the clan of the Prophet. D'Ohsson, II, 467; Bretschneider, I, 271.

20   For a general sketch of Kubilai's civil administration, based on the *Yüan Shih*, see Cordier, II, 324-30, and the ninth volume of Père de Mailla's *Histoire générale de la Chine*, Paris, 1779, 410-61, reprinted 1970.

21   According to Friar Odoric (Yule-Cordier, *Cathay*, II, 232), the emperor received in one day information from a distance of thirty days' journey.

22   Rashid ad-Din, translated in Yule-Cordier, *Cathay*, III, 115. The canal originally connected Hangchow with the Yang-tse: Kubilai extended it to Khan-Balik, thereby making its total length 1200 miles. See Lo Jung-pang, 'The Controversy over Grain Conveyance . . .', *Far Eastern Quarterly*, XIII, 1953-4.

23 Polo, II, 24. Every day 20,000 *scodelle* were distributed to the destitute. *Scodella* means porringer or rice-bowl, but the wording of the French and Latin texts of Polo imply that the figure refers to the number of *persons* fed.

24 On the *chao* or *ts'an*, paper money, see Lien-sheng Yang, *Money and Credit in China*, Cambridge, Mass., 1952, Chs 6 and 7. It originated under the T'ang, and was introduced to the Mongols by Ch'u-ts'ai, who persuaded Ögedei to make a limited issue of it in 1236. Kubilai's first issue in 1260 was in classes of notes in units of 10, 100 and 1,000, which were worth, however, only half their nominal value in silver. They were made of mulberry bark, were oblong in shape, and were stamped in red with the imperial seal. According to Polo (II, 18), they circulated all over the empire. For the unsuccessful attempt to introduce them into Persia, in 1294, see above, p. 135. For a modern economist's appraisal, see Gordon Tulloch, 'Paper Money—a Cycle of Cathay', *Economic History Review*, IX, 1956–7, and cf. H. Franke, *Geld und Wirtschaft in China unter der Mongolenherrschaft*, Leipzig, 1949.

25 The great port of Zaitun, from which the Polos sailed on their journey home in 1292, is probably to be identified with the modern Ch'uan Chow, on the coast of Fukien. Polo, II, 77; Bretschneider, I, 187, and Pelliot, *Notes on Marco Polo*, I, 583–97.

26 See, for the conditions of this trade, the handbook for merchants travelling from Europe to China compiled by Francesco Balducci Pegolotti, a factor in the Bardi Company of Florence, about 1340, and printed in Yule-Cordier, *Cathay*, III, 137–71; a critical edition by A. Evans was published in Cambridge, Mass., 1936, under the title *La Pratica della Mercatura*. Pegolotti reckoned the time taken to travel from Tana in the Crimea to Khan-Balik at between 259 and 284 days, and assures his readers that the greater part of the road is perfectly safe.

27 Yule-Cordier, *Marco Polo*, II, 328–30. The relics included two teeth of the Buddha, not the *one* tooth which the Portuguese destroyed in 1560 and which miraculously reappeared at Kandy as well as Pegu in Burma!

28 The *Kanjur*, a collection of Buddhist sacred books compiled or preserved in Tibet. Kubilai appointed a board of translators to turn it into Mongolian, a task not accomplished till after his death.

29 On Phags-pa, not a name but a title meaning 'noble', see Sarton, *Introduction*, III, 1137. His alphabet of square letters written vertically was derived from Tibetan. Pelliot judged ('Les systèmes d'écriture en usage chez les anciens mongols', *Asia Major*, 1925), that it enabled many Mongol sounds to be represented better than the Uighur alphabet, but the Mongol language continued to be written in the latter till supplanted by the Russian Cyrillic script in our own day. Cf. N. Poppe, 'The Mongolian monuments in Phags-pa script', *Gott. Asiat. Forsch.* VIII, 1957, and Igor de Rachewiltz, 'The Language Problem in Yüan China', *JOSA*, V, 1967.

30 Ssanang Setzen wrote in the seventeenth century: his work has been translated into German (I. J. Schmidt, *Gesch. der Ost-Mongolen*, St

Petersburg, 1829) and English (J. R. Krueger, *A History of the Eastern Mongols to 1662*, Bloomington, Ind., 1964).

31   De Mailla, IX, 539; cf. Quatremère's *Rashid*, 189-91.

32   He also asked the Pope to send him a hundred men of learning qualified to teach the Christian faith. Polo, I, 1. The optimism of the Polos here equals that of the Nestorians in the days of Küyük and Möngke. Yet in a later passage (II, 2) found only in Ramusio's Italian text, Kubilai is represented as hinting that a profession of Christianity on his part would be ill received by the notables of his court and might even put his life in danger.

33   Sarton, III, 1021. 'Isa' is, of course the Arabic form of Jesus. He is said to have inspired Kubilai's 1279 edict against Muslim propaganda in China, and in 1284 was sent to Persia as envoy to the new Il-khan Arghun. His four sons, also Nestorians, continued in the Mongol service. Pelliot, 'Chrétiens d'Asie Centrale' (second part), *T'oung Pao*, 1927, 159.

34   Pelliot, article cited (first part), *T'oung Pao*, 1914, 640-1. This Alan Christian community sent an embassy to Pope Benedict XII at Avignon in 1336. Yule-Cordier, *Cathay*, III, 179-88.

35   *The History of Yahballaha III*, Eng. tr. J. A. Montgomery, New York, 1927; *The Monks of Kublai Khan*, tr. E. Wallis Budge, London, 1928. The Syriac MS., preserved by the Nestorians of Irak, was published in 1888; it is the travel-diary of Rabban bar Sauma ('son of fasting'), a Nestorian priest born in Peking who went on a pilgrimage to Jerusalem along with a monk named Mark, who was appointed *Catholicos* or patriarch in 1282 under the title of Yahballaha ('God has given'). The Il-khan Arghun sent Sauma on a mission to the Pope and the western kings, which he accomplished in 1287-8; he died at Baghdad in 1293.

36   The Önguts are the Ung of Polo and the Po Ta-ta or White Tatars of the Chinese. Bretschneider, I, 184. Their land is the Tenduk of Polo (see a long note in Yule-Cordier, I, 285-9) and the Tanguth of Bar Sauma, tr. Montgomery, 34: Polo and Friar Odoric agree that it is 'the kingdom of Prester John'. See Pelliot's elucidations, 'Chrétiens d'Asie', 1914, 630-4. According to J. Dauvillier, 'Les provinces chaldéennes . . .', Toulouse, 1948, Christian remains have been found in the old Öngut country, including medals of St George, who was a popular patron among them.

37   Kubilai adopted not Mahayana Buddhism, but the debased Tantric form, shot through with superstitions and magical practices, which had long been established in Tibet. From the same source the Mongols in their homeland adopted it in 1576-7.

38   The circumstances of this anti-Muslim edict are obscure: Kubilai's Christian adviser Isa has been held responsible for it, but it ill accords with the number of high-ranking Muslims in the Khan's service. (Yule, III, 126, calls attention to the number of Muslim governors of Chinese provinces under Kubilai.) Perhaps it stemmed from the old conflict between the Muslim law and the *Yasa* about the killing of animals for ritual purposes. Yule-Cordier, *Marco Polo*, I, 422, and D'Ohsson, II, 492-3.

39   Under the Mongols, Muslims were widely scattered throughout

China. Ibn Battuta received a warm welcome from his co-religionists in Zaitun, Canton and elsewhere, and declares with some exaggeration that there was a *shaikh al-Islam* in *every* city of China. Yule-Cordier, *Cathay*, III, 119–23. On Muslims in Yunnan, see Polo, II, 39, where the province is called Karaian (Mongol-Turkish Kara-Jang), Quatremère's notes in Rashid, pp. xcii–xcviii, to his translation of a passage from the Persian historian on China, Arnold, *Preaching of Islam*, London, 1896, 298, and Marshall Broomhall, *Islam in China*, London, 1910. The Muslims in the seaports of China appear to have been, like the Christians, foreign merchants or immigrants (the names cited by Ibn Battuta are all Persian), but in the remote, mountainous frontier province of Yunnan Islam took deep root among the native population.

40 Kubilai's services were not inconsiderable. Like most of the Mongol chiefs, he was deeply interested in history and astronomy, not indeed for their own sakes, but the first for the glorification of his house and nation, and the second for astrological prediction. He had the annals of China (the revision by Chu-Hsi of a work composed in the eleventh century by Ssu-ma Kuang) translated into Mongolian and printed (from blocks, of course) in the government printing-office at Khan-Balik, whose stock was augmented by blocks brought from Hangchow, the Sung capital, after its fall. Two astronomers, the Persian Jamal ad-Din and the Chinese Kuo Shon-ching, reformed the calendar, and the latter constructed a number of astronomical instruments, two of which dated 1279 are still preserved at Peking. See Polo's chapter (II, 25) 'Of the Astrologers of the City of Kanbalu', and the Yule-Cordier notes thereon. Kubilai also prepared a new criminal code and sponsored in 1273 the compilation of a work on sericulture and agriculture. Sarton, *Introduction*, II, 980–2.

41 The history of the Il-khans is traced, with Teutonic thoroughness, by B. Spuler, *Die Mongolen in Iran*, 3rd ed. Wiesbaden, 1968, and with Gallic clarity and brevity by R. Grousset, *L'Empire des Steppes*, 4th ed. Paris, 1952, 420–68. Some additional facts may be gleaned from the third part of Howorth's massive and amorphous compilation, *The History of the Mongols*, London, 1888. All these moderns have derived their materials from Rashid ad-Din's universal history, *Jami 'al-Tawarikh*, the finest product of Persian historical literature, a portion of which Professor Boyle will shortly present in an English dress. In the meantime the reader may be referred with confidence to the fifth volume of the *Cambridge History of Iran*, London, 1968, which covers the Seljuk and Mongol periods of Persian history.

42 On Maragha, see Minorsky's article in the *EI*. Some towers dating from the time of Hülegü are still extant there, but only a faint trace remains of Nasir ad-Din Tusi's celebrated observatory.

43 He is alleged to have been subject to epileptic fits, which perhaps explains his savage outbursts of cruelty: so says the Egyptian historian Taghri-Birdi, a witness distant in time and space. The contemporary chroniclers agree that his end was preceded and predicted by a comet, whose appearance Hülegü himself correctly interpreted.

44   For Christian grief, see Stephen Orbelian, who accuses a wicked Muslim of poisoning them both! Vartan claims that Dokuz asked him if masses could be said for Hülegü's soul; he replied this would be improper for a pagan, but taxes could be remitted in his memory. Howorth, III, 209–10.

45   *History of Mar Yahballaha*, tr. Montgomery, 45.

46   Hayton, *La Flor*, 180–1.

47   The diplomacy of the Mediterranean Powers at this juncture is skilfully unravelled in Runciman's *Sicilian Vespers*, London, 1958; for the Genoese, see G. Bratianu, *Le Commerce génois dans la mer noire*, Paris, 1929. By the treaty of Nymphaeum (1261) Michael VIII granted a trade monopoly in the Black Sea to Genoa and Pisa, to the exclusion of Venice, the champion of the defunct Latin Empire.

48   The battle of Hims is noticed by the Muslim (Aba'l-Fida, 158–9), Armenian (Hayton, 183–4) and Syriac (Bar Hebraeus, 592–3) historians. The Georgians and Armenians on the right wing drove back the Mamluks, but Möngke-Temür was wounded and his withdrawal spread panic among his followers.

49   See Minorsky's article 'Tabrīz' in the *EI*. Friar Odoric, who was there about 1320, assures us that there was no city in the world 'better for merchandise' and that the Khan drew more revenue from Tabriz than the King of France from his whole kingdom. Yule-Cordier, *Cathay*, II, 103–4.

50   Hayton.

51   See the correspondence in Makrizi, II, 187–200, tr. in Howorth, III, 290–6.

52   Popular hatred of Sa'd al-Dawla is reflected in the squibs and lampoons preserved in the panegyrist Wassaf, who continued Juvaini's history but in a very inferior and bombastic style: some specimens are given in Browne, *Lit. Hist. of Persia*, III, 32–6.

53   See the letter to the Pope in Moule, *Christians in China*, 106.

54   See the fascinating details of the journey in Montgomery, 54–72. In Rome he made a profession of faith before the College of Cardinals, in Paris he was received by Philip le Bel in Saintc-Chapelle, and in Bordeaux he celebrated mass and gave communion to Edward I. Before sailing back, he spent Holy Week and Easter 1288 in Rome.

55   The details of Buscarelli's mission were first printed from the Wardrobe records by T. H. Turner, 'Unpublished Notices of the Times of Edward I', in *Archaeological Journal*, VIII, 1851. The king sent Geoffrey de Langley to Persia with his reply; he promised to co-operate with Arghun against the 'Soldan of Babylon' (i.e. the Mamluk Sultan), but the Scottish crisis detained him at home. For Arghun's letter to the King of France, now preserved in the Bibliothèque Nationale, see Mostaert and Cleaves, *Les Lettres de 1289 et 1305 des Ilkans Arghun et Öljeitü à Philippe le Bel*, Cambridge, Mass., 1962, which contains text, translation and commentary.

56   Pulad, who was presumably a sinized Mongol, was clearly a man of education and talent. During the years he resided at Tabriz as the

representative of Kubilai at the Il-khan court, he assisted the historian Rashid, who pays a warm tribute to his deep knowledge of Turco-Mongol antiquities, in those sections of his work dealing with eastern Asia. Rashid refers to him by his Chinese title *ch'eng hsiang*, or high minister. Bretschneider, I, 197; Quatremère-Rashid, 77-9.

57 The notes closely imitated their Chinese originals, even to several words in Chinese characters, which must have been wholly unintelligible in Persia. The principal difference lay in the printing on the Persian issue of the Muslim profession of faith. 'There is no god but God and Muhammad is his apostle', a significant innovation in that the khans did not yet officially profess Islam. Death was threatened for anyone defacing the notes. D'Ohsson, IV, 100-3. Cf. Smith and Plunkett, 'Gold in Mongol Iran', *JESHO*, 1968, and K. Jahn, 'Paper Currency in Iran, *JAH*, 1970.

58 The title 'il-khan' was dropped and replaced by 'khan', thereby implying independent sovereignty, whose holder ruled by the grace of God and not by favour of the Great Khan. Yet the political ties with Mongol China were not wholly severed. On Öljeitü's accession in 1304 he received a *yarlik* from Khan-Balik and the governor of Isaphan was sent to China to convey thanks, perhaps, rather than homage, but the distinction was no doubt a subtle one.

59 *The History of Mar Yahballaha* concludes with an agitated account of 'the hordes of Arabs (sic) aroused up to avenge themselves upon the Church and her children'. Tr. Montgomery, 80.

60 See the article 'Turban' in the *EI*. The date of the official adoption of the Muslim headdress was 2 November, 1297. At this point I must express my regret at not having seen I. P. Petrushevsky's *Islam in Iran*, Leningrad, 1966, which is praised by Colonel Wheeler, in an address to the Royal Central Asian Society in 1967, as 'one of the most objective and scholarly works on Islam in any language'.

61 The rise and fall of Nawruz is traced by D'Ohsson, IV, 174-90, from the evidence of Rashid.

62 The domestic reforms of Ghazan are particularized by Howorth, Part III, Ch. ix. Rashid's account of the reign has been translated into German by K. Jahn, *Geschichte Gazan-Hans*, Leiden, 1940. Rashid depicts Ghazan as the ideal Persian king, a second Chosroes, and cites in full many of the reform edicts which poured forth during the reign and which he doubtless helped to draft. Oriental historians, especially when they are also salaried bureaucrats, are much addicted to flattery, but making allowance for this, it would seem that no social abuse escaped the vigilant eye of Ghazan, who was genuinely concerned with the welfare of his people.

63 The battle of Marj al-Suffar is noticed in Hayton, *La Flor*, Bk. III, Ch. 42. *Docu. Arm.* II, 199-203. Ghazan's letter to Pope Boniface VIII, dated April 1302, is preserved in the Vatican archives: 'we are making our preparations; you too should prepare your troops, send word to the rulers of the various nations, and not fail to keep the rendezvous.' Mostaert and Cleaves, *Trois documents*, 467-78.

Chapter 8: The anti-Mongol reaction

1 For the fiscal system of Il-khan Persia, see B. Spuler, *Die Mongolen in Iran*, 3rd ed. Berlin, 1968, 306–35, and the chapter 'The Socio-Economic Condition of Iran', by the Soviet historian P. Petrushevsky, in the *Cambridge History of Iran*, Vol. 5, 1968. On the *kubchur*, see Quatremère's learned note in his *Rashid*, 256–9, and Doerfer, *Turkische und Mongolische Elemente im Neupersischen*, I, 387–91.

2 Quoted by Petrushevsky, *op. cit.*, 494, from Rashid.

3 The practice was to confer on these military officers an *ikta'*, or hereditary benefice, akin to the military fief of feudal Europe. The *ikta'*-holder collected the *kharaj* and other taxes upon it in return for the provision of a certain number of armed men. The institution dated from the tenth century, and became very common in Seljuk times. Spuler, *Die Mongolen in Iran*, 327–32; Ann K. S. Lambton, *Landlord and Peasant in Persia*, Cambridge, 1953, 53–104; C. Cahen, 'L'evolution de l'*iqta'* du ix au xiii siècle', *Annales*, 8, 1953.

4 Lambton, *op. cit.*, Chap. 4. She points out that before the *kadis* were lavishly endowed with land by the Mongol régime, they had to some extent protected the small cultivators in accordance with Islamic law, but that afterwards their economic interests were assimilated with those of the older class of landowners. When the tax-gatherer appeared, many villagers fled or hid themselves, or allowed their houses to fall into dilapidation. Runaway tax-payers were caught and whipped and the sheltering of fugitives was severely punished. Gregory of Akner, tr. Blake and Frye, 324–5.

5 Quoted by Petrushevsky, *op. cit.*, 535, from Rashid.

6 The towns of Khurasan, being in the direct path of Chingis's advance in 1220, suffered most. The highest figures for massacres, reliable or not, are given for Nishapur (1,747,000 killed) and Herat (1,600,000—only sixteen left alive!). Merv was destroyed three times, after which there were a mere hundred survivors. Balkh was still in ruins a century later, when Ibn Battuta passed by. Ray was never rebuilt. Only fifty houses were left standing in Tus. When Ögedei allowed Herat to be rebuilt in 1236, some captive weavers came back, but as the peasants had all gone, they themselves had to restore the canal and harness the plough.

7 The town life of Mongol Persia is sketched by Petrushevsky, *op. cit.*, 505–14.

8 Mazdak was a religious reformer, whose theological enemies accused him of teaching community of goods and women: he was put to death with picturesque brutality by the great Sassanid Chosroes Nushirvan in 529, and was ever after cited as a type of social subversion. E. G. Browne, *Literary History of Persia*, Cambridge, 1908, I, 166–72.

9 That modern universal historian, Professor Toynbee, has given a generous appreciation of Rashid's work, *A Study of History*, X, 71–80. Öljeitü urged him to expand his history into one of all nations, seeing that almost all the world had been made subject to the Mongols, and books

and scholars were available to provide the necessary information. Quatremère, *Rashid*, 38-9. Some unknown Latin monk, perhaps a missionary at Tabriz, supplied Rashid with the materials for the Frankish section of his history. B. Lewis, 'The Use by Muslim historians of non-Muslim Sources', in *Historians of the Middle East*, London, 1962, 180-91. It is regrettable that no English translation exists or modern critical inquiry into the sources of this part. Had any Asian before Rashid undertaken to write the history of Western Europe?

10   Edward G. Browne, who was here in 1887, was surprised to hear Öljeitü's name quoted in a piece of doggerel recited to him by an old peasant who showed him round the ruined mosque-tomb. *A Literary History of Persia*, III, 48.

11   See his *Flos Historiarum Terrae Orientis*, printed in the second volume of Armenian documents in the *Recueil des historiens des Croisades*: he presented the book to Clement V at Poitiers in 1307.

12   Rymer, *Foedera*. The envoys, as usual, were presumably Nestorian Christians who carefully concealed their master's adherence to Islam, since the English king in his reply assures the khan of their common interest in extirpating 'the abominable sect of Mahomet'!

13   That Rashid was in fact of Jewish origin appears established by the researches of Spuler, *Die Mongolen in Iran*, 247-9.

14   See the comments of Grousset, *L'Empire des Steppes*, 464.

15   See Gerhard Doerfer, *Turkische und mongolische Elemente im Neupersischen*, 3 vols, Wiesbaden, 1963-7. Significantly, the learned philologist requires two volumes to treat of Turkish words in modern Persian and only one for Mongol. I suspect that Mongol speech in Persia was extinct before the close of the fourteenth century.

16   *Temür*, Turkish-Mongol for 'iron', was a common component in the names of Kubilai's successors, and has, of course, attained lasting celebrity from Timur Lang ('Timur the Lame') or Tamerlane.

17   See F. W. Cleaves, 'Biography of Bayan . . .', *HJAS*, 19, 1956.

18   Rashid (Quatremère, 191) adds that he was much under the influence of the Tibetan lamas.

19   He was born about 1247, but where is uncertain, since there are three villages called Monte Corvino ('Raven's Hill') in southern Italy, two in the province of Salerno and one in the province of Foggia. Yule-Cordier, *Cathay*, III, 3-4.

20   The date of his arrival in China is not certainly known: the indications of time in his letters are contradictory. He may have reached Khan-Balik in 1292 or 1293, in the lifetime of Kubilai, but more probably in the reign of Temür.

21   Yule-Cordier, *Cathay*, III, 10, quoting Wadding.

22   On the economic malaise of Mongol China, see H. F. Schurmann, *The Economic Structure of the Yüan dynasty*, Cambridge, Mass., 1956, and more briefly, W. Eberhard, *History of China*, 2nd ed. London, 1960, Ch. 10.

23   See the evidence of Ibn Battuta already cited, Ch. 7, note 39.

24   One gets the impression that there were as many Italian merchants

as missionaries in early fourteenth-century China. John of Monte Corvino was accompanied by Peter of Lucalongo, who built a church for him at Peking, Yule-Cordier, *Cathay*, III, 55; Bishop Andrew of Zaitun quotes Genoese merchants on the rates of exchange, *ibid.*, III, 73; John Marignolli speaks of a *fondaco*, or depot for European merchants, at Zaitun, *ibid.*, III, 229; and Friar Odoric, describing the size and wealth of Quinsay (Hangchow), appeals for confirmation to 'the people in plenty who have been there' and who are now living in Venice, *ibid.*, II, 193–4. Among the 'seven martyrs of Almaligh', who were put to death in 1339, was William of Modena, a Genoese merchant. Cf. D. Howard Smith, 'Zaitun's Five Centuries of Sino-Foreign Trade', *JRAS*, 1958. In 1951 a marble slab was found at Yang-chou with a Latin inscription commemorating Catherine, daughter of one Dominicus de Villionis, dated 1342 and adorned with European-style carvings of the Madonna and Child. F. A. Rouleau, 'A Yang-chou Latin Tombstone', *HJAS*, 1954.

25 I borrow the economic details from Schurmann, the social from Eberhard.

26 The decline and fall of the Yüan dynasty may be traced in the fifth volume of Otto Franke (1952) and the ninth volume of Father de Mailla (1779): both are essentially paraphrases of the dynastic annals.

27 The other two were the founders of the Han and the first of the Five Dynasties.

28 This sad farewell to the sophisticated charms of China is quoted in the *Erdeniyin Tobchi*, the Mongol chronicle composed in the seventeenth century by Ssanang Setzen.

29 'Seres' is the common name for the Chinese in Ptolemy, Pomponius Mela and the Latin poets of the Augustan age: no doubt it is derived from the Chinese *szu* 'silk', *seres* merely standing for 'the people from whom silk is obtained'. Yet the name Chin, Thin or Sin is at least as old as the *Periplus of the Erythaean Sea*, which perhaps dates from the first century, and is plausibly connected with the dynasty of the Ts'in, which governed China from 255 to 207 BC. Yule-Cordier, *Cathay*, I, 1–22, and also the translated extracts from the classical authors in the Supplementary Notes; article 'Seres', in Pauly-Wissowa, II A 2, Stuttgart, 1923.

30 The letters of John of Monte Corvino and other documents relating to the Latin mission in China in the fourteenth century were first printed by the Irish Franciscan annalist Luke Wadding in his *Annales Minorum*, 8 vols, folio, Rome, 1625–52; English versions in Yule-Cordier, *Cathay*, III, and A. C. Moule, *Christians in China*, London, 1930. That these letters travelled to and fro between Europe and China says much for the efficiency of the Mongol imperial post.

31 *Didici competenter linguam et litteram Tartaricam*, says John in his first letter from Khan-Balik dated January 1305. Yule-Cordier, III, 50. But the passage is possibly corrupt, and the true reading may be *Tarsicam*, a common word for 'Christian' in medieval Asia, from the Persian *tarsa*, 'fearing', 'fearful', that is, those who fear God, Quakers! It was applied particularly to the nation, religion and script of the Uighurs, who were largely Christian.

32 See Bishop Andrew's letter to the friar warden of Perugia, dated Zaitun 1326, in Yule-Cordier, III, 71–5. On the possibility that a tomb discovered at Chuanchow is his and that he died in 1332, see J. Foster, 'Crosses from the walls of Zaitun', *JRAS*, 1954.

33 The travels of Friar Odoric fill the second volume of Yule-Cordier. Pordenone is a little town in Friuli, in the territory of Venice. The book, a lively picture of fourteenth-century Asia, was widely popular and was extensively pillaged by the notorious Sir John Mandeville. Yule gives a list of seventy-six surviving MSS. of it scattered over Western Europe.

34 He never actually entered Tibet. B. Laufer, 'Was Odoric of Pordenone ever in Tibet ?', *T'oung Pao*, 1914.

35 See the text of the letter in Yule-Cordier, III, 179–83. The embassy carried a letter from the Great Khan to the Pope, as curt as, though politer than, the celebrated letter of Küyük to Innocent IV in 1246: 'By the power of the Eternal Heaven. Our order: We send our envoy Andrew the Frank with fifteen others to the Pope, the Lord of the Christians, in Frankland beyond the seven seas, where the sun goes down, to open a way for the frequent exchange of messengers between us and the Pope, and to request the Pope himself to send us his blessing and always to remember us in his holy prayers, and to commend to him the Alans our servants and his Christian sons. Also we desire that our messengers bring back to us horses and other rarities from the sun-setting. Written in Khan-Balik in the year of the Rat, the sixth month, the third day of the moon' [July 1336]. Despite D'Ohsson's suspicions, II, 608, the genuineness of the letter is beyond question.

36 He belonged to a noble family of Florence, whose name was derived from Marignolle, a village two miles outside the city. In later life he became chaplain to the Emperor Charles IV, who asked him to write the Annals of Bohemia, which were published in Prague in 1764–8. Embedded incongruously in this work was a narrative of his Asian travels, which was not, however, recognized and extracted until 1820. Yule-Cordier, III, 177–269.

37 He carried letters of credit from Pope Benedict XII to the Khans of both these Mongol territories.

38 When the Great Khan beheld the great horses, he rejoiced exceedingly, reports the envoy, whose account is confirmed by the Chinese annals, which under the year 1342 states that the Emperor was presented with horses from the kingdom of Fulang [Frankland], one of which was eleven feet six inches long and six feet eight inches high and black all over, save the hind legs, which were white! De Mailla, IX, 579; Gaubil, *Hist. de Gentchiscan*, 279. Pelliot discovered that a picture of this noble animal was preserved in the imperial palace in Peking till the beginning of the last century.

Chapter 9: Kipchak and Chagatai

1 On Sarai, Chaucer's 'Sarray in the land of Tartarye', see Spuler, *Die goldene Horde*, 266–9: Old Sarai was on the Volga, some sixty-five miles

north of Astrakhan, and New Sarai on the Akhtuba, about thirty-five miles east of Stalingrad (now Volgograd). William of Rubruck, who passed through Old Sarai on his way back from Mongolia in 1254, refers to it as 'the new city Batu has built on the Itil (Volga)' Dawson, 207. For the early excavations there, see the German report of the Lettish archaeologist Franz Balodis, *Alt- und Neu-Sarai*, Riga, 1926.

2 Sartak's all too brief reign clouded the prospects of Christianity in Kipchak: his conversion is the best attested of any Mongol prince, and is admitted by the Muslim historians. He was actually succeeded by a son or brother named Ulaghchi, who was perhaps a child, and on whose early death Berke took the throne. Spuler, 33.

3 Spuler, 34–6. Alexander IV's letter to King Bela is printed in Mosheim, *Hist. Eccles. Tart.* 1741, No. 16, from Raynaldus. The Mongols offered alliance to Bela, who on being warned by the Pope against making agreements with perfidious heathens, complained of the poor support he had received from the Holy See and the Christian powers at the time of the invasion in 1241.

4 D. A. Ayalon, 'The Wafidiyya [i.e. immigrants] in the Mamluk Kingdom', *Islamic Culture*, Haidarabad, XXV, 1951.

5 The term 'Golden Horde' is unknown to the orientals, who speak instead of the Kipchak Khanate. The adjective 'golden' was perhaps applied because the khan's tent was covered with gold tiles or else from Mongol-Turkish colour symbolism. *EI* article 'Batu'ids'.

6 Berke involved himself in three wars against his fellow Mongols: (1) against the Great Khan Kubilai because of his support of the pretender Arik-Böke; (2) against Hülegü and the Il-khans of Persia; (3) against Alghu the khan of Chagatai. Between 1261 and 1265 Alghu seized Khwarizm and Utrar from Kipchak: the loss of Utrar, an important caravan station, was probably a severe blow to the commercial life of Berke's realm.

7 From the reign of Töde-Möngke (1280–7): Spuler, 288–9. All the so-called 'Tartars' of modern Russia speak Turkish.

8 Spuler, 289.

9 G. Bratianu, *Recherches sur le commerce génois dans la Mer Noire au xiiie siècle*, Paris, 1929.

10 Makrizi (tr. Quatremère), I, 214–15.

11 Vernadsky suggests (*The Mongols and Russia*, New Haven, 1953, 174–5) that Nogai was khan of his own Horde, the Mangkit tribe, but there was surely a special reason why he never succeeded to the supreme headship of Kipchak. The name of this celebrated prince is Mongol for 'dog': such an identification deceived the evil spirits, who fancying the possessor was an animal, refrained from molesting him at the time of his birth.

12 Yet the Mongol devastation here was so bad that Lithuania, which escaped them, was able to establish an ascendancy over Poland and Galicia. Vernadsky, 182.

13 'Tsar' was the common Russian title for the Khan: only later was it transferred to the native sovereign, the grand duke of Muscovy. M. Cherniavsky, 'Khan or Basileus', *Journal of the History of Ideas*, 1959.

14 Vernadsky, 187. Toktu is the 'Toctai' of Marco Polo, whose book concludes with an account of the war between him and Nogai.

15 I follow Vernadsky, 188, in his identification of this battlefield, but Spuler claims, 76, that it was on the Terek, in the northern Caucasus. The Muslim historians spell the name 'Kukanlik'.

16 Vernadsky, p. 195.

17 Nuvairi, in D'Ohsson, IV, 575.

18 She was later given permission to visit her father and was escorted to Constantinople by the celebrated traveller Ibn Battuta, but never returned.

19 For the career and achievements of Ivan, surnamed Kalita ('money-bags', from his avarice), and the significance of the choice of Moscow, see Vernadsky, 199–202.

20 On the formation of the Uzbek confederacy, see Barthold, *Histoire des Turcs d'Asie Centrale*, Paris, 1945, 185–6.

21 Spuler suggests (*The Mongol Period*, Eng. tr. Leiden, 1960, 54) that Janibeg's stroke against Tabriz was a deliberate riposte to the seizure of the Dardanelles by the Ottoman Turks in 1355. Realizing that the Golden Horde was now cut off from contact by sea with Egypt and the south, he made an effort to break through Azerbaijan and Syria to the Mediterranean. This may be too sophistical: Azerbaijan had long been a bone of contention between Persia and Kipchak.

22 In Turkish, Ak-Ordu. It was sometimes known as the Blue Horde. Its boundaries and its history are alike obscure.

23 See Barthold's article 'Toktamish' in the *EI*.

24 Sighnak lay on the Jaxartes, twenty or thirty miles north of Otrar; it was among the places captured by Jochi in 1219. Bretschneider, I, 170, 278; Howorth, II, i, 289.

25 'Kulikovo Pole' is the field of curlews or snipes; the victory is a proud event in Russian history. Dmitri received his surname 'Donskoy', of the Don, from the great river on whose banks the action was fought. The Russian losses were, however, heavy: when amidst the corpse-strewn field, the roll was called, there was no response to many a noble name. Vernadsky, 259–63.

26 The campaigns of Timur, which are as renowned as those of Chingis and quite as bloody, are narrated, with a wealth of lurid detail, in the *Zafar-nama*, or book of victory, by Sharaf ad-Din, from the French (1722) and English (1723) translations of which Western knowledge was for long exclusively drawn.

27 *Zafar-nama*, II, 127.

28 The *Zafar-nama*, I, 761, alleges that he took Moscow, but the Russian chroniclers are positive that he turned back at Elets or Yeletz, on the frontier between Kipchak and the Russian principalities. Vernadsky, 277; Spuler, 134–6.

29 *Zafar-nama*, II, 382.

30 The verdicts of modern Russians on the Golden Horde episode of their history are summarized in Grekov, *La Horde d'Or*, Leningrad, 1937; Fr. tr. Paris, 1939, Ch. 7.

31 On the obscure circumstances in which firearms made their appearance in the Mongol age, see above, Appendix 2.

32 For the religious history of the Horde, see Spuler, 209–41.

33 Spuler, 231, gives a list of the Orthodox bishops of Sarai. Möngke-Temür issued in 1267 the first *yarlik* protecting the Orthodox clergy in his dominions and thrice despatched Bishop Theognost on embassies to the Emperor Michael VIII.

34 The activities of the Franciscans are set forth as usual in the *Annales* of Luke Wadding, under the appropriate years: a contemporary glimpse of them is afforded by the letter of Pascal of Vittoria, printed in Yule-Cordier, III, 81–8. This friar spent a year at 'Sarray, a city of the Saracens of the Tartar empire' in 1337, before going on to 'Armalec', that is, Almaligh in Chagatai.

35 Ibn Battuta met *Turkish* Christians, apparently Cumans, in the Crimea in 1333. *Travels*, Hakluyt Society, II (1962), 470.

36 Kaffa was made a bishopric by John XXII in 1318, the same year as Sultaniya in the Il-khanate.

37 See the text of three papal letters to Özbeg in Mosheim, Nos 52, 63 and 88.

38 The last Catholic bishop of Sarai was nominated by Urban V in 1370. The Latin hierarchy in the Crimea continued as long as the Genoese were there. Spuler, 240.

39 Sultan Baybars had contacts with the *futuwwa*, Muslim guilds or associations, in the Horde's territory. Muslim travellers and merchants from Asia Minor also contributed to the spread of Islam. By 1333 there were a dozen mosques in Sarai, according to Ibn Battuta, II, 515, and in 1334 a young friar, Stephen of Peterwardein, who had apostatized to Islam and then publicly announced his return to the Christian faith, was lynched there by an angry Muslim mob. Spuler, 217.

40 The history of Chagatai, so far as it can be recovered, is sketched in Grousset, *L'Empire des Steppes*, 397–420, Barthold, *Hist. des Turcs d'Asie Centrale*, Ch. 8, and his article 'Čagatay Khanate' in the *EI*, and Spuler, *Mongol Period*, 43–6. The spelling 'Chagatai' seems now to have superseded the older 'Jagatay', except perhaps in Russia, where, however, the well-known family name Chaadayev is probably derived from the original form Cha'adai. Barthold, *Four Studies*, II, 11. For the not inconsiderable literature in Chagatay Turkish, see H. F. Hofman, *Turkish Literature, a Bio-Bibliographical Survey*, Section III, Leiden, 1969.

41 No explanation of the name and origin of these people is forthcoming: Bretschneider, II, 225, and Toynbee, *Study of History*, II, 145, confess their ignorance, while tentatively suggesting a link with the *Getae* of the classical writers and the *Jats* who plundered northern India in the weakness of the Mogul Empire. Pelliot (*Notes on Marco Polo*, I, 187) connects the word with modern Turkish *çete*, 'band of brigands'. As a term of abuse, it was applied by the people of Transoxiana to their nomadic tyrants, from whom they were delivered by Timur, perhaps the most meritorious achievement of that bloodstained destroyer. The

nomads called themselves Moghuls (Mongols) and their country, the eastern half of the Chagatai khanate, received the Persian name of Moghulistan: their term for the sedentary population was *karaunas*, bastards or mongrels, on which see a note in Yule-Cordier's *Marco Polo*, I, 98. They were long a terror to the peasants and oasis-dwellers: on one occasion the Jetes carred off 5,000 children. Barthold, *Hist. des Turcs*, 153. Polo says the 'Caraonas', who by devilish enchantments caused darkness to fall at noon, butchered the older men and enslaved the women and young men till the land became a desert.

42 For this extraordinary proposal of a federal Mongol Empire, see W. Kotwicz, 'Les Mongols, promoteurs de l'idée de la paix universelle', *Rocznik, Orient*, XVI 1950. Cf. *Cambridge History of Iran*, V, 398–9.

43 Le Strange, *Lands*, 470–71.

44 Barthold, *Four Studies*, II, 8. The coins were silver dinars and dirhams, the first minted in Chagatai. Notwithstanding the similarity of name, there appears to be no evidence that the *kebeki* was the prototype of the Russian *kopek*, as some have supposed.

45 India was the only major Asian land to escape Mongol devastation: the occasional raids were destructive but transitory. The principal contemporary source on Indo-Mongol relations is Juzjani, for many years chief *kadi* of the Sultan of Delhi Nasir ad-Din (1246–65), in whose honour he wrote about 1260 his historical work *Tabakat-i Nasiri*, Eng. tr. H. G. Raverty, London, 1881. See also J. A. Boyle, 'The Mongol Commanders in Afghanistan and India', *Islamic Studies* (Karachi), II, 1963.

Chapter 10: The Mongol age in retrospect

1 Azerbaijan, because of its rich pastures, was colonized by Turkish-speaking nomads in the Seljuk age. The Cumans, who came from the upper Obi in Siberia, borrowed their alphabet from the Uighurs on their way to the West: through them Turkish speech was carried to the borders of Hungary in the early 13th century. J. Richard, 'La limite occidentale de l'expansion de l'alphabet Ouigour', *JA*, 1951. For the Codex Cumanicus, a short Latin-Persian-Cuman dictionary compiled in 1303 and now in St Marks, Venice, see Sarton, *Introduction to the History of Science*, III, 1015.

2 I have already noticed (p. 146) the small number of Mongol words taken into Persian, compared with the large percentage of Turkish.

3 Early Chinese Buddhism is treated in F. Zurcher, *The Buddhist Conquest of China*, Leiden, 1959, which does not go beyond the fifth century. A more comprehensive view is given in A. F. Wright, *Buddhism in Chinese History*, Stanford, 1959, which unfortunately passes over the Mongol period in silence.

4 I may perhaps refer again to Arthur Waley's delightful *Travels of an Alchemist*, London, 1931, for the celebrated interview between the Conqueror and the Taoist philosopher.

5 On Mukali, see Pelliot and Hambis, *Hist. des campagnes de Genghis Khan*, Leiden, 1951, I, 362–72.

6 For these defectors, see I. de Rachewiltz, 'North China in the Early Mongol Period', *JESHO*, 1966. They were not all Han Chinese: many were sinized Ch'i-tan, who hated the ruling Chin dynasty as much as did the native Chinese.

7 Tibet entered history with Buddhism in the eighth century: L. Austine Waddell, *The Buddhism of Tibet*, London, 1895.

8 For the rapid acceptance of Lamaistic Buddhism by the Mongol leaders after 1240, see P. Demiéville, 'La situation religieuse en Chine au temps de Marco Polo', *Oriente Poliano*, Rome, 1957, and P. Ratchnevsky, 'Die mongolischen Grosskhane und die Buddhistische Kirche', *Asiatica Festschrift F. Weller*, Leipzig, 1954. See also Quatremère's note on the role of the *bakshis* or lamas in the Mongol Empire in his *Rashid*, 184–99.

9 On the obscure question of Buddhism in Il-khan Persia, see Spuler, *Die Mongolen in Iran*, 178–87, and Bausani's chapter, 'Religion under the Mongols', in the *Cambridge History of Iran*, V, 1968. Bausani remarks of the Buddhist temples in Persia that we hear of them only when they were destroyed by Ghazan in 1295–6.

10 Spuler, *Die goldene Horde*, 216, 224; Quatremère, *Rashid*, 186.

11 The farthest westward limit of Buddhism in pre-Mongol days appears to have been Bamiyan in the Hindu Kush in present-day Afghanistan, which once possessed ten Buddhist monasteries but was islamized as early as the ninth century. *EI* article 'Bāmiyān'.

12 H. F. Schurmann, 'Mongolian Tributary Practices of the 13th century', *HJAS*, XIX, 1956, 389. If the fall of the Manchus in 1912 occasioned a temporary collapse of state power, the Communists since 1949 have re-established it on an even more formidable basis.

13 E. H. Parker, *Studies in Chinese Religion*, London, 1910, 292–6.

14 Orthodox communities in the Mongol Empire included Russians, Georgians and at one time Alans, but Nestorian hostility drove the Alans over to Rome. J. Dauvillier, 'Byzantins d'Asie Centrale et d'Extrême Orient', *Revue des Études Byzantines*, XI, 1953.

15 The passage of nearly a century has added little to the exhaustive researches of F. Zarncke, 'Der Priester Johannes', two learned papers printed in the *Proceedings* of the Saxon Academy, Leipzig, 1879, 1883.

16 See p. 153 for the quarrels of Nestorians and Latins in Peking. There is little or no trace in Monte Corvino's letters of *Chinese* converts, but he translated the New Testament and the Psalter into 'Tartar' (Mongol or Turkish?) and had the captions to pictures of Old Testament scenes engraved in Latin, 'Tarsic' (probably Uighur Turkish) and Persian, but not Chinese. Yule-Cordier, *Cathay*, III, 50, 53.

17 Notwithstanding the high encomiums which have been bestowed in Kievan Russia, I cannot believe that its cultural level was as high as that of the contemporary Latin West. The absence from Russia of anything comparable to the cathedral schools of Catholic Europe is, I think, decisive in this respect.

18 No systematic Muslim suppression of Christianity is in evidence: occasional mob outbreaks, as at Arbil in Irak, Tana in India, Almaligh in Central Asia, and Sarai, betray the strength and violence of popular anti-Christian feeling after the Crusades, but the sole official action on a nation-wide scale that I know of was that taken by the Mamluk Government of Egypt, which punished the native Copts by forcing them to pay for the damage done by Peter of Cyprus's sack of Alexandria in 1365. A. S. Atiya, *The Crusade in the later Middle Ages*, London, 1938, 377.

19 *Hui-hui* is the common Chinese name for Muslims throughout the medieval period. The basic meaning is to return, come again, and the derivation from the Uighurs, whom the Chinese called *hui-ho*, was asserted in the eighteenth century by Liu chih, the foremost Chinese Muslim scholar of his time. Bretschneider, I, 264–74; Sarton, *Introduction*, III, 1586–90.

20 The earliest Muslim converts or colonists in Yunnan were therefore not Han Chinese but Tibeto-Burmans. Islam has never spread far beyond the province. Marshall Broomhall, *Islam in China*, London, 1910. Before the Communist conquest in 1949, Chinese Muslims numbered 48,000,000 indistinguishable from other Chinese except in their refusal to eat pork. I am ignorant of their present numbers and situation.

21 The literary and artistic renaissance of Persia in the Mongol age is treated with his usual sympathetic insight and wealth of illustration in the third volume of E. G. Browne's *Literary History of Persia*, Cambridge, 1920.

22 Pelliot, 'Les Mongols et la Papauté', *Revue de l'Orient chrétien*, XXIV, 310, note, comments that the only Muslim inscription found at Karakorum is in Persian. Elsewhere he notes that Persian was still employed in parts of China as late as Ming times.

23 Grousset severely condemns the Latins for missing so heaven-sent a chance and responding coldly to 'the smile of destiny'. *Hist. des Croisades*, III, 530. I cannot accept his criticism: the memory of the frightful horrors of the invasion of Europe in 1240–2 was still vivid, Mongol cruelty and treachery were notorious, and at the very moment when Hülegü made the first official approaches to the Pope in 1260, Berke and Nogai had let loose a fresh Mongol assault on Poland. It is absurd to suppose that in these circumstances the Mongols could or would be welcomed as allies by Catholic Europe.

24 The widespread abandonment of the Christian faith in the lands of its birth and early expansion was due less to persecution than to the slump in *morale* occasioned by Muslim victories and the final expulsion of the Crusaders, and the social and material benefits accruing to the profession of Islam. There was something of a literary campaign against Christianity in Egypt and Syria: see M. Perlmann, 'Notes on anti-Christian propaganda in the Mamluk Empire', *BSOAS*, 1940.

25 *The Chronography of Bar Hebraeus*, Eng. tr. Wallis Budge, 2 vols, Oxford, 1932. He himself translated into Arabic a part of this work, which early became known in Europe through Pococke's Latin version, *Historia Dynastiarum*, Oxford, 1663. His father was a Jewish convert:

hence his nickname 'son of the Hebrew'. See T. Nöldeke, *Sketches from Eastern History*, Eng. tr. London, 1892, Chap. 8; *EI* article 'Ibn al-'Ibrī'.

26   P. Hitti, *History of Syria*, London, 1951, 546.

27   The curious phenomenon of 'the transference of civilization' from Islam to Western Europe, which was not completed till the seventeenth century, is only now beginning to be investigated: see *Classicisme et déclin cultural dans l'histoire de l'Islam*, Paris, 1957, and my article, 'Problem of Islamic Decadence', *JWH*, VII, 1963.

28   C. R. Beazley, *The Dawn of Modern Geography*, III, Oxford, 1906, 413–19.

29   J. R. Partington, *A History of Greek Fire and Gunpowder*, Cambridge, 1960, assembles painstakingly the tantalizingly inconclusive evidence concerning the time and place of origin of the new weapons which revolutionized war and society. See a brief summary in Appendix 2.

30   The standard monograph on the compass is still A. Schuck, *Der Kompass*, 3 vols, Hamburg, 1911–18, the third volume of which is devoted to the Chinese claims.

31   See the text and translation of this inscription in Prince Roland Bonaparte, *Documents de l'époque mongole*, Paris, 1895.

Appendix 1

1   According to Pelliot, Köde'e-aral ('Köde's Island') was in Chingis's *ordu* at the confluence of the Sengur and Kerulen rivers in Mongolia: it was the scene of the elections of Ögedei in 1229 and Möngke in 1251. *Notes on Marco Polo*, I, 322.

Appendix 2

1   The most comprehensive recent study of the origin of firearms, a book crammed with references, is J. R. Partington, *A History of Greek Fire and Gunpowder*, Cambridge, 1960.

2   As, for instance, the Ghent MS. which speaks of cannon in 1313. Partington, 97.

3   A statue of him was erected at Freiburg im Breisgau in 1854 giving 1353 as the date of his discovery. That the new firearms troubled the mind of the age as much as nuclear weapons have troubled ours is indicated by the fact that he was sometimes represented as being instructed by the Devil. G. Sarton, *Introduction to the History of Science*, Washington, 1948, III, 1581.

4   Studies in Europe of Chinese firearms are not numerous, partly no doubt because of the language difficulty. Pioneer work was done by French Jesuit missionaries in the eighteenth century, e.g. J. Amiot, *Art militaire des Chinois*, Paris, 1772, and in articles by W. F. Mayers, 'On the Introduction and Use of Gunpowder and Firearms among the Chinese', *Journal of the North China Branch of the Royal Asiatic Society*, 1869–70,

and G. Schlegel, 'On the Invention and Use of Firearms and Gunpowder in China', *T'oung Pao*, 1902. Two valuable discussions, solidly based on Chinese sources, Goodrich and Feng, 'The Early Development of Firearms in China', and Wang Ling, 'On the Invention and Use of Gunpowder and Firearms in China', appeared in *Isis*, Vols 36 and 37, 1946–7. A full bibliography is given by G. Sarton, *Introduction to the History of Science*, Vol. II, 1931, 1036–40, III, 1948, 722–6. Partington's chapter has already been noted. The volume on Chinese physics, due to appear shortly as part of Dr Joseph Needham's great work *Science and Civilization in China*, will presumably contain the fullest discussion: meanwhile we can only refer to the brief account in his paper on Chinese science in *The Legacy of China* (ed. R. Dawson), Oxford, 1964, 242–52.

5 An alternative suggestion is that gunpowder was discovered by *Taoist* alchemists. But when? If we could be sure of the authenticity of the *Wu Ching Tsung Yao*, a manual of military techniques whose preface is dated 1044, and which contains recipes for making *huo yao*, 'fire-drug', the existence of gunpowder in China in the eleventh century would be proved. Partington, Ch. 6, 'Pyrotechnics and Firearms in China', especially pp. 261–3.

6 This work, the most valuable single source of Chinese history, was translated into French in the eighteenth century by Father Joseph de Mailla under the title *Histoire générale de la Chine*, 12 vols, Paris, 1777–83. The passages relating to the 'thunder-bomb' are cited in Partington, 241–3, and commented on in the *Isis* articles by Wang Ling, 170, and Goodrich and Feng, 117.

7 M. Prawdin, *The Mongol Empire*, Eng. tr. London, 1940, 259–60; L. Goodrich, *Short History of the Chinese People*, New York, 1943, 149. No references are given, and Partington remarks acidly (p. 291): 'I have wasted a good deal of time trying to find the source of Goodrich's statement; it may be in Voltaire.'

8 Neither Jan Długosz, the 'Polish Livy', who describes the 'gas attack' at Liegnitz (*Historia Polonica*, 2 vols, Leipzig, 1711–12, I, 679) nor John de Thurocz, who details the Mongol ravaging of Hungary in his *Chronicon Rerum Hungaricarum*, printed in the collection *Scriptores Rerum Hung.* (ed. J. G. Schwandtner, Vienna, Vol. I, 1746) makes any reference to gunpowder, still less to cannon, nor are there any in the many contemporary documents quoted in Matthew Paris.

9 Partington, p. 246, who calls it 'a large Roman candle projecting pellets by some composition analogous to gunpowder'. The year before the Mongols had used fire-arrows and naphtha pots at the siege of Baghdad, but the Persian historian Rashid ad-Din, our chief authority for this event, says nothing of explosives.

10 On the siege of Hsiang-yang, see Marco Polo, Book II, Ch. 62: he alleges that his father and uncle constructed mangonels which battered down the walls. Rashid ad-Din more plausibly brings engineers and engines from Persia. Partington, 247–8.

11 It is reproduced in Goodrich and Feng's *Isis* article. Partington, p. 275, notes that three different accounts say the Mongols used iron

cannon against the Japanese, but cautiously adds, 'These statements need investigation by linguistic and military experts'. This is sensible enough, since the only reference he gives is to a general work by F. S. Mason, *A History of the Sciences*, 1953, 62–3.

12 Wang Ling, article cited, 162. The arsenal was Sung Government property, which had perhaps just been taken over by the Mongols.

13 On Roger Bacon, see Partington, 65–79; Sarton, *op. cit.*, II, 952–67. The cipher is in the eleventh of the *Epistola*, Eng. trans T. L. Davis, Easton, Penn., 1923. Bacon's authorship has been doubted, it does not seem on strong grounds, and Sarton's statement (p. 958) that 'this cipher has no MS. authority whatever' is incorrect.

14 See the article 'Bārūd' in *EI*. The word is said to have been first used by Ibn al-Baitar, the Spanish-Arabic physician who died in 1248, as a synonym for 'Chinese snow': its etymology is unknown. From the fourteenth century onwards it was the common word for 'gunpowder' throughout Islam.

15 *The Legacy of China*, 248.

16 The earliest representation of a European gun is in the MS. of Walter de Milemete, chaplain to Edward III, dated 1326, and now at Christ Church, Oxford. The picture shows a pear-shaped gun mounted on a support being fired by a redhot iron at the touch-hole. Cannon were probably used at the battle of Crécy in 1346 and certainly at the siege of Calais in 1346–7, when ten guns were sent from London. Partington, 105–9.

17 Sarton, III, 1549. It has been noted that the great traveller Ibn Battuta was in China between 1333 and 1347, but says nothing of guns or gunpowder. The argument from silence is never conclusive, but this omission reinforces the belief that guns were known in China much later than in the West.

18 'The birth of chemical warfare had occurred in the T'ang but it didn't find wide military use before the Sung, and its real proving-grounds were the wars between the Sung empire, the Chin Tartars and the Mongols in the 11th to the 13th centuries.' Needham, in *The Legacy of China*, 252.

Bibliography

Primary sources

a Mongol

1   *Yüan Ch'ao pi-shih* (*Secret History of the Mongols*)
The capital original source; part-history, part-legend; basically a life of Chingis, but deals also with early part of Ögedei's reign; date and author uncertain (see Appendix 1); Mongol text no longer fully extant; what survives is a Chinese transcription. German translation by E. Haenisch, *Die geheime Geschichte der Mongolen*, 2nd ed. Leipzig, 1948; partial French translation by P. Pelliot, *Histoire secrète des Mongols*, Paris, 1949; partial English translation by A. Waley, *The Secret History of the Mongols and Other Pieces*, London, 1963.

2   Ssanang Setzen: *Erdeniyin Tobchi* (*Precious Summary*)
A later Mongol chronicle; author was Prince of Ordos in the seventeenth century. German translation by I. J. Schmidt, *Geschichte der Ost-Mongolen*, St Petersburg, 1829; partial English translation by J. R. Krueger, *A History of the Eastern Mongols to 1662*, Bloomington, Ind., 1964.

b Chinese

3   *Yüan Shih* (*History of the Yüan or Mongol Dynasty*)
The official annals of the dynasty, not abundantly rich in historical information; compiled about 1370. Certain chapters have been translated and published with commentaries:
Chs 93 and 94 by H. F. Schurmann as *The Economic Structure of the Yüan Dynasty*, Cambridge, Mass., 1956.
Chs 102 and 103 (on law) by P. Ratchnevsky as *Un Code des Yüan*, Paris, 1937.

255

Ch. 107 (on genealogies) by L. Hambis, in supplement to *T'oung Pao*, 1945.
Ch. 108 (on fiefs), also by L. Hambis, as *Le chapitre CVIII du Yüan che*, I, Leiden, 1954 (no more published).
4 *T'ung Chien Kang Mu (Annals of the Empire)*
The fullest collection of Chinese historical records, compiled by Ssu-ma Kuang (died 1086); remodelled by Chu Hsi about 1200, and continued by other hands. French translation by Father Joseph de Mailla, *Histoire générale de la Chine*, 12 vols, Paris, 1777–83, reprinted 1969. Vol. 9 deals with the Mongol dynasty.
5 *Sheng-wu ch'in-cheng lu*
French translation by Pelliot and Hambis as *Histoire des campagnes de Genghis Khan*, I, Leiden, 1951 (no more published). Compiled under Kubilai about 1285.
6 *Ch'ang Ch'un*
A. Waley: *The Travels of an Alchemist*, London, 1931. Report of the Taoist Sage Ch'ang Ch'un's journey across Asia to Chingis Khan's camp in the Hindu Kush, written by his disciple Li Chih-ch'ang.
7 E. Bretschneider: *Medieval Researches from Eastern Asiatic Sources*, 2 vols, London, 1888; reprinted 1967
A valuable collection of translated Chinese records of the Mongol age.

c Japanese

8 Yule-Cordier: *The Book of Ser Marco Polo*, II, 260.

d Chagatay Turkish

9 Abu'l-Ghazi Bahadur Khan: *Histoire généalogique des Tartares*, Leiden, 1726; *Histoire des Mongols et des Tatares*, tr. Desmaisons, 2 vols, St Petersburg, 1871–4
The author was khan of Khiva in the seventeenth century; he died in 1663. His book contains much semi-legendary material about Chingis Khan. Two Swedish prisoners in captivity in Siberia after Pultava (1709) found a copy and translated it into German; from this the 1726 French translation was made. It was a useful source of information in the eighteenth century, but has lost its value now that more reliable sources are available.

e Persian

10 Juvaini: *Ta'rīkh-i jahān gushā (History of the World Conqueror)*
A life of Chingis and his successors to 1256 by a Persian official who served the Il-khans. A most valuable and well-documented work. English translation by J. A. Boyle, 2 vols, Manchester, 1958.
11 Rashid ad-Din: *Jami 'al-Tawarikh (Compendium of Histories)*
A world history by a vizier of the Il-khans who was executed in 1318 on a trumped-up charge of treason. Deals with the history of China and

Europe as well as the Islamic world. A great deal of it is available in Russian, but there is no complete edition or translation. French translation by E. Quatremère of the reign of Hülegü, *Histoire des Mongols de la Perse*, Paris, 1836, reprinted 1968. French translation by K. Jahn of the European portion, *Histoire des Francs*, Leiden, 1951. Translations of other sections are planned. The most valuable single source of Mongol history.

12 Juzjani: *Tabaqāt-i Nāsiri*
English translation by H. G. Raverty of the Mongol portion of this history as *A general history of the Muhammadan dynasties of Asia*, 2 vols, London, 1881.

13 Wassaf ('panegyrist'), Persian official who continued Juvaini's *History* from 1257 to 1328. Partial German translation by von Hammer, *Geschichte Wassafs*, Vienna, 1856.

14 Ibn Bibi, author of a Persian chronicle dealing with the Seljuks of Rum from 1192 to 1280. German translation of an epitome of it by H. W. Duda as *Die Seltschukengeschichte*, Copenhagen, 1959.

f Arabic

15 Ibn al-Athir: *Kamil* ('perfect' chronicle), a universal history to 1231, giving a vivid glimpse of beginning of the Mongol invasions. No complete translation; extracts translated into French in *Recueil des historiens des Croisades: Hist. Orient*, II, 1887.

16 Nasawi, secretary of Khwarizm-Shah Jalal ad-Din, whose life he wrote about 1241. French translation by O. Houdas as *Vie de Djelel ed-Din Mankobirti*, Paris, 1895. Striking picture of the Mongol sweep into Western Asia.

17 Sadeque, S. F.: *Baybars I of Egypt*, Dacca, 1956. Contains an English translation of Ibn Abd al-Zahir's Life of Baybars, which comes down to 1265.

18 Makrizi: Egyptian historian, died 1442, author of *Khitat*, encyclopaedic survey of the history and geography of Egypt, and *Suluk*, a chronicle of the Ayyubids and Mamluks
French translation by E. Quatremère of the part dealing with the Mamluks as *Histoire des sultans mamelouks*, 2 vols, Paris, 1837–45. Useful work, based on older sources.

g Armenian

19 Gregory of Akner: *A History of the Nation of Archers* (i.e. the Mongols)
English translation by Blake and Frye, Cambridge, Mass., 1954.

20 *Documents arméniennes*, I, 1869, in *Recueil des historiens des Croisades*
Some references to the Mongols in this collection of extracts from Armenian chroniclers of the thirteenth century. For Hayton, see under 'French'.

h Syriac

21 Bar Hebraeus or Abu'l-Faraj: *Chronography*
English translation by Wallis Budge, 2 vols, Oxford, 1932. The author, who was Primate of the Jacobite Church, lived mostly at Maragha and died in 1286; he gives the Oriental Christian standpoint.
22 Rabban Sauma: *Travel Diary*
English translation by J. A. Montgomery as *The History of Yahballaha III and Bar Sauma*, New York, 1927, reprinted 1966, and by Wallis Budge as *The Monks of Kublai Khan*, London, 1928. The author was a Nestorian churchman who accompanied his patriarch (Mar Yahballaha III) to Irak and later travelled to Western Europe in 1287–90.

i Georgian

23 *K'art'lis Chovreba* (Georgian Chronicle)
French translation by M. Brosset as *Histoire de la Géorgie*, 4 vols, St Petersburg, 1849–58, reprinted 1969.

j Russian

24 *The Chronicle of Novgorod*
English translation Camden Society, London, 1914. Of the numerous medieval Russian chronicles extant, this is the only one available in translation. Those who read Russian should consult the full bibliography in B. Spuler, *Die goldene Horde*, 2nd ed. 1965.

k Latin

25 Matthew Paris: *Chronica Majora*, Rolls series, 7 vols, London, 1872–83
English translation by J. A. Giles, Bohn series, 3 vols, London, 1852–4. The fullest Western source on the Mongols, containing many original documents. Though primarily a history of England in the reign of Henry III, it covers European affairs at some length. The author was a monk at St Albans, near London; he died in 1259.
26 Vincent of Beauvais, *Speculum Historiale*, Douai ed. 1624
World history to 1254.
27 John of Plano Carpini, William of Rubruck, etc.
The reports of these Franciscan missionaries of Mongolia are available in several forms:

W. W. Rockhill: *The Journeys of William of Rubruck and John of Pian de Carpine*, English translation, Hakluyt Society, London, 1900.
C. Dawson (ed.): *The Mongol Mission*, London, 1955; reprinted as *Mission to Asia* (Harper Torchbook), 1966.
R. Skelton and others (ed.): *The Vinland Map and the Tartar Relation*,

New Haven, 1965. Text and translation of a new MS. believed to be the report of Benedict the Pole.

There is useful material in the old collections:

28   Luke Wadding: *Annales Minorum*, 8 vols, Rome, 1626–54 Reprinted Rome, 1731–47. Documents relating to Franciscan history, arranged in annalistic form.
29   J. L. Mosheim: *Historia Eccles. Tart.*, Helmstadt, 1741 Includes a collection of papal letters to and about the Mongols.

1 French

30   Sieur de Joinville: *Histoire de Saint Louis* Many editions; English translation by Marzials, Everyman's Library, 1908. The famous life of Louis IX by his old comrade, who died in 1319 at 95.
31   Hayton the Monk: *La Flor des Estoires, Documents armén.* II, 1906 The author was a nephew of King Hayton (Hethum) of Armenia, long resident in France; he died about 1310. A Latin version, also printed in *DA*, was made at the same time as the French.
32   Jean Dardel: *Chronique d'Arménie*, in *Documents armén.* II, 1906 By a French Franciscan, secretary to last king of Little Armenia; died 1384.
33   Mostaert and Cleaves, *Les Lettres de 1289 et 1305 des Ilkans Arghun et Öljeitü à Philippe le Bel*, Cambridge, Mass., 1962 Correspondence between the Mongol Il-khans of Persia and the French king.

Secondary sources

a General Histories

Grousset, René: *L'Empire des Steppes*, Paris, 1939; 4th ed., 1952 A lucid survey of nomadic imperialism from the Scythians onwards.
Howorth, Sir Henry: *History of the Mongols*, 3 vols in 4, London, 1876–88 Supplementary volume with indices to the whole work, 1927. Reprinted 1965. Laboriously detailed; uncritical and undiscriminating, but still the fullest account in English.
Ohsson, Mouradja d': *Histoire des Mongols depuis Tchinguiz-Khan jusqu'à Timour Bey*, 4 vols, Amsterdam, 1824, later editions 1834, 1852 Critical scholarly work, based on the Perso-Arabic sources; not superseded.
Prawdin, M. (pseud. of Michael Charol): *The Mongol Empire, its Rise and Legacy*, 1938; Eng. tr. London, 1940 Popular; not always accurate.
Spuler, Bertold: *The Mongol Period*, Eng. tr. Leiden, 1960

BIBLIOGRAPHY

Part of a larger work *The Muslim World, a Historical Survey*. Deals only with Islam in the Mongol age; so omits China.
———: *Les Mongols dans l'histoire*, Paris, 1961
Good short sketch by the leading German Mongolist of our time.
———: *History of the Mongols*, Eng. tr. 1971.

b The Eurasian Steppe

Jettmar, K.: *The Art of the Steppes*, 1964; Eng. tr. 1967. Best recent survey.
Krader, L.: *The Social Organization of the Mongol-Turkic Pastoral Nomads*, Bloomington, Ind., 1963.
Lattimore, Owen: *Inner Asian Frontiers of China*, New York, 1940; 2nd ed. 1951
Valuable study, part historical, part geographical.
———: *Studies in Frontier History*, London, 1962
A selection of papers on China's frontier lands by a leading expert on the region.
Mongait, A.: *Archaeology in the USSR*, 1955; Eng. tr. Pelican, 1961
Useful summary of Soviet archaeological work in Central Asia down to 1955.
Phillips, E. D.: *The Royal Hordes*, London, 1965
———: *The Mongols*, London, 1969
Two popular and well-illustrated short summaries of recent research in Central Asian antiquities.
Sinor, Denis: *Introduction à l'étude de l'Eurasie centrale*, Wiesbaden, 1963
Indispensable work of reference; lists hundreds of books and articles on Central Asia in many languages published up to 1961

c Chingis Khan

Fox, Ralph: *Genghis Khan*, London, 1936
A biography which utilized Russian work on the Conqueror's life.
Gaubil, F.: *Histoire de Gentchiscan*, Paris, 1739.
The first European life to make use of the Chinese sources.
Grousset, René: *Le Conquérant du monde*, Paris, 1944; Eng. tr. 1966
Popular, but well grounded on the *Secret History*.
Lamb, Harold: *Genghis Khan, Emperor of All Men*, New York, 1927, often reprinted
Popular, but not inaccurate.
Martin, H. Desmond: *The Rise of Chingis Khan*, Baltimore, 1950
Valuable for its analysis of Mongol military organization and methods.
Pétis de la Croix, F.: *Histoire du grand Genghiscan*, Paris, 1710
The first Western life; based on the Persian and Arabic sources.
Vladimirtsov, B. J.: *Life of Chingis Khan*, 1922; Eng. tr. 1930, Fr. tr. 1948
The standard modern life, by the distinguished Russian Mongolist.
———: *Le Régime social des Mongols*, 1934; Fr. tr. 1948

Though much criticized, this acute analysis of Mongol society on the eve of the conquests is still indispensable.

d The Mongols in China

The literature on Mongol China is growing but there is little in English and the Chinese sources have by no means been thoroughly sifted. The standard history of ancient and medieval China to 1368 is by Otto Franke: *Geschichte des chinesischen Reiches*, 5 vols, Berlin, 1930–52, of which the fourth and fifth volumes cover the Mongol period. This work, though well-documented, is perhaps too narrowly political. The old eighteenth-century work by Father Joseph de Mailla, *Histoire générale de la Chine*, summarizes the Chinese annals: Vol. 9 (Paris, 1777) deals with the Mongols. The whole work is now being reprinted.

Chapman, Walter: *Kublai Khan, Lord of Xanadu*, New York, 1966
Of no scholarly value. No satisfactory study of Kubilai exists in any European language.

Eberhard, W.: *Conquerors and Rulers: Social Forces in Medieval China*, 2nd revised ed., Leiden, 1965
Discusses rather briefly the complex problem of the interaction of Chinese and barbarian culture.

Franke, H.: *Geld und Wirtschaft in China unter der Mongolenherrschaft*, Leipzig, 1949
Useful monograph on the economic life of Mongol China.

——: *Beiträge zur Kulturgeschichte Chinas unter der Mongolenherrschaft*, Wiesbaden, 1956
Translation of a fourteenth-century scholar's notebook; glimpses of social and intellectual life in Yüan China.

Herrmann, A.: *Historical Atlas of China*, 1935; revised ed. 1966
The maps are accompanied and explained by a valuable commentary.

Olbricht, P.: *Das Postwesen in China unter der Mongolenherrschaft*, Wiesbaden, 1954
Valuable study of the famed Mongol post-system.

Rachewiltz, Igor de: 'Yeh-lü Ch'u-ts'ai', in *Confucian Personalities*, Stanford, 1962
Fullest study in English of this Ch'i-tan adviser to Chingis and Ögedei.

——: 'Personnel and Personalities in North China in the early Mongol period', *JESHO*, 1966.

Reischauer and Fairbanks: *East Asia, the Great Tradition*, I, 1958
A textbook, but useful as a general survey not confined to China.

Schurmann, H. F.: *The Economic Structure of the Yüan Dynasty*, Cambridge, Mass., 1956
The introduction to this translation of Chs 93 and 94 of the *Yüan Shih* contains an illuminating analysis of economic conditions in Mongol China.

Wittfogel and Feng: *History of Chinese Society: Liao 907–1127*, Philadelphia, 1949

Deals with an earlier part of Chinese history, but much of the analysis also applies to the Mongol age.

e The Mongols in Persia

Browne, E. G.: *A Literary History of Persia*, 4 vols, Cambridge, 1902–24
Classic survey of Persian culture; Vols 2 and 3 cover the Mongol period.
Cambridge History of Iran, Vol. 5, the Saljuq and Mongol Periods, Cambridge, 1968
Includes chapters on the economic life of Mongol Persia by the Soviet historian I. P. Petrushevsky, the leading authority in this field.
Lambton, Ann K. S.: *Landlord and Peasant in Persia*, London, 1953
Good social analysis.
Spuler, B.: *Die Mongolen in Iran*, 3rd ed., Berlin, 1968
The standard monograph.
Vambéry, A.: *History of Bokhara*, London, 1873
Somewhat antiquated, but still useful as giving one city's experience of the Mongols.

f The Mongols in Russia

Grekov and Yakubovsky: *La Horde d'Or*, Leningrad, 1937; Fr. tr. 1939
Short but authoritative account by two leading Soviet Mongolists.
Pelliot, P.: *Notes sur l'histoire de la Horde d'Or*, Paris, 1950
A learned commentary on Spuler, mostly philological.
Spuler, B.: *Die goldene Horde*, 1943; 2nd ed. Wiesbaden, 1965
Standard comprehensive account.
Vernadsky, G.: *The Mongols and Russia*, New Haven, 1953
Best available recent study in English.

g Mongol Relations with the West

Bréhier, L.: *L'Eglise et l'Orient au Moyen Age*, Paris, 1921
Valuable summary of papal diplomacy and missionary effort in Asia.
Moule, A. C.: *Christians in China before 1550*, London 1930
Standard account of Christian missions in medieval China, with much material translated from Chinese sources.
Olschki, L.: *Marco Polo's Asia*, Los Angeles, 1960
A useful miscellany.
Oriente Poliano, Rome, 1957
Collection of papers by experts on various aspects of thirteenth-century Asia and the links with Europe.
Pelliot, P.: 'Les Mongols et la Papauté'. Three articles in the now defunct *Revue de l'Orient chrétien*, 23 (1922), 24 (1924) and 28 (1931)
Masterly study of the first Mongol-Western contacts.
——: *Notes on Marco Polo*, 2 vols, Paris, 1959–63
Indispensable.
Polo, Marco: *The Book of Ser Marco Polo*, ed. Yule and Cordier, 2 vols, London, 1903

Valuable notes and commentaries; a volume of *Addenda* was published by Cordier in 1920.

Soranzo, G.: *Il Papato, l'Europa cristiana e i Tartari*, Milan, 1930
Good general survey; occasionally inaccurate.

Strakosch-Grassmann, G.: *Der Einfall der Mongolen in Mitteleuropa*, Innsbruck, 1893
Still the only scholarly monograph on the Mongol invasion of Europe; very detailed on the campaign in Hungary; now inevitably outmoded in part. Nothing is more urgently needed than a new critical study of the events of 1241–42, taking into account recent specialist research in Russian, Polish, Czech and Hungarian.

Sykes, Sir Percy: *The Quest for Cathay*, London, 1936
Popular sketch.

Wallis Budge, E.: *The Monks of Kublai Khan*, London, 1928
Nestorian contacts with the West.

Yule, Sir Henry: *Cathay and the Way Thither*, 4 vols, 1913–16, revised by Henri Cordier, reprinted 2 vols, Taipeh, 1966
A precious collection of reports on medieval Asia and Mongol China by missionaries and travellers, enriched by notes and commentaries.

Zarncke, F.: 'Der Priester Johannes'. Two papers in the *Proceedings* of the Saxon Academy, Leipzig, 1879, 1883
The most exhaustive study of the Prester John myth in all its ramifications.

h The Mongols in Central Asia

The leading authority here is Wilhelm Barthold: the following works of his are models of painstaking erudition.

Turkestan down to the Mongol Invasion, St Petersburg, 1900; Eng. tr. 3rd ed., 1968, which includes a new chapter, covering the years 1227–69, translated from the second (1963) Russian edition.

12 Vorlesungen über die Geschichte der Türken Mittelasiens, Berlin, 1935; Fr. tr. *Histoire des Turcs d'Asie Centrale*, Paris, 1945.

Four Studies on the History of Central Asia, Eng. tr., 2 vols, Leiden, 1956.

i Mamluk Egypt

Lane Poole, S.: *Egypt in the Middle Ages*, London, 1901; 4th ed., 1924
Standard work; strictly political.

Muir, Sir William: *The Mameluke or Slave Dynasty of Egypt*, London, 1896; reprinted 1968
Rather antiquated, but still useful.

Poliak, A. N.: *Feudalism in Egypt and Syria* 1250–1900, London, 1939
Short study of the Mamluk military fiefs.

Wiet, G.: *L'Égypte arabe*, Paris, 1932
Fuller on the social and economic side than Lane Poole or Muir.

For the role of the Frankish Crusaders in the Mongol-Mamluk contest, see the third volume of Sir Steven Runciman, *History of the Crusades*, Cambridge, 1954.

Index

ch'ao (paper money): introduced into Persia from China, 135, 236, 240

Chapar: proposes Mongol Empire be made a federation, 171-2, 248

Charlemagne, 20

Charles of Anjou, 131, 233

Charles IV (emperor), 244

Cherkes/Cirassians (Caucasian people), 59, 167, 214

Chernigov, 83

Cherson, 23

Chi-lu-ku (Gun-khan), 55

Chin (kingdom founded by Ju-chen), 37; Later Chin, 34, 53, 54, 62, 74; destroyed by Ögedei, 75-6, 77

China, 9, 18, 20; relations with Turks, 24-6, 31; invasions after fall of T'ang, 34-7; invaded by Chingis, 53-4; invaded by Ögedei, 75-6; conquest of Sung China by Kubilai, 122; government under Kubilai, 121-8, 234-8; government under later Mongols, 146-52, 242-4; Ming revolution (1368), 152; Christian missions, 152-4, 182; Buddhism, 179, 248; Islam, 183, 250; gunpowder and firearms, 197-9, 251-3; defeat of nomadism, 191; links with Persia, 125, 189

Chingis Khan: birth, 211; career, 44-70, 212; conquest of the steppes, 49-52; meaning of title 'Chingis', 212; campaign in the west, 55-61, 213-15; meeting with Ch'ang Ch'un, 62, 215; death and burial, 63, 216; military leader, 63-6, 216; civil administrator, 66-70, 217; law-giver, 69, 217; family, 73, 75, 218; personal appearance, 63

Chinkai (Mongol adviser), 98, 100, 219

Ch'i-tan/Khitan (barbarian rulers of North China under name of Liao), 35, 36, 37, 39, 54, 209

Chmielnik, 85

Choban (Mongol commander in Persia), 145

Chormagan (Mongol commander in Persia), 78, 79

Chu river, 19, 25, 36

Ch'ung-shui (place of Chingis's death), 63

Chu yuan-chang (founder of Ming dynasty), 151

Ch'u-ts'ai (adviser to Chingis), 67, 76, 77, 93, 217

classes, social, in Mongolia, 50, 212

Clement V (pope), 147, 153

Clovis the Frank, 37

Coloman, 87

Conrad (king of Germany), 86

Conrad (Polish duke), 92

Confucian classics, examinations in, 124, 147, 235

Constantinople, 21, 22, 79, 102, 131, 157; recaptured by Greeks 1261, 116, 157, 159

Cracow, 85, 157

Crimea: Turks, 23, 59, 102, 157, 162, 182; Genoese, 159, 167, 170, 247

Croatia, 87

Cumans, 83, 84, 86, 214, 221, 247; *see also* Kipchaks

cycle, 12-year animal, xiii, 28, 207

Cyprus, 97, 102

Dalai (ocean), 225

Dalmatia, 87

Damascus, 113, 115, 232

Daniel (Russian prince), 101, 156, 160

Dardanelles, 246

Daruga/Darukhachi: Mongol commissioner in occupied territory, 77, 123, 143

Dandankan, battle of, 39

David (king of Georgia), 79

Delhi, 172

Diyar Bakr, 78

Dobun the Wise (ancestor of Mongols), 45